In this remarkable work of comparative economic history, Stephen _
activities and economic significance of the Indian mercantile communities which traded in Iran, Central Asia and Russia in the seventeenth and eighteenth centuries. The author uses Russian sources, hitherto largely ignored, to show that these merchants represented part of the hegemonic trade diaspora of the Indian world economy, thus challenging the conventional interpretation of world economic history that European merchants over-whelmed their Asian counterparts in the early modern era. The book not only demonstrates the vitality of Indian mercantile capitalism, but also offers a unique insight into the social characteristics of an Indian expatriate trading community in the Volga–Caspian port of Astrakhan.

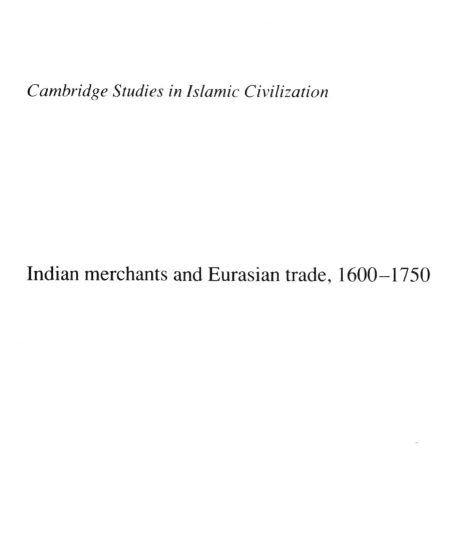

Cambridge Studies in Islamic Civilization

Indian merchants and Eurasian trade, 1600–1750

Cambridge Studies in Islamic Civilization

Editorial board
DAVID MORGAN (general editor)
JOSEF VAN ESS   BARBARA FLEMMING   METIN KUNT   W. F. MADELUNG
ROY MOTTAHEDEH   BASIM MUSALLAM

Titles in the series

Indian merchants and Eurasian trade, 1600–1750

STEPHEN FREDERIC DALE

Ohio State University

CAMBRIDGE
UNIVERSITY PRESS

PUBLISHED BY THE PRESS SYNDICATE OF THE UNIVERSITY OF CAMBRIDGE
The Pitt Building, Trumpington Street, Cambridge, United Kingdom

CAMBRIDGE UNIVERSITY PRESS
The Edinburgh Building, Cambridge CB2 2RU, UK
40 West 20th Street, New York NY 10011–4211, USA
477 Williamstown Road, Port Melbourne, VIC 3207, Australia
Ruiz de Alarcón 13, 28014 Madrid, Spain
Dock House, The Waterfront, Cape Town 8001, South Africa

http://www.cambridge.org

© Cambridge University Press 1994

First published 1994
Reprinted 1997
First paperback edition 2002

A catalogue record for this book is available from the British Library

Library of Congress Cataloguing in Publication data
Dale, Stephen Frederic.
Indian merchants and Eurasian trade, 1600–1750 / Stephen Frederic Dale.
          p.   cm. – (Cambridge studies in Islamic civilization)
Includes bibliographical references.
ISBN 0 521 45460 3
1. India – Commerce – Eurasia – History.   2. Eurasia – Commerce –
India – History.   I. Title.   II. Series.
HF3788.E83D35   1994
382′.095405–dc20   93-31404   CIP

ISBN 0 521 45460 3 hardback
ISBN 0 521 52597 7 paperback

Contents

Illustrations

Preface

This work is a study of economies and trade routes, of merchants and their capital in Mughul India, Safavid Iran, Uzbek Turan and Muscovite Russia. It is, more particularly, a study of the characteristics and significance of the Mughul-Indian trade diaspora in Iran, Turan and Russia. The underlying purpose of the work is to use new evidence and employ a new perspective to amend radically the persistent Eurocentric bias that continues to characterize most research on Eurasian trade in the sixteenth, seventeenth and eighteenth centuries. A remarkable number of articles and books have been published on this commerce in the last two decades, and many have focused on India, but nearly all of them have been primarily concerned with aspects of European maritime expansion. Two prevalent assumptions of this historiography have been that Indian commerce with its neighboring territories was comparatively insignificant when measured against European trade, and that Indian merchants themselves, to the extent that they ever had been involved in this trade in the first place, were by the seventeenth century in full-scale retreat in the face of European competition. As far as Mughul India's trade with Iran, Turan and Russia was concerned, these assumptions are incorrect.

I began this study in order to correct this erroneous, one-sided view of Eurasian commerce by examining the role of large numbers of merchants from Mughul India who lived semi-permanently and conducted business in Iran, Turan and Russia in the seventeenth and eighteenth century. I would not have attempted to do so had not an adolescent interest in understanding the angst of characters in nineteenth-century Russian novels at least left me with the ability to use more than eleven hundred pages of published Russian documents that illumine the business activities of a little-known settlement of Indian merchants in the Russian Caspian port of Astrakhan. These records provide a uniquely detailed insight into the commercial and financial activities of Indian merchants, not merely in Astrakhan itself, but in Iran as well. They offer the only means that I know to discuss specific Indian business practices in the diaspora in the early modern era, and they contain at least one set of data for evaluating the economic significance of the larger emigré Mughul-Indian merchant population. Unfortunately, I was not able to convince the Soviet government that I should be able to visit Astrakhan itself, but my disappointment in not being able to use the district and city archives there was somewhat diminished by the discovery of several fine historical studies of Astrakhan city and region by Soviet scholars. In addition I have benefited from a wide variety of other Soviet studies of the socio-economic characteristics of merchants and urban societies.

Anyone who studies commerce or mercantile life in the pre-modern era is quickly made aware of two inescapable realities. First, statistics are rarely available to document even long-term economic trends, and most conclusions about commercial life have to be tentatively apprehended from the braille of occasional coin finds, scattered records and anecdotal evidence. Basic customs and financial data are almost never available. These are problems too for most aspects of the economic history of India, Iran, Turan and Russia between 1600 and 1750, the century and a half during which the Astrakhan Indian community first prospered and then decayed. However, an exceptional number of administrative manuals, histories and travelers' accounts are extant for this period of Mughul and Safavid history, and in Astrakhan itself a significant number of customs records have been preserved. Second, just as it has been practical to write only about a relatively brief time span out of centuries of commercial interaction between Indian and adjacent territories, so too I have been compelled artificially to limit my study of expatriate South Asian merchants to those who emigrated from Mughul India to Safavid Iran, Uzbek Turan and Muscovite Russia. Yet Mughul India did not exist in a state of autarky within the South Asian subcontinent, and the diaspora of Mughul Indian merchants was not confined to these three states or regions. It extended throughout the Indian Ocean region, was highly visible in the Ottoman empire and penetrated into Chinese Turkistan. At the very least, though, this work will offer clues and analogies for understanding the significance of South Asian merchants throughout the wider diaspora and in so doing encourage the study of regional economic history of Asia in the early modern era.

I have an enormous intellectual debt to a large number of accomplished scholars who have written studies of commerce or merchant classes in India, Iran, Turan and Russia in the early modern era. For India I have particularly benefited from the writings of Christopher Bayly, K. N. Chaudhuri, Irfan Habib and his justly influential Aligarh school, Muzaffar Alam, Tapan Raychaudhuri and John Richards. I would also like specially to acknowledge the work of Surendra Gopal, the first non-Soviet scholar who recognized the potential scholarly importance of the Russian Astrakhan records. My understanding of Iranian history of the Safavid era has been especially influenced by the interpretations of Bert Fragner, Edmund Herzig, Mehdi Keyvani, Rudolph Matthee, R. Roemer and R. W. Ferrier. E. A. Davidovich, N. M. Lowick, R. D. McChesney and R. G. Mukminova have produced works that have been crucial to my understanding of the trade of South Asian merchants in the Uzbek states or appanages of Turan.

I began my tutorials on Russian merchants by reading the articles and books of Samuel H. Baron and Paul Bushkovitch, but learned most about the particular subject of South Asian merchants in Russia by immersing myself in the uniquely valuable document collections that were carefully edited by K. A. Antonova, N. M. Gold'berg and others. My debt to N. B. Golikova will be especially evident in the notes, for her use of unpublished Astrakhan customs records has allowed me to make some statistically verified conclusions that could only be inferred from the published records. I have also benefited from the criticisms and suggestions of Thomas Allsen, Paul Bushkovitch, John Masson Smith Jr. and my colleague Alam Payind. I must also record my debt for the second time in my scholarly life to the exceptional scholarship of the late S. D. Goitein, whose work on the Cairo Geniza documents has incalculably enriched my understanding of pre-modern commerce in the Mediterranean and Islamic world.

Finally, I would like to thank Professor Tosun Aricanli for inviting me to present a paper at the "Workshop on the Political Economies of the Ottoman, Safavid and Mughal States during the 17th and 18th Centuries," that was held in Istanbul, Turkey, 16–20 June, 1992. The final revision of this manuscript was influenced by several of the participants at that conference, particularly Suraiya Faroqhi, Ashraf Ghani, Edmund Herzig and Rudolph Matthee. While this manuscript was begun well before that meeting it is, in a way, a testimony to the wisdom of studying the early modern Islamic world from a comparative perspective.

Cindy Gray and Jon Fehrman helped with the design of the maps and Jon Fehrman prepared the final version of each map.

Note on transliteration

I have chosen to follow R. D. McChesney's sensible modifications of the *Encyclopaedia of Islam* system of rendering the Cyrillic alphabet that he employed in his recent study, *Waqf in Central Asia*. I found it difficult to decide how to present Russian renderings of Indian names that were generally unfamiliar to their officials, particularly those who first encountered Indian merchants in the early seventeenth century. They rendered some names correctly and others are recognizable. Others, though, have been a matter of anguished speculation. After consulting with several Indian colleagues and getting as many variant suggestions for one or two names I decided to transliterate them from Russian without change. I have, however, usually placed the Russian personal suffix, -ov, -ev, etc. in parenthesis to enable others to more easily recognize Hindu and Jain names. Muslim names were not usually a problem. Not only were Russians more familiar with Muslims, but few Indian Muslims were present in the Astrakhan settlement.

Abbreviations

AA   *A'in-i Akbari*, Abu'l Fadl 'Allami, trans. and ed. by
            H. Blochmann and D. C. Phillott, repr. (New Delhi:
            Crown Publications, 1988), 3 vols.
AN   *Akbar Nama*, Abu'l Fadl 'Allami, trans. by H. Beveridge,
            repr. (New Delhi: Ess Ess Publications, 1987), 3 vols.
Antonova, I *Russko-Indiiskie Otnosheniia v XVII veke*, K. A.
            Antonova *et al.*, ed., *Sbornik Dokumentov* [Russian–
            Indian Relations in the 17th Century, A Collection of
            Documents] (Moscow: Nauka, 1958).
Antonova, II *Russko-Indiiskie Otnosheniia v XVIII veke*, K. A.
            Antonova *et al.*, ed., *Sbornik Dokumentov* [Russian–
            Indian Relations in the 18th Century, A Collection of
            Documents] (Moscow: Nauka, 1965).
CEHI   *The Cambridge Economic History of India*, Tapan
            Raychaudhuri and Irfan Habib, eds., I: *c. 1200–c. 1750*
            (Cambridge: Cambridge University Press, 1982).
CHI   *The Cambridge History of Iran*, I, W. B. Fisher, ed., *The
            Land of Iran*; V, J. A. Boyle, ed., *The Saljuq and Mongol
            Periods*; VI, Peter Jackson and Laurence Lockhart,
            ed., *The Timurid and Safavid Periods* (Cambridge:
            Cambridge University Press, 1965–86).
Golikova, *Essays* *Ocherki Po Istorii Gorodov Rossii kontsa XVII–nachala
            XVIII v*, N. B. Golikova [Essays on the History of
            Russian Cities from the End of the 17th to the Beginning
            of the 18th Century] (Moscow: Moscow University,
            1982).
Mukinova,   *Sotsial'naia Differensiatsiia Naseleniia Gorodov
Social Differentiation Uzbekistana v XV–XVI vv* [Social Differentiation of the
            Urban Population of Uzbekistan in the 15th and 16th
            Centuries] (Tashkent: Fan, 1985).

CHAPTER 1

An Indian world economy

Have we not Indian carpets dark as wine,
  Turbans and sashes, gowns and bows and veils,
And broideries of intricate design,
  And printed hangings in enormous bales?
                              James Elroy Flecker: "The Golden Journey to Samarqand"

The Indian Diaspora

In a discussion of the commerce and business classes of Safavid Iran (1501–1722), Mehdi Keyvani has remarked that the presence and proliferation of Indian "moneychangers" in several major Iranian cities during the later Safavid period is "an astonishing and unexplained episode of Iranian economic history."[1] Keyvani would have been justified in adding that the increased settlement of these Indians in Iran has also remained an unexplained aspect of Indian economic history in this period when Mughul emperors ruled the northern half of the South Asian subcontinent (1526–1739). If no more than a few Indians had been involved their presence might justifiably be dismissed as an intriguing anomaly that had no fundamental significance for the economic history of either Iran or India, but thousands and perhaps tens of thousands of Indian businessmen lived and worked in Iran in the seventeenth and early eighteenth century. Some of these men were moneychangers and/or moneylenders, but many of the same individuals also worked as retail and wholesale merchants, commodity brokers and financiers. Taken as a whole they constituted an influential but rarely noticed trade diaspora that also encompassed the Uzbek khanates of western Turkistan or Turan (c. 1500–1920). In the early seventeenth century the diaspora extended its mercantile activities to include the Russian Caspian port of Astrakhan, the Volga basin and, for a brief period, Moscow itself. This expanding sphere of Indian mercantile influence thus represented far more than a transitory episode for Safavid Iran, far more even than an important moment in Mughul–Safavid

---

[1] Mehdi Keyvani, *Artisans and Guild Life in the Later Safavid Period* (Berlin: Klaus Schwarz, 1982), 228.

1

economic relations. It was a climactic moment of an important phase in Eurasian economic history.

The concept of a trade diaspora has been widely publicized by the African historian, Philip Curtin, who, along with Fernand Braudel, is also one of the few scholars who have alluded to the presence of Indian merchants in Russia.[2] "Trade diaspora" is a useful descriptive tool for the phenomenon of merchant migrations from one cultural zone to another, and in his book, *Cross-cultural Trade in World History*,[3] Curtin applies it to a multitude of examples that range from the Middle East in the fourth century BC to the "tightly controlled trade diasporas of the chartered European trading companies in eastern seas."[4] By itself, though, the concept is not sufficient to convey the economic significance of this wide-spread dispersal of Indian merchants in Iran, Turan and Russia. This particular diaspora reflected an asymmetrical economic relationship in which Indians marketed agricultural products, textile manufactures and their own financial expertise throughout a broad region where they enjoyed a competitive advantage in both goods and services – or, in visible and invisible exports. In brief, the diaspora manifested in the persons of these merchants the Mughul empire's stature as a regionally dominant economic power or, in Fernand Braudel's phrase, a regional "world economy."[5]

One of the best known and clearest examples of this type of regionally dominant diaspora in the early modern era, the sixteenth through the eighteenth century, is that of the western European economic penetration of Russia. The phenomenon is particularly obvious in this instance because these two societies had been largely isolated from one another before representatives of the nascent European world economy in the person of English merchants literally stumbled over the primitive Muscovite state while searching for a northwest passage to the orient. T. S. Willan has examined the early English phase of discovery and Jonathan Israel has written an exceptionally lucid account of the later Dutch phase in his overall analysis of their hegemonic diaspora, *Dutch Primacy in World Trade, 1585–1740*.[6] The settlement of English and Dutch merchants and entrepreneurs in Archangel and Moscow is particularly apropos since it represented virtually the same process as the nearly simultaneous extension of

---

[2] Fernand Braudel is the only scholar to hint at the economic significance of these Indian merchants. *The Perspective of the World*, Vol. III of *Civilization and Capitalism 15th–18th Century*, trans. by Siân Reynolds (London: Collins, 1984), 461.

[3] Philip D. Curtin, *Cross-cultural Trade in World History* (Cambridge: Cambridge University Press, 1984), 189.

[4] Curtin, *Cross-cultural Trade*, 8.

[5] Braudel, *Perspective of the World*, 22, 24–45. See also Frederic Mauro's rhetorical question about the relationship of merchant communities to the idea of world economy in his essay, "Merchant Communities, 1350–1750," in James D. Tracy, ed., *The Rise of Merchant Empires* (Cambridge: Cambridge University Press, 1990), 286.

[6] T. S. Willan, *The Early History of the Russia Company, 1553–1603* (Manchester: Manchester University Press, 1956), and Jonathan Israel, *Dutch Primacy in World Trade, 1585–1740* (Oxford: Clarendon Press, 1989).

Indian economic influence to Astrakhan, the Volga cities and Moscow. The significance of these two diasporas differed only in that western Europeans were just beginning their world-wide expansion whereas in retrospect it is obvious that the arrival of Indian merchants and financiers represented the western highwater mark of the Indian world economy. Unfortunately, it has been impossible even to guess at the scope and implications of the Indian diaspora because so little attention has been devoted to it. Until now more has been written about the Russian career of one Dutch entrepreneur, André Vinius (1605–1662/63), than about all of the Indian merchants in Iran, Turan and Russia over the entire course of the seventeenth century.[7]

The vestigial credit network of this Indian mercantile presence was still operating effectively in the early nineteenth century. Alexander Burnes, one of the best informed and precisely accurate British observers who visited northwestern India, Afghanistan, Turan and Iran, found out while visiting Kabul in 1832 that much of the trade of Central Asia was in the hands of Hindu merchants, who had "houses of agency from Astracan and Meshid to Calcutta." These merchants offered to give him bills of exchange on Nizhnii Novgorod, on the upper Volga, Astrakhan or Bukhara.[8] Yet the magnitude and influence of the Indian diaspora has remained virtually unknown in modern scholarship because of well-entrenched Eurocentric biases in historical studies on Eurasian commerce in the early modern era, although the nature of available sources has also discouraged research on this topic.

To understand how this Indian world economy functioned it will be necessary to alter fundamentally some of the traditional approaches to and conclusions about Eurasian economic and commercial history in the early modern period. First of all it is essential to discuss Indian economic history as a provincial segment of a much broader South Asian–Near Eastern regional history. Such a regional perspective is a commonplace in cultural historiography of the region, but it is still rare in scholarly studies of the economic history of the Middle East and South Asia, which tend to be conceptualized in terms of modern political boundaries.[9] Thus no one who is familiar with Mughul or Safavid historiography would be surprised to learn that a recent Iranian publication, *Karvan-i Hind*, *The Caravan of India*, dealt

---

[7] For a summary of the career of Vinius see Joseph T. Fuhrmann, *The Origins of Capitalism in Russia* (Chicago: Quadrangle Books, 1972), 55–91.

[8] Alexander Burnes, *Travels into Bokhara* (London: John Murray, 1835), II, 144–45. The operation of bills of exchange or *hundis* within Mughul territories is well known, but for a recent description of the practice in the seventeenth century see Irfan Habib, "The System of Bills of Exchange (Hundis) in the Mughal Empire," in Satish Chandra, ed., *Essays in Medieval Indian Economic History* (New Delhi: Munshiram Manoharlal, 1987), 207–21. It is quite typical of sources for the period that most of Habib's information comes from English East India Company documents rather than Persian or other Indian language materials.

[9] This approach is exemplified, for example, by the *Cambridge Economic History of India* and the *Cambridge History of Iran*. Authors of chapters on commerce or economic history in both volumes tend to write with very little knowledge of regional commercial ties or the economic history of contiguous states.

with the emigration of poets from the Safavid to the Mughul court rather than the passage of prosaic camel caravans.[10]

The two most important exceptions to this narrow, politically defined historiography are the recent dissertations of Rudolph P. Matthee, "Politics and Trade in Late Safavid Iran: Commercial Crisis and Government Reaction Under Shah Solayman (1666–1694)," (UCLA, 1991), and Edmund Herzig, "The Armenian Merchants of New Julfa, Isfahan: A Study in Pre-Modern Asian Trade" (Oxford, 1991). Both Matthee and Herzig are nominally scholars of Safavid Iran, but they locate their works within the broader context of Eurasian economic history, and Professor Matthee's summary of his thesis characterizes both their approaches. "This study then views Iran as an early modern state embedded in a commercial network stretching from the Levant and the emerging Russian state to India."[11] Both too use a wide variety of European and Iranian sources that illuminate the economic relationships of a broad Eurasian region. Both scholars also understand the crucial nexus between government policy and commerce. Professor Matthee's work is especially important for the present study, because he appreciates that Mughul–Safavid commerce was a major factor in the economic history of both states, and his sophisticated knowledge of commercial and monetary history complements K. N. Chaudhuri's massive history of British East India Company trade in the Mughul–Safavid era.[12] Professor Herzig's pioneering study of the famous Armenian commercial community of Isfahan offers crucial new data on a mercantile diaspora that co-existed with that of the Indians in Iran and Russia. His research illumines aspects of Armenian merchant organization and practice that corroborates and supplements the available data on Indian merchants.

Throughout most of the sixteenth, seventeenth and eighteenth centuries India's most important markets were located in the countries bordering the Indian Ocean and the contiguous land mass of the Iranian plateau and the Central Asian steppe. Equally important, the Mughuls were one of three major early modern Muslim dynasties, along with the Safavids and Ottomans, who established a fairly effective pax Islamica throughout the traditional civilizational centers of the Near East and South Asia. From the sixteenth century most rulers of these dynasties consistently implemented standardized political–economic policies that were designed to stimulate both internal and external trade. These policies, which will be discussed below primarily in terms of Mughul India's commercial relations with Safavid Iran and Uzbek Turan, were particularly effective in securing the overland routes between northern India and the Iranian plateau. By the early seventeenth century Mughul and Safavid monarchs had jointly created what were probably the most effective conditions for commerce that had ever existed in the

---

[10] Ahmad Golchin Ma'ani, *Karvan-i Hind* (Mashad: Astan-i quds-i razavi, 1991), 2 vols.

[11] Matthee, "Politics and Trade," xii.

[12] K. N. Chaudhuri, *The Trading World of Asia and the English East India Company, 1660–1760* (Cambridge; Cambridge University Press, 1978).

history of the Indo-Persian region. This was an economic "conjuncture," largely obscured by scholars' traditional preoccupation with European maritime trade, that favored the steady increase of long-established trading patterns and the substantial expansion of the Indian mercantile diaspora.

The general assessments of Tapan Raychaudhuri on Mughul India and H. R. Roemer on Safavid Iran convey an impressionistic sense of conditions in these countries around 1600, although they are discussing different facets of Mughul and Safavid rule. After discussing the Mughul regime's efficient land revenue extraction mechanisms Raychaudhuri writes:

If the Mughuls were ruthless in their expropriation of surplus, their rule beyond doubt brought a high level of peace and security. From the 1570s – by which time Akbar had consolidated his empire – for more than a hundred years the greater part of India enjoyed such freedom from war and anarchy as it had not known for centuries . . . The economy of the empire derived direct benefits from this altered state of peace and security. Substantial increases in trade, both inland and foreign, was rendered possible by this development. It would perhaps be an exaggeration to say that the Mughul age saw the emergence of an integrated national market. Still, the commercial ties which bound together different parts of the empire had no precedents.

Roemer in depicting the achievements of the pivotal Safavid monarch, Shah 'Abbas, writes:

At the end of the 10th/16th and the beginning of the 11/17th century, Shah 'Abbas had mastered the crises which had shaken his country at the time of his accession . . . After security had been restored in the country 'Abbas turned his attention to establishing an effective administration. In the development of transport routes, which he pursued with energy, particularly noteworthy is the network of caravansarais he created . . . These and other measures invigorated trade and industry so that the broad masses of the population also found that their standard of living was at first improved and ultimately reached a level never known up to that time.[13]

It is possible to paraphrase Raychaudhuri's comments on Mughul India and apply them to both India and Iran so that they read: "It would perhaps be an exaggeration to say that the Mughul–Safavid age realized an integrated regional market, but the commercial ties which now bound these two empires together had no precedents." By the second decade of the seventeenth century Muscovite Russia also became part of this market as its rulers aggressively stimulated foreign trade by encouraging the settlement of foreign merchants. The settlement of Indian merchants in Astrakhan was one of the results of this policy.

To understand the operation of this world economy it is also necessary to appreciate that the Indian merchants who conducted business throughout Iran, Turan and Russia were members of a sophisticated trading network that in most

---

[13] Raychaudhuri, "The State and the Economy: The Mughal Empire," CEHI, I, 184 and H. R. Roemer, "The Safavid Period," CHI, VI, 269.

respects mirrored the commercial and financial characteristics of the Armenian mercantile diaspora. European scholars have generally seen Indian and other Asian merchants as archaic commercial artifacts of the early modern world. The term peddler has frequently been used to categorize and implicitly denigrate the economic effectiveness of Asian merchants in this period.[14] As it is usually used, peddler represents a kind of economic orientalism in which Asian merchants are viewed as a quaint and ineffective commercial "other." The implicit standard of comparison is, of course, the British and Dutch East India companies. It has been relatively easy for scholars to hold this view because there is a lack of data on non-western merchants before the twentieth century. Apart from S. D. Goitein's monumental study of Middle Eastern commerce and Jewish society, *A Mediterranean Society*, there has been no study of Asian merchants that is comparable in biographic and economic detail to Sylvia Thrupp's work, *The Merchant Class of Medieval London*, or equal to the voluminous, richly detailed literature on Italian Renaissance merchants.[15]

The data on Indian merchants in Iran, Turan and Russia is itself not strictly comparable to the relatively lavish sources that are extant for medieval and early modern Europe. This information is, however, remarkably full when compared to existing knowledge about India's mercantile communities in the early modern period, whether within South Asia itself or in the broader South Asian commercial diaspora. The Astrakhan documents especially represent a unique collection of sources for a single community of Asian merchants, second only perhaps to the data that Edmund Herzig has obtained for the Isfahan Armenians.[16] In contrast to the records of the Dutch and English East India companies, which contain only limited data on Asian traders, these Russian sources were compiled by an autocratic regime whose representatives closely monitored customs transactions, recorded details of partnerships and other contracts, adjudicated commercial disputes and in census reports and taxation records offered insights into the cultural and social characteristics of the Indian Community. These data make it possible to see that apart from the exceptional case of the two great European companies, Indian merchants closely resembled their well-known European contemporaries – particularly those in Genoa, Florence and Siena. In

[14] The classic statements of the peddler thesis are the original formulation by J. C. van Leur, *Indonesian Trade and Society* (The Hague: W. van Hoeve, 1955), and the more recent restatement of van Leur's ideas by Niels Steensgaard, *The Asian Trade Revolution of the Seventeenth Century, The East India Companies and the Decline of the Caravan Trade* (Chicago: University of Chicago Press, 2nd ed., 1974).
[15] S. D. Goitein, *A Mediterranean Society* (Berkeley: University of California Press, 1967–88), 5 vols., and Sylvia Thrupp, *The Merchant Class of Medieval London* (Chicago: University of Chicago Press, 1948).
[16] Analyses of pre-modern Indian firms have never really been attempted because of the scarcity of sources, but even the discussion about mercantile organization is still carried on at a fairly elementary level. For an introduction to modern studies of firms, see Oliver E. Williamson and Sidney G. Winter, *The Nature of the Firm* (New York: Oxford University Press, 1991), a book that contains a collection of articles by Ronald H. Coase and other scholars writing on Coase's now famous essay, "The Nature of the Firm."

fact, one of the secondary purposes of this study is to suggest that there was a common Eurasian mercantile type and characteristic Eurasian firm in the early modern era.

The Eurasian context

Mughul-Indian merchants who migrated to conduct business in Iran, Turan and Russia operated in four different states, whose policies and structure directly or indirectly influenced the diaspora's prosperity and prospects for growth. All four states were successors of the Mongol–Timurid nomadic empires of the thirteenth, fourteenth and fifteenth centuries. Mughul India, Safavid Iran and Uzbek Turan were also immediate heirs to the administrative and cultural traditions of the Timurids, Timur's descendants who ruled in Turan from 1405 to 1506. Nevertheless, the legacies of these empires that Marshall Hodgson has characterized as "military patronage states" differed in each instance.[17] Rulers of Uzbek Turan were direct descendants of Chingiz Khan and their dynastic legitimacy appears to have been generally accepted by the Turco-Mongol inhabitants of that region who spoke Turkic dialects and shared their Sunni Muslim faith. Uzbek rulers inherited Mongol assumptions that territorial conquests belonged to and should be shared among clan members.[18] Unlike Chingiz Khan, though, the Uzbek grand khan, who normally ruled in Bukhara, rarely functioned as more than a primus inter pares, a first among Chingizid equals. With the exception of the last quarter of the sixteenth century Uzbek rulers usually functioned as a patchwork of agnatically related but largely autonomous appanages. Yet despite the fragmented structure of Uzbek polity it survived essentially intact from the time of the decisive Uzbek victories over the last Timurid rulers in Turan in the early sixteenth century throughout the early modern period.

The Mughuls were members of one of those Timurid lineages. Their founder, Zahir al-Din Muhammad Babur (1483–1530), had lost two battles to Uzbek forces that caused him to take refuge in the impoverished Timurid outpost of Kabul in 1504. He ruled from there until 1526 when he was able to reestablish Timurid

---

[17] It is difficult to see that Hodgson's concept of the "military patronage state" explains very much about the characteristics of the Mughuls, Safavids or Ottomans, although it is often used as a convenient label. Hodgson himself only tentatively suggested that there was a connection. He wrote: "what I have called 'military patronage state' never formed a single pattern, but at some point I think I can see common effects on such states [Ottoman, Safavid and Mughul] from the special circumstances of the age," *The Venture of Islam*, III: *Gunpowder Empires and Modern Times* (Chicago: University of Chicago Press, 1974), 27. For a discussion of the diverse Timurid heritage of the Mughul, Safavid and Uzbek states see Stephen F. Dale, "The Legacy of the Timurids," in David Morgan and Francis Robinson, eds., *The Legacy of the Timurids* (New Delhi: Oxford University Press for the Royal Asiatic Society, forthcoming, 1994).

[18] The best introduction to Uzbek polity and political thought is R. D. McChesney's *Waqf in Central Asia* (Princeton: Princeton University Press, 1991). For a political history of the Uzbeks in this period see the same author's article, "Central Asia, VI. In the 10th–12th/16th–18th Centuries," in E. Yarshater, ed., *Encyclopaedia Iranica* 5, fasc. 2 (Costa Mesa., Calif.: Mazda, 1990), 176–93.

fortunes by seizing northern India from a disunited Afghan dynasty.[19] Like Uzbek rulers Mughul emperors were Sunni Muslims, but Babur and his successors based their dynastic claims on Timurid rather than Chingizid descent. Unlike the Uzbeks, Mughul emperors were able to transcend their own appanage tradition that had previously doomed the continued rule of Timur's descendants in Turan. By the end of the sixteenth century they had established an indigenously tinged Perso-Islamic absolutism in northern India that for a century and a half enjoyed paramountcy over a diverse, predominantly non-Muslim population and a bewildering variety of regional and local rulers.

Based partly on the achievements of their Afghan predecessors, Mughul rulers were able to assert direct control over most cities and much of the agricultural heartland of the north Indian plains. The family's Timurid legitimacy, which exerted only modest influence in India, was reinforced by the Mughuls' significance as a Muslim dynasty among northern India's substantial but still minority Indo-Muslim population. Still, the acquiescence of many South Asian Muslims was tentative and conditional. Even if they were temporarily co-opted into the imperial system, groups such as the clan-centered Afghans never offered the Mughuls more than temporary cooperation. The loyalty of subordinate Hindu lineages was almost entirely pragmatic and temporary. Therefore, while weak Uzbek appanages survived in Turan, Mughul imperial rule weakened quickly after the death of the last great emperor Aurungzeb (r. 1656–1707). It virtually ceased to exist after the Iranian invader and heir to Safavid power, Nadir Shah, administered the coup de grace to the system when he sacked Delhi and seized the Mughul treasury in 1739.

The Safavids were also heirs to a common Timurid legacy, but they differed from the Mughuls and Uzbeks even more than these two states were distinct from one another. Originally leaders of a militarized *sufi* order, Safavid rulers succeeded in establishing a state that covered areas of eastern Anatolia and north-western Iran by 1501.[20] They largely relied for military power on Turkic tribes in the region who were known as the Qizilbash, or "redheads," after their distinctive headgear, who had been attracted to the Safavid cause by the family's quasi-Shi'i messianic preaching. In the following decade Safavid forces conquered much of the Iranian plateau and also began their systematic conversion of the population to Shi'i Islam. Their successful persecution of Sunni Muslims permanently altered

---

[19] For an introduction to the history of the Mughul empire, see J. F. Richards, *The Mughal Empire* (Cambridge: Cambridge University Press, 1993). Peter Hardy offers an insightful introduction to questions of Mughul legitimacy and sovereignty in his work, *The Muslims of British India* (Cambridge: Cambridge University Press, 1972), 1–30; and for brief articles on various aspects of Mughul culture and administration see M. Athar 'Ali *et al.*, "Mughuls," *Encyclopaedia of Islam* new ed., VII, fasc. 119–20 (Leiden: E. J. Brill, 1991), 313–46.

[20] The best introduction to various aspects of Safavid history is found in the various articles in volume VI of *The Cambridge History of Iran*. See also H. R. Roemer, *Persien auf dem Weg in die Neuzeit: Iranische Geschichte von 1350–1750* (Beirut: Franz Stiner, 1989), and Klaus Michael Röhrborn, *Provinzen und Zengralgewalt, Persiens im 16. und 17. Jahrhundert* (Berlin: Walter De Gruyter, 1966).

the religious landscape and clerical organization of Iran, but Safavid military and political fortunes sharply declined after 1514 when they lost the battle of Chaldiran to Ottoman forces. Following this defeat Safavid Iran not only ceded most of its northwestern provinces, but the dynasty's charismatic authority was compromised and Qizilbash tribes increasingly asserted control over the state's remaining territories and periodically usurped the power of the Safavid family itself. The sixteenth century was the Qizilbash century in Safavid Iran, even if Iranian bureaucrats and *'alims* dominated the administration and the religious hierarchy.

The Safavid state experienced a genuine renaissance under Shah 'Abbas I (r. 1588–1629). 'Abbas reestablished dynastic control over the central government, reconquered lost territories and radically restructured the state. He transformed it from what had been almost a tribal confederation led by formerly charismatic Safavid shaikhs to a more traditional Perso-Islamic absolutism that was increasingly supported by a reorganized military system independent of Qizilbash leadership. Following 'Abbas' death, though, the Safavid state entered into an almost century-long period of stasis, a result in large measure of his policy of immuring potential heirs in the haram. This policy, which his descendants also followed, almost guaranteed that the pillars of a dynastic, patriarchal state, the princes, would be inexperienced or incompetent monarchs. Symptomatic of this problem was the shift in spending patterns of late Safavid Iran. Finances that had earlier gone for the army and such commercial infrastructure as caravansarai were diverted in the second half of the seventeenth century to construction of palaces and mosques for the increasingly powerful Shi'i clergy.[21] While the court managed to sustain much of its splendor and appearance of central authority throughout the seventeenth century, by the accession of Shah Husain in 1694 the decay of the dynasty had left the state vulnerable to the slightest external threat. In 1722 it dissolved almost overnight in the face of an Afghan revolt that inadvertently culminated in the conquest of Shah 'Abbas' splendid capital, Isfahan.

The Muscovite state of the late sixteenth century had emerged from Mongol vassalage only a century earlier, but unlike the Mughul, Safavid and Uzbek regimes it exhibited few long-term effects of its subordination.[22] The Mongols had ruled Russia's northeastern forest zone indirectly, so their administrative and cultural legacy in the Moscow–Novgorod heartland was slight. The most obvious permanent legacy was the tsars' assumption of the title "autocrat," which proclaimed their independence of the "Tatar yoke." Mongol rule has sometimes been blamed for Russia's autocratic character, but when compared with Mughul, Safavid or Uzbek polities it is impossible to discern, as many Russian historians

[21] Matthee, "Politics and Trade," 78–79 and 123.
[22] See Nicholas V. Riasanovsky, *A History of Russia* (New York: Oxford University Press, 1984), and for social and economic history, Jerome Blum, *Lord and Peasant in Russia* (Princeton: Princeton University Press, 1961).

have traditionally done, any specifically Mongol or "Asiatic" features in its governmental traditions, only the continuous development of an implacable absolutism. The success of one line of Muscovite princes in extinguishing the independence and then the autonomy of the area's other princely appanages was virtually assured by the reign of Vassili III (1533–55), and it was climaxed by Ivan the Terrible's extraordinary administrative and military policy known as the *oprichina*. Ivan (r. 1533–84) discernibly directed this reign of terror at potential princely opponents of his rule, but he also loosed a destructive and seemingly indiscriminate assault on large regions of the countryside that he evidently suspected of disaffection.

It is a remarkable feature of Russian history that their autocrats, however terrible, enjoyed a legitimacy of indisputable Russian princely birth that was bolstered by the almost unwavering support of the orthodox church and the ideological underpinnings of Roman and Byzantine absolutist precedents. Their success in creating a true absolutism that none of their European or Asian contemporaries could possibly hope to emulate was a reflection of Russia's political and socio-economic primitiveness rather than its Asiatic sophistication. As Nicholas Riasanovsky has persuasively argued in his comparison of Lithuania and Moscow:

the princedom of Moscow arose in a relatively primitive and pioneer northeast, where rulers managed to acquire a dominant position in a fluid and expanding society . . . Lithuania, in contrast, always had to deal with different peoples and cultures and formed a federal, not a Unitary state.[23]

Absolutism and primitiveness are two features of the Muscovite state that must be appreciated in order to understand the situation of the Indian diaspora in that country, for they help to explain the Indian merchants' initial success and partly account for their eventual stagnation.

Merchants from Mughul India who traded in Safavid Iran or Uzbek Turan operated within a broadly similar commercial and linguistic environment. While merchants in these states did not possess the urban autonomy that many of their western European contemporaries had achieved, they still enjoyed almost unrestricted freedom to carry on their trade within the general framework of Islamic contractual law.[24] What Goitein has said about mercantile life in the Mediterranean region from the mid-tenth to the mid-thirteenth century is also applicable to the conduct of commerce in Mughul India, Safavid Iran and Uzbek Turan in the early modern era. According to Goitein, "during the High

---

[23] *Ibid.*, 138–39.

[24] Unfortunately, the unanswered question that is implicit in this statement, that is, did non-Muslims receive equal treatment in cases of contract disputes with Muslims, cannot be answered in any satisfactory way. For an introduction to the theory of Islamic commercial law see Abraham L. Udovitch, *Partnership and Profit in Medieval Islam* (Princeton: Princeton University Press, 1970), and for discussions of the functions of certain officials who typically dealt with contracts, such as *qadis* and *muhtasibs*, Emile Tyan, *Histoire de l'organisation judiciare en pays d'Islam* (Leiden: E. J. Brill, 1960).

Middle Ages men, goods, money and books used to travel far and almost without restrictions throughout the Mediterranean area. In many respects the area resembled a free-trade community."[25] Edmund Herzig has written in a similar vein about the Armenians in the early modern period, observing that "From the Mediterranean ports of the Ottoman empire to the harbours of the Indonesian archipelago Armenians were free to travel and trade without obstruction."[26]

Indo-Muslim merchants particularly were able to travel and conduct business almost as comfortably in Iran and Turan as they could within the Mughul empire. Virtually all of them knew Persian, which was the most widely used administrative and cultural language throughout the entire region, and Central Asian immigrants to the Mughul empire also knew Turkic dialects that were widely spoken in Iran and southern Russia as well as in Turan itself. While Chaghatai Turkish – or old Uzbek – may have been spoken by the majority of Central Asian inhabitants, the urban mercantile class in Turan, commonly identified as Sarts, also used Persian, as members of the *'ulama* usually did when they recorded commercial contracts.[27] Nor were Indian Sunni Muslims subject to the kind of harassment or danger in Safavid territories that Iranian Shi'is could experience in aggressively Sunni Uzbek Turan. Shi'i–Sunni differences were never a significant issue in Mughul–Safavid relations, whose conflicts were almost entirely confined to military struggles for the control of the Afghan marches between their respective empires.

Most substantial non-Muslim merchants also knew Persian, a language that gradually became established as one of the principal spoken and written languages of the Panjab during Mughul rule.[28] If merchants had direct dealings with the court or its administrative apparatus, as many of them commonly did, they often absorbed aspects of Mughul court culture. At least two members of the large Khattri caste-group that dominated commerce in many parts of the Panjab and northwestern India became high-level Mughul officials and one of them thoroughly absorbed Indo-Persian literary culture.[29] Khattri merchants established especially close relations with Mughul provincial officials in the

[25] Goitein, *A Mediterranean Society*, 66.
[26] Edmund Herzig, "The Armenian Merchants of New Julfa, Isfahan: A Study in Pre-Modern Asian Trade," unpublished Ph.D. dissertation, Oxford, 1991, 27.
[27] For Chaghatai and "old Uzbek" see Ilse Laude Cirtautas, "On the Development of Literary Uzbek in the last Fifty Years," *Central Asiatic Review* XXI (1977), 36–51. V. Barthold discusses the Sarts, *Four Studies on the History of Central Asia*, trans. by V. and J. Minorsky (Leiden: E. J. Brill, 1962), 63. Examples of contracts can be found in Mukminova, *Social Differentiation*, 53–61.
[28] Prakash Tandon, *Punjabi Century* (Berkeley: University of California Press, 1960), 14–15.
[29] The best known of these Khattri officials was Todar Mal (d. 1589), who became *diwan*, or chief revenue officer, of the emperor Akbar, who is, though, well known for adamantly remaining an orthodox Hindu. Less well known is Iklas Khan Iklas Kish (Kishn Chand), who served under the last great Mughul emperor, Aurungzeb, and his successors and wrote a Persian biography of the emperor Farruksiyar and a *tazkirah*, a biographical dictionary of Mughul poets. T. W. Beale, *An Oriental Biographical Dictionary*, repr. (New Delhi: Manohar Reprints, 1971), 176 and 223.

Panjab.[30] Therefore, in linguistic terms at least Khattris and other non-Muslim Indian merchants could extend their commercial operations to Iran and Turan almost as easily as non-Muslim merchants. Hindus and Jains may have experienced petty harassment on caravan journeys, encouraging them to use intermediaries for the transport of their goods, and they were occasionally persecuted or even attacked in these predominantly Muslim countries in times of economic hardship or political chaos. However, Hindus or Jains apparently never suffered as much as Jews and Armenians in Iran.[31] Hindus may not have suffered official religious persecution because they wielded so much economic power, and/or because they were not regarded as Iranian citizens.[32] The one Hindu merchant whose complaints about Iranian treatment of Indian merchants have been preserved never suggested that Hindus had been singled out for abuse or excessive duties.[33]

Conditions in Russia were different for all mercantile groups. Turkic speakers enjoyed a decided advantage in dealing with the predominantly Turkic population of the former Astrakhan khanate,[34] and Armenians were granted special privileges because of their uniquely influential role as marketers of Iranian silk. Otherwise Iranian, Central Asia and Indian merchants were linguistically and legally on an equal footing. Unless they knew Russian, which many long-term residents did acquire, they had to use the mediatory services of local translators, who were usually local Turks, and each community enjoyed the same legal rights as members of ethnically defined, semi-autonomous mercantile corporations. Merchants of all communities could depend upon judicial authorities to enforce the letter of their commercial and financial contracts. They did so even to the extent that other Russian officials in the city sometimes complained that Indian merchants in particular contributed to depopulation and a lowered tax base in the city when they attempted to enforce their agreements against defaulting Turks, some of whom fled into the steppe if they were pressed for payment.[35] While

[30] Muzaffar Alam has provided important evidence and thoughtful discussions of the Khattris' relations to Mughul officials in the Panjab in the early eighteenth century in his book, *The Crises of Empire in Mughal North India, Awadh and the Punjab, 1707–1748* (Delhi: Oxford University Press, 1986); see especially pp. 169–74.

[31] Edmund Herzig usefully observes of Shah 'Abbas, "It is surprising that 'Abbas I, generally remembered as the Protector of the Christians, was in fact responsible for more instances of anti-Christian persecution than any of his successors." "Armenian merchants," 83.

[32] For the situation of Iranian Jews see Vera Basch Moreen, *Iranian Jewry During the Afghan Invasion* (Stuttgart: Franz Steiner, 1990) and *Iranian Jewry's Hour of Peril and Heroism* (New York: American Academy for Jewish research, 1987). Professor Moreen specifically mentions that none of her seventeenth-century sources alludes to persecution of Hindus in Iran, even though Jews and Armenians were certainly being mistreated. I am indebted to her for these references. The question of suffering monetary extortion is, of course, a separate issue.

[33] Antonova, II, 1647, 84–85.

[34] B. Spuler briefly describes the history of the Astrakhan khanate. "Astrakhan," *Encyclopaedia of Islam*, new ed. (Leiden: E. J. Brill, 1960), I, 721–22. See also Golikova, *Essays*, 7–35 and V. P. Nikitin, *Astrakhan' i ee Okrestnosti* [Astrakhan and its Environs] (Moscow: Iskusstvo, 1981), which has numerous pictures of what used to be a closed city.

[35] Antonova, II, nos. 109–11, 204–5.

merchants undoubtedly welcomed Russian enforcement of their contractual rights they were not pleased to have to accept relatively strong centralized monitoring and control of their own commercial affairs. All aspects of foreign merchants' life in Astrakhan would have reminded them that they were no longer operating within the laissez faire economic atmosphere of early modern Islamic empires. Mercantilism, not free trade, was the hallmark of Muscovite economic policy.

CHAPTER 2

India, Iran and Turan in 1600

In the beginning of the month of Day [October 1615] merchants came from Persia and brought pomegranates of Yazd and melons from Kariz, which are the best of the Khurasan melons . . . As my revered father (may God's light be his witness!) had a great liking for fruit I was very grieved that such fruits had not come to Hindustan in his victorious time.

The Mughul emperor Jahangir: *Tuzuk-i Jahangiri*, I, 270

The composition of Mughul India's trade with Safavid Iran and Uzbek Turan was determined primarily by contrasts between its economy and those of these two contiguous states, while the volume of exchange was influenced both by supply and demand and the commercial policies and political stability of their dynasties.[1] Mughul India possessed vastly greater natural and human resources than did Safavid and Uzbek territories; its economy also overshadowed its neighbors in terms of its overall size, diversity and sophistication. There was a consistent demand for Mughul India's natural and manufactured products in Iran and Turan, and the level of commerce was catalyzed in the second half of the sixteenth century by the achievements of two exceptionally able Mughul and Safavid rulers. These were the Mughul emperor Akbar (1556–1605) and the Safavid shah 'Abbas (1587–1629). Both men stimulated internal and external commerce by consolidating their dynasties' political authority, and by consciously instituting policies that stimulated trade. The relatively high level of stability and prosperity of the Mughul and Safavid states also contributed to an increase in commerce between them and Uzbek Turan, which itself was governed in the latter half of the sixteenth century by an unusually capable and ambitious ruler, 'Abd Allah Khan II (c. 1551–98). The commercial impetus of Akbar and Shah 'Abbas' accomplishments was sustained into the early eighteenth century, even though Uzbek Turan relapsed into congeries of autonomous Chingizid appanages following 'Abd Allah Khan's death, and Safavid Iran exhibited signs of impending collapse by the late seventeenth century.

---

[1] Mughuls referred to all of western Turkistan or Central Asia as "Turan." "Uzbek Turan" will be used throughout this work to refer to the territory controlled or dominated by the Chingizid khanates or appanages of Khiva, Bukhara (including Samarqand and Tashkent) and Balkh.

14

The economies

At Akbar's death in 1605 the Mughuls controlled or exercised hegemony over the Indo-Gangetic plains, one of Asia's richest agricultural regions. From Thatta in Sind northeast to Lahore in the Panjab then southeast to the Ganges–Jumna *duab* and the Gangetic valley to Bengal, the plains constituted a South Asian fertile crescent of immense agricultural potential.[2] A sense of the fertility of this region and the population it supported in the 1580s was conveyed with an almost intoxicated sense of elation by the Mughul historian and administrator, Khwajah Nizam al-Din Ahmad, who wrote of Akbar's territories that:

In a description of the countries ruled over by the servants of His Majesty, let it not remain concealed, that the length of the country, which is to-day in the possession of this powerful State, from Hindu Koh on the borders of Badakhshan to the country of Orissa, which on the further side of Bengal, from west to east is one thousand and two hundred Akbar Shahi *karohs* by the Ilahi yard measure . . . and its breadth from Kashmir to the hills of Bardah, which are at the extreme limit of the country of Sorath and Gujrat is eight hundred *karohs Ilahi* . . . At present there are three thousand and two hundred towns; and one or two or five hundred or a thousand villages appertain to each of these towns . . . Out of these there are one hundred and twenty great cities, which are now well populated and flourishing.[3]

Estimates of the number of people who lived in these thousands of villages, towns and cities have usually been based upon the cultivation and land revenue statistics that Nizam al-Din's contemporary, Abu'l Fadl 'Allami, supplied in his detailed gazetteer of the Mughul empire, the *A'in-i Akbari*.[4] Using Abu'l Fadl's figures scholars have variously calculated the Mughul population in 1598, the year when the *A'in* was essentially completed, at between 60 and 98 million people. More of a consensus exists with regard to the distribution of this population. It is generally although not universally agreed that approximately 85 percent of the inhabitants of Mughul territories lived in rural areas, while 15 percent resided in towns and cities.[5]

---

[2] O. H. K. Spate, *India and Pakistan*, repr. (London: Methuen, 1960), 33. Spate specifically refers to "The great crescent of alluvium from the delta of the Indus to that of the Ganges."

[3] Khwaja Nizam al-Din Ahmad, *The Tabaqat-i-Akbari*, trans. by Brajendranath De and ed. by Baini Prashad (Calcutta: Asiatic Society of Bengal, 1937), 811. The "Akbar Shahi *karohs*" represented about 2.5 miles. For explanations of this and other Mughul units of distance and measurement see Irfan Habib, *An Atlas of the Mughal Empire* (Delhi: Oxford University Press, 1982), xiii.

[4] Abu'l Fadl 'Allami, *The A'in-i Akbari*, trans. and ed. by H. Blochmann and D. C. Phillott, repr. (New Delhi: Crown Publications, 1988). Hereafter cited as AA.

[5] For discussions of the Mughul population see, among other works, Shireen Moosvi, *The Economy of the Mughal Empire, c. 1595. A Statistical Study* (Delhi: Oxford University Press, 1987), chapters 13 and 17; Irfan Habib, "Population," CEHI, I, 167, and Sanjay Subrahmanyam, *The Political Economy of Commerce: Southern India, 1500–1650* (Cambridge: Cambridge University Press, 1990), 14–17. Stephen Blake persuasively criticizes prevailing notions of the permanent population of Indian urban centers that also functioned as temporary administrative headquarters in his article "The Hierarchy of Central Places in North India during the Mughul Period of Indian History," *South Asia* VI/1 (1983), 1–32.

Many European travelers remarked upon the extensive agriculture and density of settlement in Mughul India. Those like Jean Chardin, later Sir John Chardin, who traveled in both India and Iran, were well aware of the comparatively scarce resources and scattered population of the Safavid state. Chardin, the French Huguenot jeweler and later English subject, visited India at least twice during his prolonged stays in Iran between 1666 and 1677, and said that the *"Indies . . . is a Country very Rich, Fruitful and populous . . . "*[6] Iran, in contrast, he characterized as

dry, barren, mountainous, and but thinly inhabited. I speak in general, the twelfth Part is not inhabited, nor cultivated; and after you have pass'd any great Towns about two Leagues, you will meet never a Mansion-House, nor People in twenty Leagues more. The *Western* side above all the rest, is the most defective, and wants to be peopl'd and cultivated the most of any, and nothing is to be met with there almost, but large and spacious Deserts. This barrenness proceeds from no other Cause than the scarcity of Water, there is a want of it in most Parts of the whole Kingdom, where they are forc'd to preserve the Rain-water, or to seek for it very deep in the Entrails of the Earth. For in all the Places where there is a good store of Water, the soil is kindly, fertile and agreeable.[7]

The productive possibilities of Safavid lands for settled agriculture were poor. Even the two largest river systems within the expanded boundaries of the state achieved by Shah 'Abbas, the Araks–Kura duab and the Arghandab–Helmand basin, were modest waterways in relation to Mughul India's great river systems. They were also inconveniently located on the state's northwestern and southeastern frontiers respectively. With the exception of its Transcaucasian and Caspian provinces most Safavid territories were situated on the Iranian plateau, a region that has been characterized in modern geographical terms as an interior basin, an "arid zone with green islets" scattered over it, a "parched country" in which "the religious and traditional value of water . . . has been magnified in Zoroastrianism" and symbolized by the association of paradise with irrigated gardens.[8] Agriculturalists in Iran also had to compete continuously with pastoral nomads for scarce resources. They often lost this struggle between the tenth and sixteenth centuries when the plateau was repeatedly inundated by migrations and invasions of Turkic and Mongol tribes and armies, and during the early period of Safavid rule particularly the Qizilbash tribal supporters of the dynasty often enjoyed virtual autonomy in many regions of the country. Throughout the Safavid period Qizilbash and other tribes made up a significant proportion of the country's population, functioned as a distinct sector of its

---

[6] (Sir) John Chardin [Jean Chardin], *Travels in Persia 1673–1677*, repr. (Mineola, N.Y.: Dover Books, 1988), 130. On Chardin see John Emerson, "Chardin, Sir John," *Encyclopaedia Iranica* V, fasc. 3 (1991), 369–77 and Anne Kroell, "Douze lettres de Jean Chardin," *Journal Asiatique* CCLXX/3–4 (1982), 295–338.

[7] Chardin, *Travels in Persia*, 128.

[8] J. Behnan, "Population," CHI, I, 470–71, and Elizabeth Moynihan, *Paradise as a Garden: In Persia and Mughal India* (New York: Braziller, 1979).

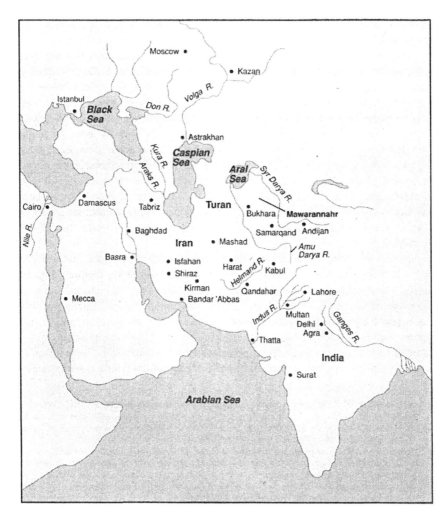

Map 1 India, Iran and Turan

economy and represented a major and often dominant force in its military and political life.[9]

Population estimates for Safavid Iran have no statistical bases that are even comparable to Abu'l Fadl's land revenue and land tenure data.[10] Scholars who have offered estimates have rarely made explicit their assumptions or sources; their calculations seem to be based variously on anecdotal accounts of European travelers or retrogressive analyses that extrapolate from twentieth-century census figures. All such calculations appear to refer broadly to the seventeenth century rather than to a particular year or decade. Implicit in the figures is the assumption that they represent the Safavid population in the period following Shah 'Abbas' conquests, which brought several regions under Safavid control that were subsequently lost to the modern Iranian state. These include districts in eastern Anatolia, Mesopotamia, Transcaucasia and most of southern and western Afghanistan, up to and usually including the city of Qandahar.[11]

Thomas Herbert, a young member of the English diplomatic mission that arrived in Iran in 1627, two years before Shah 'Abbas' death, reported that the country had ninety walled towns and approximately 40,000 villages, although considering Herbert's limited experience in the country these figures probably represented a formulaic number that he had received from an informant.[12] Some modern scholars have estimated that these sedentary inhabitants plus Iran's large nomadic population totaled between five and ten million people in the seventeenth century,[13] but others have argued that even the figure of five million is improbably

[9] I. P. Petrushevsky, "The Socio-Economic Condition of Iran Under the Il-khans," CHI, V, 489–505. An idea of the pivotal role that Qizilbash tribes played in Safavid history can be seen in Eskandar Beg Monshi, History of Shah 'Abbas the Great [Tarik-e 'Alamara-ye 'Abbasi], trans. by Roger Savory (Boulder, Colo.: Westview Press, 1986), 486.

[10] Bert Fragner, "Social and Internal Economic Affairs," CHI, VI, 491ff. passim, It is indicative of the problem that no scholar writing in the Cambridge History of Iran attempts to estimate the population of Iran, for which there is not even a citation in the index to volume VI. While the Mongols undoubtedly took some type of census in Iran during the Ilkhanid period (1218–1336), the first modern census of Iran took place only in 1956!

[11] Safavid provinces are listed in V. Minorsky, ed. and trans., Tadhkirat al-Muluk, repr. (Cambridge: Cambridge University Press for E. J. W. Gibb Memorial Series, 1980), 164–73. Mughul–Safavid struggles for Qandahar are summarized on 169.

[12] Thomas Herbert, Travels in Persia, 1627–1629, repr. (Freeport, N.Y.: Books for Libraries Press, 1972), 224. Minorsky suggests that Herbert's estimate probably represents the received tradition of Shah 'Abbas' time. Tadhkirat al-Muluk, 162.

[13] Minorsky, Tadhkirat al-Muluk, 186; Charles Issawi, The Economic History of Iran, 1880–1914 (Chicago: University of Chicago Press, 1971), 28; John Foran, "The Modes of Production Approach to Seventeenth Century Iran," International Journal of Middle Eastern Studies XX/3 (Aug. 1988), 360 and n. 39; and Firuz Tawfiq, "Census I. In Persia," in E. Yarshater, ed., Encyclopaedia Iranica, V, fasc. 2 (Costa Mesa, Calif.: Mazda, 1990), 142–52. According to the 1956 census the rural population of Iran was 13,001,141 and the urban population was 5,953,563. Tawfiq, "Census I. In Persia," 145.

Regarding the Afghan provinces of the Safavid state, the first modern census of Afghanistan took place only in the "late 1970s" when the population was listed as 13,051,358 sedentary and 771,463 nomadic. Daniel Balland, "Census II. In Afghanistan," in E. Yarshater, ed., Encyclopaedia Iranica, V, fasc. 2, 157.

high.[14] Considering the various estimates, the modern Iranian census and the country's modest agricultural potential, it seems possible that the Safavid state could have contained as many as seven to eight million inhabitants at the height of Shah 'Abbas' military successes when he controlled substantial territories in Mesopotamia.[15] A figure of between five and six million seems more reasonable after those districts were lost. Given the aridity of most of the Iranian countryside the ratio of urban to rural settlement may have been higher in Iran than it was in Mughul India. This seems especially likely if the experienced, Persian-speaking Jean Chardin was even remotely accurate when he estimated that Isfahan and Tabriz, Safavid Iran's most populous cities in the seventeenth century, each contained more than 500,000 people.[16]

Chardin's description of Iran's desiccated, thinly populated countryside might just as easily have been used to characterize the agrarian resources and population distribution in Uzbek Turan which, like Iran, was also a region of persisting competition between agriculturalists and pastoral nomads throughout the Mughul and Safavid periods. Parts of the Uzbek territories may have been more desolate than Iran's central deserts, particularly the vast region between the Amu Darya river and the Caspian that the English Muscovy Company factor, Anthony Jenkinson, described in 1557 and 1558.[17] This area was capable of supporting only a small number of pastoral nomads. Yet significant areas within the region had enough water to support intensive agriculture and/or substantial numbers of pastoralists. These included the northern slopes of the Hindu Kush mountains, especially the territory around Balkh, and extensive stretches of land within Mawarannahr, in particular the upper and lower reaches of the Amu Darya, the Zarafshan valley between Samarqand and Bukhara and the upper reaches of the Syr Darya between the Ferghana valley and Tashkent.[18] Irrigated tracts in these areas also benefited from the exceptional fertility of the soil, much of which was

---

[14] Conversation with A. S. Morton of the School of Oriental and African Studies, London, March 1991.

[15] In fact, all population estimates for Safavid Iran are sheer conjecture. Most retrogressive analyses from twentieth-century figures do not allude to territorial differences between modern Iran and the Safavid state. For a recent, refreshingly critical study of Iranian demographics see J. Guerney, "Rewriting the Social History of Late Safavid Iran," in Charles Melville, ed., *Pembroke Papers*, I: *Persian and Islamic Studies in Honour of P. W. Avery* (Cambridge: Centre of Middle Eastern Studies, Cambridge University, 1990), 43–57.

[16] W. Barthold, *An Historical Geography of Iran*, trans. by Svat Soucek and ed. by C. E. Bosworth (Princeton: Princeton University Press, 1984), 177 and 222.

[17] Anthony Jenkinson, *Early Voyages and Travels to Russia and Persia*, ed. by E. Delmar Morgan and C. H. Coote (London: Hakluyt Society, 1886), II, 66–82. See also "Puteshestvie v Sredniaia Aziiu [Antoni Dzhenkinsona] [Journey to Central Asia [of Anthony Jenkinson]] in B. A. Akhmedov, *Istoriko-geograficheskaia literatura Srednei Azii*, XVI–XVII vv [Historical-geographical literature of Central Asia of the sixteenth and seventeenth centuries] (Tashkent: fan, 1985), 194–200. For a recent survey of the population and geography of the region see Ian Murray Matley, "The Population and the Land," in Edward Allworth, ed., *Central Asia* (Durham, N.C.: Duke University Press, 1989), 92–130.

[18] E. D. Murzaev, ed., *Srednaia Azia* [Central Asia])Moscow: Akademii Nauk, 1968), maps 73 and 78; and W. Rickmer Rickmers, *The Duab of Turkistan* (Cambridge: Cambridge University Press, 1913), 44–55 and map 2.

formed from the same loess deposits that made China's Yellow river basin so remarkably productive.[19]

The relative strength of Uzbek Turan's agrarian and nomadic economies depended upon the degree to which a state could protect and expand irrigation systems.[20] In the second half of the fifteenth century, for example, Timurid rulers presided over an expansion of irrigation canals in the Bukhara region. Uzbek conquests and subsequent succession disputes among their leaders devastated segments of the region's agricultural economy in the sixteenth century, but 'Abd Allah Khan II presided over sharply increased irrigation work in the latter half of the century.[21] The reassertion of autonomous tribal authority after 'Abd Allah Khan's death in 1598 undoubtedly meant that the total amount of irrigated land and settled agriculture increased only slowly throughout the seventeenth and eighteenth century. Even within Mawarannahr it is unlikely to have exceeded 10 percent of the total land area, an estimate that was made for the region in the early twentieth century.[22] Yet income from settled agriculture probably still generated the largest amount of revenue for various rulers in Uzbek Turan, as it was reliably estimated to do for the independent appanage of Qunduz in the early nineteenth century.[23]

Population estimates for Uzbek Turan in the seventeenth century are equally as conjectural as those for Safavid Iran. The earliest Russian census of 1897 counted 7,746,818 inhabitants in Russian Turkistan, with the largest concentrations found in the Ferghana and Syr Darya provinces, each of which held about 1.5 million people at that time. This census did not include the still autonomous khanates of Bukhara and Khiva, but these were estimated to have a combined population of three million at this period.[24] None of these figures, though, included the Balkh

---

[19] Rickmers, *The Duab of Turkistan*, 36–39 and Arminius Vambery, *Sketches of Central Asia*, repr. (Taipei: Ch'eng Wen Publishing Co., 1971), 237.

[20] See, for example, the description of nomadic attacks in Balkh by B. A. Amhmedov, *Istoriia Balkha* [The History of Balkh] (Tashkent: Fan, 1982), 124 and McChesney, *Waqf in Central Asia*, 28–29.

[21] A. R. Mukhamedzhanov, *Istoriia Orosheniia Bukharskogo Oazis* [History of Irrigation of the Bukhara Oasis] (Tashkent: Fan, 1978), 108–14.

[22] Rickmers, *The Duab of Turkistan*, 25. Rickmers, who traveled widely in Mawarannahr, wrote that "It will greatly simplify the reader's conception of the Duab if he looks upon the whole of it as one tract of desert and steppe, whether flat or mountainous, high or low, and upon fields and gardens as nothing but oases content with a small portion of the entire surface. On a liberal estimate, all patches of cultivation with villages and cities occupy a tenth of the total land area."

[23] (Sir) Alexander Burnes, "A Memoir on the Uzbek State of Kunduz," No. XI, "Political," in Sir Alexander Burnes et al., *Reports and Papers, Political, Geographical and Commercial* (Calcutta: Military Orphan Press, 1839). See also McChesney's comments on irrigated agriculture in the Balkh oasis, *Waqf in Central Asia*, 21–26 and Mir Izzet Ullah, "'Travels Beyond the Himalayas', from *The Calcutta Oriental Quarterly Magazine*, 1825," in *Journal of the Royal Asiatic Society* VII (1853), 336–37.

[24] Lawrence Krader, *Peoples of Central Asia* (Bloomington, Indiana: Indiana University Press, 1963), 171–72 and 198. In 1832–33 Alexander Burnes estimated the population of Bukhara to be 150,000. *Travels into Bokhara*, III, 159–60. Jean-Paul Roux offers a very interesting, positive assessment of the level of urbanization of Mawarannahr in the Timurid period: "Urbanisation et villes timourides: comparison avec l'Europe et l'Empire ottoman," *Histoire des Grands Moghols, Babur* (Paris: Fayard, 1986), 371–76.

region that was then part of Afghan territory. The same census estimated that 86 percent of the population of Turkistan lived in rural areas with 14 percent resident in towns and cities,[25] but unfortunately no attempt seems to have been made to differentiate between agriculturalists and nomads. This latter figure must still have been quite high given the decentralized political structure of the Uzbek territories. Considering these data, including the fact that Bukhara and Khiva were desert oasis cities, it seems unlikely that the early seventeenth-century population of Uzbek Turan, including Balkh, could have exceeded five million people. Then as in the late nineteenth century the rich Ferghana valley and the Zarafshan and the Amu Darya river systems must have supported the largest population concentrations.

When compared with the meagre agricultural potential and a modest number of inhabitants in Safavid Iran and Uzbek Turan the disparate size of Mughul India's agrarian resources and population is an unmistakable clue to its stature as a regional "world economy."[26] Northern India possessed enormous agrarian and human resources that generated a diverse agricultural and manufacturing economy. These resources allowed it to become a net exporter of goods to these neighboring areas, a trade imbalance that is best documented in the case of Mughul commercial relations with Iran. Mughul India's exports primarily consisted of bulky staples, rather than the luxury items that are commonly thought to have predominated in this intra-Asian commerce. The most valuable commodities in this trade were a variety of food and non-food crops, some of which could only be grown easily in India's subtropical climate, and cotton textiles, India's premier export since Roman times. Imported into Mughul territories were a number of specialty crops and luxury manufactures, most of them destined for the Mughul elite, and the one commodity that both elite and Mughul emperors regarded as a necessity, central Asian horses for their cavalry, the backbone of the imperial army.

All three of these regions appear to have been largely self-sufficient in most basic foodstuffs, but a number of agricultural products were exchanged between them. From India some specialty crops were exported to these neighboring areas. Saffron grown in Sind and pan and betel leaf coveted at the Safavid court would have been sold abroad in relatively small amounts.[27] More significant was tobacco. While it only began to be cultivated in India during the Mughul period tobacco quickly became an important export to Iran and probably Turan as well.[28] These commodities were overshadowed in both amount and value, though, by

[25] Krader, *Peoples of Central Asia*, 202.
[26] Fernand Braudel, *Perspective of the World*, 25 and 484.
[27] R. W. Ferrier, "An English View of Persian Trade in 1618," *Journal of the Economic and Social History of the Orient* XIX/2 (1976), 207, for saffron exports and Riazul Islam, *A Calendar of Documents on Indo-Persian Relations, 1500–1750* (Karachi: Institute of Central and West Asian Studies, 1979), I, 443 for pan exports.
[28] Irfan Habib, "The Systems of Agricultural Production, Mughul India," CEHI, I, 217 and R. W. Ferrier, "Trade from the mid-14th Century to the End of the Safavid Period," CHI, VI, 475.

Mughul India's most important agricultural exports, sugar and indigo.[29] It was probably a measure of the cost of indigo imports and its potential importance as a cash crop for Iran that Shah 'Abbas attempted to introduce the cultivation of this widely used textile dye into his Mazandaran province, along the Caspian shore, where the humid climate was suited to its cultivation.[30] The Safavid ruler's efforts were apparently unsuccessful in substantially curtailing the flow of Indian indigo into the country, but they show that he was fully aware of the restricted export potential of the Iranian economy, with its modest natural and human resources.

Mughul India's agricultural imports were primarily specialty rather than staple crops. They included the widely used food flavoring and medicinal gum resin asafoetida that was grown in the Safavids' eastern provinces, and varieties of fresh and dried fruits and nuts that complemented those found in the Mughuls' Afghan territories. These latter imports may have had as great a cultural as an economic significance, for they were prized by the Mughul elite and especially by members of the ruling family. The Mughuls' nostalgic taste for melons, dried apricots and almonds echoes their political irredentism for Timurid homelands in Turan. Mughul rulers' well-known longing for Central Asian or similar Iranian fruits that Zahir al-Din Muhammad Babur, the founder of the Mughul empire, affectingly expressed in his memoirs,[31] was powerful enough to trigger a minor diplomatic contretemps between the Mughul emperor Shah Jahan (1628–56) and Safavid officials in the early 1640s. In 1641 or 1642 the Mughul emperor ordered that caravans from Iran should be prohibited from entering Mughul territory, because he had learned from his governor of Qandahar that Iranian officials had banned the export of an especially coveted variety of Iranian melon known by the name of the principal village where it was cultivated as *kharbuzah-i kariz*.[32] In the eyes of the governor the Iranian actions were "very unfriendly proceedings."[33] Upon being informed that only a poor harvest had caused the supply to be interrupted Shah Jahan relented and permitted caravan traffic to resume.

Considering the crops involved, Mughul India probably enjoyed a favorable balance in agricultural goods with both Iran and Turan; it unmistakably did so when it came to the marketing of textiles, and especially the sales of cotton cloth.

---

[29] One of the earliest references to the export of Indian sugar is that by the founder of the Mughul empire, Zahir al-Din Muhammad Babur, during a period when he was still merely the ruler of Kabul and knowledgeable about the transit commerce through the city. See Annette Susannah Beveridge, trans. and ed., *The Babur-nama in English* (London: Luzac, 2nd ed., 1969), 202. Sugar and indigo are both listed as Indian exports to Iran in Ferrier's useful summary of an English East India Company factor's early evaluation of Anglo-Iranian and Indo-Iranian commerce: "An English View of Persian Trade," 182–214. One of the first detailed reports of Indian indigo exports to Bukhara was by Alexander Burnes, *Reports and Papers*, "Commercial," 56.

[30] Islam, *Calendar of Indo-Persian Relations*, I, 164.

[31] Beveridge, *The Babur-nama in English*, 645, among numerous other references.

[32] J. P. Ferrier, *Caravan Journeys and Wanderings in Persia, Afghanistan, Turkey and Beloochistan*, trans. by William Jesse (London: John Murray, end ed., 1857), 138. It was evidently this melon that Jahangir mentioned in his memoirs. See also AA, I, 69.

[33] Islam, *Calendar of Indo-Persian Relations*, I, 285–86. It is, of course, probable that this incident was related to the Mughul–Safavid struggles over Qandahar.

Cotton was cultivated in all three areas, but northern India's extensive tracts of arable land and comparatively large population had generated a proportionate-sized and diverse cotton textile industry that dwarfed the productive capacity of those arid, thinly populated neighboring regions.[34] In lieu, as usual, of statistics that could conclusively document this relationship, the relative strengths of Mughul, Safavid and Uzbek cotton textile industries are indicated by the lack of references to Mughul imports of Iranian or Central Asian fabrics and the multiplicity of references to the sales of Indian cloth in those regions.

In the case of Safavid Iran an idea of the volume of cotton cloth exports from Mughul territories is suggested by the English estimate that in 1661 the value of cotton fabrics shipped to Iran only from the Gujarati port of Surat was one million rupees.[35] It is conceivable that a comparable amount was shipped overland via Qandahar in the same year. Little more than a decade later Chardin offered both a general explanation for the sale of Indian cotton textiles in Iran and a specific reason for the successful marketing of certain varieties. He observed, first of all, that "The *Persians* do not understand to make cloth [although] they make very fine and very light Felt Tufts." He went on to add that

They make also *Calico Cloth* very reasonable; but they make none fine, because they have it cheaper out of the *Indies* than they can make it [and] . . . they understand also the painting of Linnen, but not so well as the *Indians*, because they buy in the Indies the finest painted Linnen so cheap, that they would get nothing by improving themselves in that Manufacture.[36]

Chardin's comments summarized the competitive advantage in price and quality that Indian cotton textiles enjoyed over those of the entire Middle East and Europe at this period, and like the English Iranians also sought to lessen their dependence on Indian textiles by stimulating local production.[37] However, as was true of Shah 'Abbas' attempt to grow indigo, he apparently also failed to increase significantly Iran's cotton cloth output.[38] It seems unlikely that it could have been raised very quickly without first substantially expanding the amount of irrigated land available for cotton production, an expensive, long-term undertaking.

---

[34] This is not to say that neither area produced some competitively priced, high-quality cotton goods. The Russians located a Bukharan "master-dyer" in Astrakhan when they were searching for experts to improve their cloth production in the 1660s. Antonova, I, nos. 78–80, 1665, 156–57. In the nineteenth century cotton cloth from certain Iranian cities such as Bam in the southeast and cotton fiber from towns in Mawarannahr were famous for their high quality. See Barthold, *Historical Geography*, 139, Vambery, *Sketches of Central Asia*, 246–49 and Fragner, "Social and Internal Economic Affairs," CHI, VI, 494.

[35] Chaudhuri, *Trading World*, 196–97. See also pp. 243–45 for a list of Indian exports to West Asia, although note that this list of production centers in India and the accompanying map omit an important southern Panjabi manufacturing city and entrepôt, Multan. This omission is then repeated by Braudel, since he uses Chaudhuri as his source for this topic. *Perspective of the World*, 507.

[36] Chardin, *Travels in Persia*, 278–79.

[37] For an excellent summary of English attempts to respond to Indian textile imports see Chaudhuri, *Trading World*, 237ff. *passim*.

[38] Ferrier, "An English View of Persian Trade," 206.

Exports of Indian cloth from Mughul territories to Uzbek Turan are well documented in contemporary sources. When Anthony Jenkinson finally fought his way into Bukhara in December 1557 after a perilous journey across the desert from the Caspian with an armed caravan, he reported that Indian merchants were selling textiles in the city. Jenkinson said that Indian merchants, some of whom came from as far away as Bengal, "doe bring fine whites which serue for apparell being made of cotton wooll and crasko [coarse linen], but gold and siluer, pretious stones, and spices they bring none."[39] Forty years later another Indian merchant who worked in the neighboring city of Samarqand showed that some Indians had taken the next logical step in the export of Indian textiles by moving production to the market. This man, Darya Khan Multani, had evidently used his capital to bring Indian textile artisans to Samarqand, where they manufactured cloth using locally produced yarns and wool.[40]

Indians did import some silk from both Iran and Turan throughout the Mughul period and into the nineteenth century. Silk was Iran's premier export to Europe as well as Asia, and sales of the cloth generated most of Safavid Iran's foreign exchange.[41] As early as 1618 English East India Company factors learned that "bannyans," a term that Europeans used to refer either to Indian merchants or moneylenders, carried Khurasan silk to India via Lahore or, more rarely, via Hurmuz. According to these Englishmen, while Indians had formerly imported mainly raw silk or silk thread they were then purchasing cloth.[42] It is likely, though, that Indian merchants imported thread as well as cloth throughout the Mughul period, for they were bringing both into India in the early nineteenth century via Shikarpur, the small entrepôt situated at the eastern entrance of the Bolan pass.[43] Bukhara was also a source of both raw silk and silk cloth for India. Jenkinson said that Indian merchants bought "wrought silks" in that city,[44] although early nineteenth-century European observers primarily refer to the importation of silk thread which was then woven into cloth at Shikarpur or Multan.[45]

---

[39] Jenkinson, *Early Voyages and Travels*, II, 87.

[40] Mukminova, *Social Differentiation*, 53–68. This important, unusually well-documented example of a South Asian merchant's business will be discussed in detail in chapter 2.

[41] It is surprising that there is still no comprehensive study of Iran's silk industry, considering its importance during the Safavid period. For a preliminary, unpublished study see Linda K. Steinmann, "Shah 'Abbas I and the Royal Silk Trade, 1599–1629," unpublished Ph.D. dissertation, New York University, 1986. Professor Rudolph P. Matthee is currently working on a major study of the Safavid silk trade.

[42] Ferrier, "An English View of Persian Trade," 203. See AA, I, 98–102, for types of Iranian silk and satin textiles imported into Mughul India.

[43] T. Postans, "Miscellaneous Information Relative to the town of Shikarpoor . . . In the Years 1840 and 1841," India Office Library, 92.

[44] Jenkinson, *Early Voyages and Travels*, II, 88.

[45] G. T. Vigne, *A Personal Narrative of a Visit to Ghuzni, Kabul and Afghanistan*, repr. (Lahore: Sang-e-Meel Publications, 1982), 21–22. Vigne wrote about his visit to Multan in 1836 that "Seven hundred maunds of raw silk are brought to Multan every year by the Lohanis [an Afghan tribe], chiefly from Bokhara and Turkistan; these are manufactured in one hundred and fifty workshops."

Silk, like fruit and nuts, was a luxury import whose end products were destined for a small stratum of the Indian population, and while the value of imported silk thread and cloth has to remain a matter of conjecture it could not have balanced India's staple exports of cotton cloth, indigo and sugar. Apart from carpets, another luxury manufacture that the Mughul elite particularly coveted,[46] only two commodities were available in sufficient quantities to offset Mughul India's favorable trade balance with Iran and Turan, horses and precious metals. Nomads of both areas raised a surplus of horses that Mughul rulers, commanders and cavalrymen valued as mounts. In this they were only perpetuating Indians' historic preference for the tough steppe horses over indigenous stock.[47] Whatever the value of such local animals as the famous light Maratha ponies, India's climate and lack of proper grazing land seems to have made it impossible to develop brands with the endurance of Turkic or mixed Turkic and Iranian animals that both Mughuls and members of the English East India Company preferred.[48] Chinese emperors exhibited a similar, well-known preference for Central Asian mounts throughout most of recorded Chinese history.[49]

Mughul rulers themselves frequently ordered small numbers of animals directly from Iran or Turan, as did Jahangir in 1607 when he instructed his commercial agent, Kamran Beg, to buy superior quality horses when he visited the Safavid court.[50] An especially droll instance of the lengths to which emperors would go to acquire additional Central Asian mounts occurred when Jahangir's father, Akbar, ordered that members of two heterodox sects of "shaikhs and faqirs" be deported to Qandahar and sold there in exchange for Turkic horses.[51] Akbar evidently attempted to exercise a measure of control over major horse dealers who sold animals to the imperial stables in Agra, but neither he nor any of his successors seem to have felt the need to adopt the Chinese system of establishing a government department that dealt directly with pastoral nomadic suppliers.[52] The actual commerce appears to have been left mainly in the hands of Afghan, Iranian and Turkic merchants who, in the last decade of Akbar's reign, supplied as

---

[46] See among other references Ferrier, "An English View of Persian Trade," 203. By Akbar's day, however, most carpets were being manufactured in India. AA, I, 57.

[47] The clearest statement of the rationale for and the number of horses that were imported into India from Turan in pre-Mughal times is that of the Arab traveler, Ibn Battuta. H. A. R. Gibb, ed., *The Travels of Ibn Battuta* (Cambridge: Cambridge University Press, 1936), II, 478–79.

[48] Richard Meixsel, "Horses and Empire in Muslim India," unpublished seminar paper, Department of History, Ohio State University, 1989, 6–9 and William Foster, *The English Factories in India, 1670–1677* (Oxford: Clarendon Press, 1936), 178.

[49] C. H. G. Creel, "The Role of the Horse in Chinese History," *American Historical Review* LXX/3 (April 1965), 647–72.

[50] Islam, *Calendar of Indo-Persian Relations*, 152.

[51] al-Bada'uni ['Abd al-Qadir ibn Muluk Shah], *Muntakhabu-T-Tawarikh*, trans. by G. Ranking and ed. by B. P. Ambashthya, repr. (Patna: Academica Asiatica, 1973), II, 308–9.

[52] Moosvi, *Economy of the Mughal Empire*, 242 and Morris Rossabi, "The Tea and Horse Trade with Inner Asia during the Ming," *Journal of Asian History* XLII (1970), 136–68.

many as 1,000 Iranian and 21,000 Turkic horses for the imperial cavalry every year.[53]

The sales of Indian cotton textiles, indigo and sugar in Uzbek Turan were evidently sufficient to pay for thousands of Turkic horses that merchants purchased every year for the Indian market. At least little evidence exists to show that Mughul currency or bullion was used to purchase these animals, for only a few Mughul coins, and those of the first two emperors Babur (r. 1526–30) and Humayun (r. 1530–40, 1555–56), have been discovered in Central Asian coin hoards.[54] In Iran, though, which exported fewer expensive cavalry horses to India, imports of Indian agricultural and textile goods produced a large deficit that could not be bridged with sales of Iran's premier export, silk cloth. Edward Pettus, an English East India Company agent in Isfahan, summarized the economic relationship succinctly in 1614 when he wrote that "The Banians, in return for their linens, carry most of the silver and gold out of the country," although some of this drain was also due to the profits that Indian merchants made from their financial operations and currency manipulations.[55] A microcosm of this trade relationship can be seen in the way that English East India Company factors in Surat sold Indian goods in Iran to generate specie for their trade in India and elsewhere. Typical of the cargoes that their ships brought from Iran in the seventeenth century were the 1,000 *tumans*, three horses and some unspecified "freight goods" that arrived in India abroad the *Francis* in April 1637.[56] The

[53] Moosvi, *Economy of the Mughul Empire*, 378 and Rossabi, "Tea and Horse Trade," 146. The Ming purchased about 14,000 horses from Central Asian suppliers each year in the fourteenth century for the limited purpose of frontier defense. This suggests that Moosvi's figures might be, if anything, too conservative since the Mughuls used horses for the principal striking forces of their armies.

[54] E. A. Davidovitch, "Klad serebrianykh Monet XVI v. iz Tadzhikistana [Hoard of Silver Money of the XVIth century of Tajikistan], in E. B. Shelov, ed., *Numizmatika i Epigrafika* [Numismatics and Epigraphics], III (Moscow: Nauka, 1970), 77 and Davidovitch, *Klady Drevnikh i Srednevekovykh Monet Tadzhikistana* [Hoards of Ancient and Medieval Money of Tajikistan] (Moscow: Nauka, 1979), no. 78, 380–934, especially n. 2, pp. 392–3.

[55] Quoted by Rabino di Borgomale, *Coins, Medals, and Seals of the Shahs of Iran, 1500–1941* (Oxford: Oxford University Press, 1951), 33. No systematic study of Safavid–Mughul gold/silver ratios has been done, and care should be taken when making generalizations on this complex subject. See also Ferrier, "The Armenians and the East India Company in Persia in the Seventeenth and Early Eighteenth Centuries," *The Economic History Review*, 2nd ser., XXVI/1 (1973), 56 n. 1 for the Armenian currency trade. Fragner, "Social and Internal Economic Affairs," CHI, VI, 564–65, show how greatly the gold/silver ratios within Iran fluctuated in the seventeenth century alone. Rudolph Matthee argues that extreme caution must also be used when discussing the relation between exchange rates and Iranian exports to India. Matthee, "Politics and Trade," 275. See chapter 2 for discussions of Indian moneylending profits in Iran.

[56] Foster, *The English Factories in India, 1637–1641*, 242. The *tuman* was not a coin but a "money of account." In 1664 a tuman equaled fifty silver 'abbasis. In the seventeenth century its ratio to the rupee varied from 24 to 30 rupees per tuman. Borgomale, *Coins, Medals, and Seals*, xv and 4. For discussion of "moneys of account," which also included the Russian rouble in the seventeenth century, see E. E. Rich and C. H. Wilson, *The Cambridge Economic History of Europe*, V, *The Economy of Expanding Europe in the Sixteenth and Seventeenth Centuries* (Cambridge: Cambridge University Press, 1967), 378–91, and Herman Van der Wee, *The Growth of the Antwerp Market and the European Economy* (The Hague: Martinus Nijhoff, 1963), chapter 3, "Money and the History of Prices."

overall trade imbalance with India helped to produce a chronic silver shortage in Iran throughout much of the seventeenth century.[57] The problem was already so acute in Shah 'Abbas time it was reported to be a capital crime for Indian merchants to export currency from the country,[58] but these draconian restrictions, if indeed they were ever systematically enforced, had no evident effect, and the currency hemorrhage continued down to the collapse of the Safavid dynasty in 1722.[59]

Safavid Iran's chronic currency shortage was undoubtedly due in part to its lack of workable precious metal deposits, although that problem did not distinguish it significantly from Mughul India or Uzbek Turan. None of these states are known to have possessed significant gold or silver reserves; silver deposits in the Hindu Kush that produced large amounts of coins in the Samanid period (819–1005) were evidently exhausted by the sixteenth century.[60] Iran still had workable copper deposits in Khurasan but its gold and silver mines had been depleted by Safavid times.[61] Copper was also found in Mughul territories, but like the Safavids the Mughuls possessed no significant gold or silver deposits. However, it is a well-known feature of Mughul economic history that the state benefited from the enormous currency influx from both Europe and the Middle East to pay for purchases of Indian cloth, indigo and other products.[62] The state's surplus of precious metals allowed it to produce the heavy, exceptionally pure and finely designed gold and silver coins that were emblems of the dynasty's prosperity.

Turan's resources, like virtually every other aspect of the economy in that region in the early modern period, are more difficult to assess. Gold was apparently obtainable in significant amounts in Ferghana in the sixteenth and seventeenth century,[63] and it was present in the bed of the Zarafshan and other rivers of the area. W. Rickmer Rickmers, who toured Mawarannahr in the late

---

[57] Ferrier, "An English View of Persian Trade," 193. Note that Richard Steel and John Crowther, who traveled overland from India to Iran in 1616, reported only that the export of all currency except that of the reigning monarch was prohibited. Richard Steel and John Crowther, "Journey of Richard Steel and John Crowther, from Ajmeer in India, to Isfahan in Persia, in the Years 1615 and 1616," in Robert Kerr, ed., *A General Collection of Voyages and Travels* (Edinburgh: Blackwood, 1824), IX, 206–19. See also Borgomale, *Coins, Medals, and Seals*, 39, for an extreme statement on the outflow of Iranian currency to India.

[58] Borgomale cites an example of an Englishman executed for exporting currency. *Ibid.*, 33.

[59] Mr. Stephen Album states that the assertion of some British and Dutch sources that Safavid currency shortages led to a severe debasement of the coinage is not borne out by numismatic studies of extant Safavid coins. Personal letter to the author, 4 November 1991. However, Professor Matthee cogently argues that the opinion of experienced British and Dutch merchants ought to be taken seriously, even if no examples of debased coins are currently known. "Politics and Trade," 289.

[60] John S. Deyell, *Living Without Silver* (Delhi: Oxford University Press, 1990), 58 n. 2.

[61] Fragner, "Social and Internal Economic Affairs" CHI, VI, 498 and J. V. Harrison, "Minerals," in *ibid.*, I, 489–517.

[62] John S. Deyell, "The Development of Akbar's Currency System and Monetary Integration of the Conquered Kingdoms," in J. F. Richards, ed., *The Imperial Monetary System of Mughal India* (Delhi: Oxford University Press, 1987), 20 and 64–65 n. 17 on copper supplies, and Om Prakash, "Foreign Merchants and Indian Mints in the Seventeenth and Early Eighteenth Century," in *ibid.*, 171–72, for examples of the European currency influx.

[63] Mukimova, *Social Differentiation*, 79.

nineteenth and early twentieth century, "heard" that as much as £30,000 a year of gold ore could be sifted from the rivers in the mountainous eastern areas of the Bukhara khanate.[64] Whether this ore had ever been systematically extracted in the Uzbek period is not known. None of the Uzbek states or appanages appear to have possessed workable silver deposits.[65] In the sixteenth and seventeenth century Uzbeks may have plundered some silver from their expeditions into Safavid Khurasan, but it is likely that they, like the Safavids, suffered from a persistent shortage. At least silver was among the commodities that Bukhara wanted to obtain from Mughul India in 1671.[66] The khanate may have procured significant amounts of the metal through its large horse trade with Russia; both Russian specie and Dutch coins were imported into Bukhara in the early nineteenth century, when some of this money was also being re-exported to India.[67]

All three states issued gold, silver and copper currency, but gold coins rarely circulated in any of them in the seventeenth century. Gold coins appear to have been minted most frequently in India at this period, where they were even occasionally used to pay salaries, but the finely designed and stamped *muhr* (10.9 g, 1584–1605) rarely circulated.[68] The muhr was used instead as a convenient form of accumulation in royal treasuries and for private savings.[69] The Safavid gold coins, either Ashrafis or, under Shah 'Abbas the 'Abbasi (9.33 g–7.776 g, 1588–1629), were entirely ceremonial coins that rulers used as gifts.[70] The Uzbek gold *tilla* probably fell into the same category in the

---

[64] Rickmers, *The Duab of Turkistan*, 426. Henry Lansdell, on the other hand, asserted in the late nineteenth century at least gold ore was not available in commercial quantities. *Russian Central Asia*, repr. (New York: Arno Press, 1970), 381–82.

[65] In the nineteenth century different opinions on possible silver resources were given by Vambery, *Sketches of Central Asia*, 254, who reported that some silver might be found in Khiva, and Nikolay Murav'yov, *Journey to Khiva through the Turkoman Country*, repr. (London: Oguz Press, 1977), 108 and 137, who stated that no significant amounts of gold and silver were obtainable in the area at that time.

[66] Antonova, I, no. 93, 1671, 171.

[67] V. G. Volonikov and N. A. Khalfin, *Zapiski o Bukharskom Khanstve* [Notes on the Bukharan khanate], ed. P. I. Demezona and I. V. Vitketicha (Moscow: Eastern Literature, 1983), "Indian, Lohhani and Afghan merchants bring products of India, the Punjab and Afghanistan to Bukhara and carry from here only a small amount of goods. All the money remaining to them they change into Bukhara *tillas* [gold coins] and Dutch ducats which they yearly send into Kabul and India," 82. This source refers to a period when the collapse of the Mughul empire had led to a marked reduction in the import of Central Asian horses, so the trade imbalance described here would not necessarily have been true of the seventeenth century. Burnes specifically mentions the reduced horse trade and also the substantial importation of Bukhara gold tillas: Burnes, *Reports and Papers*, "Commercial," No. 4, 26, for the horse trade and No. 8, 86, where he mentions that 40,000 rupees worth of Bukhara gold tillas were being imported yearly into Kabul. Mir Izzet Ullah, "Travels Beyond the Himalaya," 339 mentions the import of silver from Turan into India in 1812.

[68] Deyell, "Akbar's Currency System," in Richards, ed., *The Imperial Monetary System of Mughal India*, 36–37. This discussion does not include the gold coinage produced in many South Indian states.

[69] Irfan Habib, "A System of Trimetallism in the Age of the 'Price Revolution': Effects of Silver Influx on the Mughal Monetary System," in Richards, ed., *The Imperial Monetary System of Mughal India*, 145, citing AA and Deyell, "Akbar's Currency System," 23 and 45.

[70] Fragner, "Social and Internal Economic Affairs," CHI, VI, 563, and Borgomale, *Coins, Medals and Seals*, 14–15.

seventeenth century, even though it appears to have been traded frequently in the region two hundred years later.[71]

Silver currency was the most common medium of exchange for commercial transactions in all three states in the seventeenth century, with copper coins largely confined to local markets, except in Mughul India where they circulated widely.[72] In all three states, too, silver currency had been based originally upon a fifteenth-century Timurid unit established by Shah Rukh (1405–47), known as the *tanka-i shahrukhi*.[73] In India the nearly pure Mughul silver rupee (11.6 g, 1584–1605) was minted instead of the Timurid coin that had been used in the early sixteenth century, and the rupee gradually displaced the copper *dam* as the principal medium of commercial exchange throughout the empire. Safavid Iran went through a similar evolution with specifically Safavid issues replacing the Timurid *tanka* and during Shah 'Abbas' reign the 'Abbasi became established as the most commonly used coin in commerce.[74] The 'Abbasi was initially minted at 9.3 g, but its standard weight through most of the century was 7.77 g,[75] although this fell slightly in the last two decades. In Uzbek Turan Shah Rukh's *tanka* remained the standard silver coin and weighed an average of slightly more than 5 g throughout the sixteenth century.[76] Under 'Abd Allah Khan's successors its weight fell slightly to an average of about 4.25 g, but this reflected a drastic reduction of silver content from about 96 percent in the early sixteenth century to around 56 percent in Balkh and Bukhara in the seventeenth century.[77]

As Mughul, Safavid and Uzbek rulers all had to acquire their specie from abroad the weight, purity and production of coins was by itself one general measure of their states' relative economic status. Mughul India stood at one end of the spectrum, largely self-sufficient in both foodstuffs and textiles and the

[71] Jenkinson reported on the basis of a brief residence that no gold coins were circulating in Bukhara in 1558. *Early Voyages and Travels*, II, 85. See above, n. 67, for references to the circulation of Bukharan gold tillas at a later period.

[72] For an introduction to the currency of these regions, which has been analyzed most extensively for Mughul India, see the articles included in Richards, ed., *The Imperial Monetary System of Mughul India*; for Timurid and Safavid Iran, Fragner, "Observations on the Monetary System," CHI, VI, 556–65; for Safavid Iran, Borgomale, *Coins, Medals, and Seals*; and for Uzbek Turan, N. M. Lowick, "Shaybanid Silver Coins," *The Numismatic Chronicle*, 7th ser., VI (1966), 251–339; E. A. Davidovitch, *Istoriia Denezhnogo Obrascheniia Srednevekovoi Srednei Azii* [History of Monetary Circulation of Medieval Central Asia] (Moscow: Nauka, 1983) and E. A. Davidovitch, *Klady Drevnikh i Srednevekovykh Monet Tadzhikistana*.

[73] Lowick, "Shaybanid Silver Coins," 257.

[74] Borgomale, *Coins, Medals, and Seals*, 33.

[75] Sibylla Schuster-Walser, *Das Safawidische Persien im Spiegel Europäischer Reiseberichte (1502–1722)* (Baden-Baden: Bruno Grimm, 1970), 43 and 47.

[76] Lowick, "Shaybanid Silver Coins," 258.

[77] E. A. Davidovitch, "Klad serebrianykh monet Sheibanidov (XVI v), Velikikh Mogolov (XVI v) i Dzhanidov (XVII)" [Hoard of Silver Money of the Shaibanids (XVI) and the Great Mughuls (XVI) and the Janids (XVII)] and "Klad serebrianykh Dzhanidskikh monet XVII v" [Hoard of Silver Janid Money XVII]," in *Klady drevnikh i Srednevekovykh Monet Tadzhikistana*, 380–94 and 396–402. Note that these figures are based on a relatively small number of hoards described by Davidovitch.

beneficiary of foreign specie generated by the export of both commodities. Safavid Iran occupied a middle position. Its coins retained a high level of purity but were slightly less heavy and production declined when trade imbalances reduced supplies of imported specie. Some Iranian coins may also have been debased in the late Safavid period.[78] At the opposite end from India was Uzbek Turan whose coins weighed less than half the Mughul rupee even in the sixteenth century and were radically debased after the death of 'Abd Allah Khan II in 1598. This debasement, though, may have been partly due to a fragmentation of resources that accompanied the reassertion of appanage power in the seventeenth century. Such an association between weakness of centralized political control, and variations in the coinage may also have been at the root of the "distinct coinage standard" that was maintained in eastern Safavid lands throughout the dynasty's history.[79]

Commerce and the state

Coinage was from one perspective a commodity whose exchange compensated for other trade imbalances, in this instance especially those between Mughul India and Safavid Iran. Minting of coins was also an aspect of economic policy over which early modern Islamic rulers usually asserted absolute authority, even if their ability to choose the size and purity of coins was determined by economic and political circumstance. Apart from the important use of currency for state propaganda, Mughul, Safavid and Uzbek rulers all had an interest in maintaining a stable, high-quality coinage in order to facilitate revenue collections and catalyze commercial transactions.[80] It is impossible to measure separately the effect that the currency system had on commerce because monetary policy was only one of a larger set of measures that these rulers adopted to increase both internal and external trade. The policies are well-documented for Mughul India and Safavid Iran, although in the Mughul case they have been largely overlooked because of the distorting bias that has influenced much modern scholarship on the economic history of Mughul India.

Jean Chardin, himself a jeweler who was familiar with merchant classes in both the Mughul and Safavid states, knew that commerce was a high-status occupation in both, partly because it was more secure than other professions and partly, because Turco-Mongol and Iranian elites who governed these states all engaged in trade themselves.

---

[78] Letter to the author from Mr. Stephen Album, 4 November 1991.

[79] *Ibid.*

[80] Deyell attributes Akbar's revision of his mint system to a specific ministerial meeting in 1577–78. "Akbar's Currency System," 30–31. Marie H. Martin argues of Akbar's reforms that "The government's probity in regard to monetary matters was an integral part of the founding, development, and prosperity of the Mughul Empire under Akbar." "The Reforms of the Sixteenth Century and Akbar's Administration: Metrological and Monetary Considerations," in Richards, ed., *The Imperial Monetary System of Mughal India*, 98.

Trading is a very honourable Profession in the *East* as being the best of those that have any Stability, and are not so liable to change . . . Another Reason why it is valu'd is, because the Noblemen profess it and the Kings also; they have their Deputies, as the Merchants have, and under the same Denomination: They have most of them their Trading-Ships and their Store-Houses. The King of *Persia*, for Instance, sells and sends to the Neighbouring Kingdoms, Silk, Brocades, and other rich Goods, Carpets and Precious Stones. The Name of Merchant, is a Name much respected in the *East*, and is not allowed to Shop-keepers or Dealers in trifling Goods; nor to those who Trade not in foreign countries: . . . In the *Indies* the Laws are still more favourable to Traders, for tho' they are much more numerous than in *Persia*, they are nevertheless more set by. The Reason of this additional Respect is, because in the *East* Traders are Sacred Persons, who are never molested even in time of War; and are allowed a free Passage, they and their Effects, through the Middle of Armies: 'Tis on their account especially that the Roads are so safe all over *Asia*, and especially in *Persia*.[81]

Chardin overstates the sanctity of merchants but otherwise his portrayal accurately reflects conditions in the century. His opinion is partly corroborated by the comment of the early eighteenth-century Panjabi Khattri merchant, Anand Ram 'Mukhlis, who wrote that "Trade is many times better than nobility: nobility makes one subject while in [the profession of] trade one leads the life of a ruler."[82] His observation is also a useful reminder of the symbiotic relationship between Safavid and Mughul nobles and merchants.

The measures that the rulers of both dynasties took to stimulate trade were variants of orthodox economic policies that were norms in the early modern Islamic world. It was usual for the ideas to be transmitted in standardized form in "mirror for princes literature," which itself, of course, merely schematized existing practice. Often contained in *nasihat namas*, literally, letters of advice, the economic theory was relatively simple. Monarchs were enjoined to create an infrastructure of roads, bridges and caravansarais, and to protect travelers and merchants.[83] One Ottoman treatise urged them specifically to

Look with favour on the merchants in the land; always care for them; let no one harass them; let no one order them about; for through their trading the land becomes prosperous, and by their wares cheapness abounds in the world; through them, the excellent fame of the sultan is carried to surrounding lands, and by them the wealth within the land is increased.[84]

The major difference in the way that these policies were instituted in the Mughul Safavid empires stemmed from the relative economic strength of each state.

[81] Chardin, *Travels in Persia*, 279–80. For a brief survey of Mughul emperors' trade see Satish Chandra, "Commercial Activities of the Mughul Emperors During the Seventeenth Century." in Chandra, ed., *Essays in Medieval Indian Economic History* (New Delhi: Munshiram Manoharlal, 1987), 163–69.

[82] Muzaffar Alam, *The Crises of Empire in Mughal North India* (New Delhi: Oxford University Press, 1986), 174 n. 154.

[83] Halil Inalcik, "Capital Formation in the Ottoman Empire," *Journal of Economic History* XXXIX/1 (March 1969), 97–98.

[84] *Ibid.*, 102.

Mughul rulers had the luxury of being able merely to preside over a powerful laissez faire economy that allowed them to have what was essentially a free-trade foreign economy policy, while Shah 'Abbas instituted a kind of state capitalism and an Iranian mercantilism to develop and protect his state's more fragile economic circumstance.[85]

Akbar might have been sitting with one such nasihat nama in hand when he formulated Mughul commercial policies, were it not for the general conviction that he was, at best, only semi-literate. As described in detail by Abu'l Fadl and other Mughul historians, his policies represented a textbook case of Muslim rulers who presided over predominantly agrarian states. It is remarkable, therefore, that this exceptionally well-documented case has been consistently misinterpreted. One possible reason why a policy which is so clearly described in Mughul historical literature has been overlooked by modern scholars is that historians of the period generally use the moral or religious idiom of "mirror for princes" literature when describing economic decisions.

A case in point is the story that the founder of the Mughul empire, Babur, relates about his father, Umar Shaykh (d. 1495), a minor Timurid prince who ruled over a small state in the Ferghana valley, east of Samarqand. As an illustration of his father's exemplary character, he gives an anecdote that could have been taken from or intended for a nasihat nama. According to Babur, during his father's reign a caravan once passed through his territories on its way to China and was trapped in a snow storm resulting in the deaths of many merchants. Umar Shaykh is then said to have ordered the goods of the dead men to be stored until relatives could claim them. Babur explains his father's actions by saying that it was motivated by his sense of justice. What he fails to mention is that these merchants were traveling along the principal overland route, the so-called silk route, linking the Middle East and Uzbek Turan with China, which ran through the Ferghana valley. Umar Shaykh had good practical reasons for his solicitous treatment of these unlucky men apart from his concern for his reputation as a just sultan, a traditional legitimizing characteristic of Islamic rulers, for customs duties undoubtedly generated a major proportion of his small state's annual revenue.[86]

---

[85] At the "Workshop on the Political Economies of the Ottoman, Safavid and Mughal States during the 17th and 18th Centuries" held in Istanbul, Turkey, 16–20 June, 1992, there was vigorous debate as to whether Shah 'Abbas' policies could be termed mercantilist. Some participants thought that the term was totally inappropriate for Iran while others felt that the Iranian ruler at least had mercantilist "impulses." Rudolph Matthee writes about this issue that "What was true for mercantilist Europe was equally so for seventeenth-century Iran where scarcity . . . was even more endemic and financial dependence on outside sources of specie much greater." "Politics and Trade," 245. For a discussion of the various meanings of the term see Leonard Gomes, *Foreign Trade and the National Economy, Mercantilist and Classical Perspectives* (London: Macmillan, 1987).

[86] Beveridge, *The Babur-nama in English*, 15. For an early nineteenth-century estimate of the revenue of the Uzbek appanage of Qunduz see Burnes' memoir on Qunduz cited in n. 23 above. See also Mohan Lal on the revenues of the western Afghan city of Harat in the same period: "A Brief Description of Herat," *Journal of the Asiatic Society of Bengal*, III, no. 25 (January 1834), 9–18.

Another reason why Mughul commercial policies may be so poorly understood is related to this story, in that historians of Mughul India write almost entirely without reference to or an understanding of the Mughuls' Central Asian background. In consequence these scholars have little appreciation for the traditional political economy of the Turco-Mongol rulers of the region. Yet even Mongols, or especially the Mongols, who are often viewed from the South Asian as well as the Chinese perspective as little more than an inchoate plundering rabble, not only protected trade routes carefully but formed trading partnerships known as *ortays* with merchants of adjacent sedentary societies.[87] These were similar in many respects to the business alliances that Mughul and Safavid rulers and nobles made with indigenous merchants of their societies. In view of this background it is scarcely surprising that more sedentarized, more urbanized Turco-Mongol dynasties such as the Mughuls would be at least equally attuned to commerce, both personally and as rulers.

It is well known that Mughul rulers and their families commonly invested in ambitious commercial ventures, although it is not quite so generally appreciated that most of the Mughul elite did so as well. Abu'l Fadl's contemporary, the 'alim, courtier and historian, al-Badauni, confirmed the accuracy of Chardin's observation about nobles' commercial and financial interests. He showed how carefully Mughul nobles looked to their own financial affairs when he reported how Akbar had responded to their criticism of his appointment of a Hindu, the Punjabi Khattri Todar Mal, as the revenue minister. According to al-Badauni, Akbar pointedly remarked to them in reply that "Everyone of you has a Hindu to manage his private affairs. Suppose we too have a Hindu, why should harm come of it?"[88] Akbar was alluding to the Mughul nobles' habit of appointing Hindus as *vakils*, or economic managers, a custom that often gave these Hindus considerable de facto political power.[89] Akbar's own attitude towards merchants as a class may have been partly reflected in Abu'l Fadl's allusion to the fact that merchants were present both day and night at the Mughul court. Akbar after all is known to have approved what Abu'l Fadl wrote about the history of his reign in the *Akbar-nama*, so his own opinions probably informed Abu'l Fadl's narrative when the latter wrote admiringly of the "body of energetic men of mercantile disposition" who knew that it was in their interest to attend the emperor at all times.[90]

Mughul commercial policies can be documented more easily than those of their contemporaries in Iran or Turan because of a relative wealth of extant late sixteenth- and early seventeenth-century sources. It is possible to see, for example, how their adherence to the nasihat nama ideal of commercial orthodoxy

[87] Thomas T. Allsen, "Mongolian Princes and their Merchant Partners," *Asia Major*, 3rd ser. II/2 (1989), 83–125 and Elizabeth Endicott-West, "Merchant Associations in Yüan China: The Ortay," in *ibid.*, 127–54.
[88] al-Badauni, *Muntakhabu-T-Tawarikh*, II, 65.
[89] Alam, *Crises of Empire*, 173–75.
[90] AN, III, 208.

varied directly with their sense of military and political security, describing an arc of solicitous concern that rose from a nadir during Babur's insecure, impecunious years as ruler of Kabul between 1504 and 1526 towards the comparative wealth and security of Akbar's later years. As a young refugee from his unsuccessful power struggles with Timurid cousins and Uzbeks in Turan, Babur unabashedly plundered caravans to generate income in his first years in Kabul.[91] His son Humayun was even more pressed toward the end of his fifteen-year exile from India, and during his siege of his half-brother Kamran in Kabul he extorted horses and goods from passing caravans. Yet, as Abu'l Fadl reveals in his disarmingly ingenuous narration of Humayun's actions, Mughuls of the late sixteenth century were embarrassed by these events. Abu'l Fadl felt constrained to say of Humayun's confiscations that one group of horses which he had seized had been "voluntarily" offered to him, while the goods and horses he took from a second group of merchants actually had been presented to him as gifts which he promised to repay later. In contrast Abu'l Fadl shows Kamran to have been an illegitimate ruler because he "arbitrarily" seized horses from passing Afghan merchants during this same siege.[92]

Abu'l Fadl's narration of events surrounding Humayun's siege of Kabul defined normative conduct for Islamic rulers regarding private property. While Mughul rulers might occasionally have extorted merchandise, funds or even immovable property from merchants, such actions were illegal in Islamic societies whose legal systems minutely defined contractual and property rights.[93] Mughul rulers were acutely conscious of these norms. Just as Abu'l Fadl felt that he had to offer an explanation that showed Humayun to have acted legally and Kamran illegally, so the historian of Shah Jahan's reign reported that when the emperor realized that the parcel of land near Agra where he planned to build the Taj Mahal belonged to a well-known Rajput ally, Raja Jai Singh, he refused even to accept the raja's offer of the land as a present. In the words of the historian, 'Inayat Khan, "His majesty, with that scrupulousness so requisite in worldly transactions, conferred on him in exchange a splendid mansion out of imperial properties."[94] South Asian historians, particularly those who are primarily interested in the preconditions of modern economic development, often assert that commercial

---

[91] Beveridge, *The Babur-nama in English*, 235.

[92] AN, III, 437.

[93] As Tapan Raychaudhuri points out, it is important to distinguish between Mughul policy and the interests of their subordinates. Raychaudhuri, "The State and the Economy: The Mughal Empire," CEHI, I, 190–91. The confiscation of officials' property, which is often taken as an indication of the insecurity in early modern Islamic empires, is really a separate issue. In the Mughul case this usually occurred when an official or noble died and a customary percentage of his wealth was taken by the state. According to Jahangir, no property was to be confiscated during his reign. Henry Beveridge, ed. and Alexander Rogers, trans., *The Tuzuk-i-Jahangiri*. repr. (New Delhi: Munshiram Manoharlal, 1978), I, 8. See Inalcik's discussion of this issue in the Ottoman case, "Capital Formation," 107.

[94] W. E. Begley and Z. A. Desai, eds., *The Shah Jahan Nama of 'Inayat Khan* (Delhi: Oxford University Press, 1990), 73–74.

property was perilously insecure in the Mughul empire, but this evaluation over-looks both stated Mughul policy and common practice as well as the policy and practice of other early modern Islamic states. It also discounts the Mughul elites' vested interest in maintaining a high level of business confidence so that their own investments would prosper.[95]

Abu'l Fadl wrote when the prosperous, relatively stable conditions of Mughul India made distasteful expediencies of earlier years unnecessary. He reported that Akbar's successes also led the emperor to abolish certain internal customs dues, explaining his decision to do so by observing that "ancient rulers and former potentates" collected tolls

to produce the materials of world-conquest and for administrative purposes . . . [but] the Incomparable Creator has put under my control the territories of so many great princes and has made me the keeper of such vast treasures . . . the arm of demand should be shortened and should not reach the hem of traders.[96]

Whether or not the measures that Akbar and his successors are said to have taken to eliminate internal barriers to commerce significantly increased trade cannot be determined, because it is usually impossible to ascertain whether imperial commands to abolish specific duties were effectively enforced. Abu'l Fadl himself said of Akbar's 1581 order to abolish the commercial taxes "baj and tamgha" that the emperor had issued precisely the same order at the beginning of his reign. Writing with the frankness that sometimes relieves the tedium of his hyperbolic prose, Abu'l Fadl wrote, "Yet, as the world's lord had remained behind the veil, and from the avarice of the guardians of the commands of the Caliphate it did not come into effect."[97] Abu'l Fadl continued on to say that Akbar controlled his territories much more securely in 1581 than in the early years of his reign so that no one then dared to disobey an imperial order.

The most demonstrably effective measures that Akbar took to catalyze both internal and external trade were those that comprised the typical recitatives of nasihat namas: improvement of roads, construction of bridges and caravansarais and the protection of travelers. Akbar and his successors constructed a network that ran through the heart of the empire and in the west traversed Afghan territories to the Mughul borders with Iran and Uzbek Turan. The internal system has been well publicized and was described in 1615 by the Englishmen Steel and Crowther as they made their way from Agra to Lahore.

---

[95] See Bruce Master's comments on the sanctity of private property in Islamic states in *The Origins of Western Economic Dominance in the Middle East, Mercantilism and the Islamic Economy in Aleppo, 1600–1750* (New York: N.Y. University Press, 1988), chapter 6.

[96] AN, III, 437.

[97] *Ibid.*, 437–38. See Fragner's discussion of these terms. In post-Mongol Iran tamgha was used as an all-inclusive term for urban taxes while baj referred to city customs duties: "Social and Internal Economic Affairs," CHI, VI, 540. Suraiya Faroqhi refers to "bac and damga" as Ottoman "sales dues." *Towns and Townsmen of Ottoman Anatolia, Trade, Crafts and Food Production in an Urban Setting, 1520–1650* (Cambridge: Cambridge University Press, 1984), 4.

Every five or six coss, there are serais built by the king or some great man, which add greatly to the beauty of the road, are very convenient for the accommodation of travelers, and serve to perpetuate the memory of their founders.[98]

Parts of this system, of what were in legal terms *waqfs* or religious endowments, had been constructed by the Mughuls' predecessor, Shir Shah Lodi, but the Mughuls not only improved it they also extended it to cover the most important overland routes as well.[99] The East India Company officer, Alexander Burnes, described a remnant of the caravansarai network in the 1830s when he traveled from Kabul to Balkh. He wrote: "They may even be traced across the mountains to Balkh . . . What opinion does this inspire of the grandeur of the Mughul empire? We have a system of communications between the most distant provinces as perfect as the posts of the Caesars."[100]

Akbar's policy was undoubtedly motivated in part by strategic considerations, but improving trade was always linked with these. All of the overland routes from India to Kabul, Iran and Turan ran through Afghan or Baluchi tribal territory, as did the Indus route to Thatta and the Arabian Sea. Ensuring safe passage through these regions was a consistent goal of Mughul policy. The same year that he abolished "baj and tamgha," Akbar began construction of a fort at Attock or Atak-Banaras, the northern Indus crossing between what the Mughuls distinguished as "Hindustan" and "Kabulistan," specifically in order to enforce "obedience of the turbulent of that border," that is, the Afghan tribes.[101] Abu'l Fadl went on to note that as a result of enforcing peace in the area "the helpless obtained a means of subsistence, the seekers of traffic obtained confidence and world traversers had security."[102] He might have added that Mughul customs revenues probably rose substantially as a result, a matter of considerable interest not only to the government but to individual nobles who might have administered the area.[103]

It is, indeed, worth remembering the Mughul government derived significant revenues from mint charges for coining imported specie and much greater amounts from customs duties on both imported and exported goods, even if these were normally the modest 2.5 to 3 percent ad valorem tariffs common in the early modern Islamic states. If these revenues were modest in comparison with land

---

[98] Steel and Crowther, "Journey," 208. For brief comments on Mughul infrastructure see CEHI, I, 182 and for photographs of some bridges and discussions of specific caravansarais see Ebba Koch, *Mughal Architecture* (Munich: Prestel, 1991), for example, pp. 66–68.

[99] al-Badauni, *Muntakhabut-T-Tawarikh, , 473.*

[100] Burnes, *Travels into Bokhara,* II, 109. His late-Romantic era rhetoric should not be allowed to obscure the importance of his observation.

[101] An, III, 521.

[102] *Ibid.*

[103] K. N. Chaudhuri usefully observes of the customs revenues that "The meticulous care with which imperial officials at Surat, Hugli, or Balasore recorded in writing the exports and imports of various ports is only one indication among many of the Mughal administrative preoccupations with matters of trade." "Markets and Traders in India during the Seventeenth and Eighteenth Centuries," in K. N. Chaudhuri and Clive J. Dewey, eds., *Economy and Society* (New Delhi: Oxford University Press, 1979), 144. See Fragner, "Social and Internal Economic Economic Affairs," CHI, VI, 542–45, for a discussion of customs duties in Iran at this period.

revenue collections they still represented significant sums of ready cash that were realized with very little administrative overhead. In 1644 the newly appointed Mughul governor of Ahmedabad was to draw nearly one-third of his first year's salary from Surat treasury revenues.[104] It was certainly not an accident that after the conquest of Sind the port of Lahori Bandar, or Lahore's port, on the Arabian Sea estuary of the Indus was declared to be *khalsa* or crown lands by Akbar.[105] Commercial traffic between the Panjab and other Indian or Persian Gulf ports passed through Lahori Bandar; like Surat and other ports it would have generated large annual revenues. Only collections from customs dues and mint charges could explain why the village of Attock would rank so prominently among Panjabi towns based upon taxation. Customs were assessed here and a copper mint was established at the Attock ferry to serve the large volume of overland trade that was carried across the river at this point after Akbar had secured the Khyber Pass and the route to Kabul.[106]

By 1587 after the road between Attock and Kabul had been at least temporarily secured, Akbar vowed to construct a series of caravansarais along its length to prevent Afghan attacks on passing travelers.[107] Nine years later the road was leveled, allowing wheeled vehicles to reach Kabul, and perhaps for the first time in Indo-Muslim history the Khyber Pass became the most important commercial and military route between northwestern India and Kabul.[108] The southwestern routes to Afghanistan were secured by the conquest of Sind in 1590,[109] and by the more temporary expedient of ordering punitive expeditions against the Afghan Kakar tribes, whose attacks on caravans had prevented them from traveling safely to and from Qandahar.[110] All along the roads, Abu'l Fadl writes, "The gracious sovereign cast an eye upon the comfort of travelers and ordered that in the serais on the high roads, refuges and kitchens should be established, and that articles of food should be in readiness for the empty-handed travelers."[111] Akbar's descendants pursued these same policies. Additional bridges and caravansarais were built along the Khyber route in Shah Jahan's time, and it may also have been during his reign that the caravansarais which Burnes saw were constructed along the tortuous routes over the Hindu Kush to Badakshan.[112]

[104] This was, in fact, Prince Murad Baksh. W. E. Begley and Z. A. Desai, eds., *Taj Mahal: The Illumined Tomb* (Seattle: University of Washington Press, 1990), 134.

[105] AN, III, 986.

[106] See Moosvi's map, "Towns of the Mughal Empire, Size by Taxation," *Economy of the Mughal Empire*, 311, where Attock is given unusual prominence. Customs charges based on weight are given by Antonova, I, no. 32, 1545, 81.

[107] AN, III, 792. See also Wayne E. Begley, "Four Mughal Caravansarais Built during the Reigns of Jahangir and Shah Jahan," in Oleg Grabar, ed., *Muqarnas* (New Haven, Conn.: Yale University Press, 1983), I, 167–69.

[108] AN, III, 1502.

[109] *Ibid.*, 1013.

[110] *Ibid.*, 1043.

[111] *Ibid.*, 1236.

[112] As Burnes implies, some of these may have been built when Shah Jahan's son and eventual successor, Aurungzeb, was governor of Balkh. *Travels into Bokhara*, II, 109.

Textual evidence for Iranian and Uzbek commercial policies is less piquant than that for Akbar's India. Uzbek policies in particular have to be largely inferred from references to caravansarai construction, numismatic evidence and diplomatic correspondence.[113] These show that 'Abd Allah Khan II followed orthodox economic policies while he attempted to centralize power in Turan, but the attitudes of the appanage rulers who succeeded him are difficult to ascertain. There are prima facie reasons for believing that the quasi-city states of Khiva, Bukhara and Balkh would naturally have been solicitous of merchants since they probably generated such a large percentage of their income.[114] This is borne out to some degree for a later period by Burnes, who described conditions in Bukhara in 1832 and reported that "No people could be more liberal encouragers of trade than the rulers of Bukhara." He cited as evidence the report that "During the reign of the last monarch, the duties on goods were never paid until they were sold, as in the bonding system of a British customhouse."[115] High praise indeed!

Shah 'Abbas I was more famous than any of his contemporaries for his favorable treatment of merchants. Steel and Crowther were only two of many Europeans who commented on this. When they reached Farrah, the city now in western Afghanistan where Iranian customs were assessed at a standard 3 percent ad valorem rate, they reported that "Merchants are used with much favour, lest they should make complaints to the king, who will have merchants kindly treated."[116] Shah 'Abbas also complemented Akbar's public works in India with his own systematic development of an Iranian infrastructure of roads, bridges and caravansarais, a building program that his court historian, Iskandar Beg Munshi summarized in typical mirror-for-princes moral rhetoric. In "Discourse 5" of his work, "On Shah 'Abbas' Justice, Concern for Security of Roads, and Concern for the Welfare of his Subjects," Iskandar Beg observes that:

The greater part of governing is the preservation of stability within the kingdom and security on the roads. Prior to the accession of Shah 'Abbas, this peace and security had disappeared in Iran, and it had become extremely difficult for people to travel about the country. As soon as he came to the throne Shah 'Abbas turned his attention to this problem.

---

[113] Mukimova has a brief discussion of 'Abd Allah Khan's policies. *Social Differentiation*, 121. For his monetary reforms see Akhmedov, *Istoriko-geograficheskaia Literatura Srednei Azii*, 198 n. 76. For an example of "mirrors for princes" literature in the Timurid period that emphasizes the importance of creating this infrastructure, see Wheeler Thackston, "Sultan Husayn Mirza's 'Apologia'," in Thackston, ed. and trans., *A Century of Princes* (Cambridge, Mass.: Aga Khan Program for Islamic Architecture, 1989), 375.

[114] Mir Izzet Ullah reported in 1812 that customs represented the second largest source of revenue for Bukhara at that time: "Travels Beyond the Himalaya," 336–37. For the idea of Tashkent in the eighteenth century as a city-state see O. D. Chekovitch, "Gorodskoe samoupravlenie v Tashkente XVIII v," [City Self-government in Tashkent in the 18th century], in B. G. Gafurov and B. A. Litvinskii, eds., *Istoriia i Kul'tura Narodov Srednei Azii* [History and Culture of the Peoples of Central Asia] (Moscow: Nauka, 1976), 149–60.

[115] Burnes, *Travels into Bokhara*, II, 248–49.

[116] Steel and Crowther, "Journey," 214.

He called for the principal highway robbers in each province to be identified, and he then set about eliminating this class of people ... With security restored to the roads, merchants and tradesmen traveled to and from the Safavid empire.[117]

Even if Iskandar Beg exaggerated the contrast in public safety before and after his patron's accession, by the end of Shah 'Abbas' reign security for travelers had reached an exceptional level even when compared with conditions in the relatively well-managed Mughul and Ottoman empires.

All European merchants reported that Iranian roads were the most secure in the entire region of the three early modern Islamic empires in the seventeenth century, although some breakdown was apparent in the later part of the period.[118] *Rahdars*, highway police, patrolled roads in every province to protect travelers and merchants and arrest robbers. Foreign merchants found that in Iran they could travel without the protection of arms or large caravans. Rahdar salaries were defrayed by modest fees in addition to customs duties charged to merchants, but the fees also appear to have represented state-sponsored commercial insurance, since merchants were normally compensated by local officials if their goods were stolen.[119] In addition to this institution 'Abbas also built important roads, the most famous of which was the *sang farash* metalled highway across a swampy stretch of desert north of Isfahan that "at a single stroke ... made Isfahan the centre of Iranian internal trade."[120] As was true of the Mughuls, Shah 'Abbas built, or encouraged his nobles to build, caravansarais along roads and major trade routes and erected caravansarai and bazar complexes in such major commercial centers as Isfahan and Kirman. Even though most of the caravansarais in the countryside have no inscriptions, "the existence of several very similar caravansarais at intervals along a given route is ample testimony – on grounds of expense alone – of exalted patronage."[121]

---

[117] Eskandar Beg Monshi, *History of Shah 'Abbas the Great*, trans. by Roger Savory (Boulder, Colo.: Westview Press, 1978), II, 523.

[118] Rudolph Matthee gives details of increasing rates of highway robberies in the later Safavid era: "Politics and Trade in Late Safavid Iran," 132–34. Several European travelers reported that Iran was much safer than the Ottoman empire. See the references in the article by John Emerson and Willem Floor, "Rahdars and their Tolls in Safavid and Afsharid Iran," *Journal of the Economic and Social History of the Orient* XXX (1987), 319. Some Europeans also knew that it was more dangerous to travel in Mughul India, even in the heart of the empire, than in Safavid Iran. Steel and Crowther said that it was dangerous to travel at night along the Agra–Lahore road, "Journey," 208; and while danger of night travel is hardly conclusive even the Russian ambassador to Bukhara in 1646, one A. Gribov, knew, presumably from Indian merchants, that the road between Delhi and Agra was plagued by armed robbers, who probably were Jats. Antonova, I, no. 32, 1646, 82.

[119] Emerson and Floor, "Rahdars and their Tolls in Safavid and Afsharid Iran," 318–27. This institution existed in Mughul India but is rarely commented on by travelers.

[120] Fragner, "Social and Internal Economic Affairs," CHI, VI, 527.

[121] Robert Hillenbrand, "Safavid Architecture," CHI, VI, 817–19. For a first-hand description of many Iranian caravansarais in the last years of Shah 'Abbas' reign see Herbert, *Travels in Persia*, for example, p. 51. Maxime Siroux describes several Iranian caravansarais from an art historical perspective in her article, "Les caravansareis routiers safavids," *Iranian Studies* VII/1–2 (winter-spring 1974), 348–75.

Plate 1 Caravansarai and Akbar's fort at Attock (Atak-Banares)

The simultaneous pacification of trade routes and construction of roads and caravansarais throughout northern India, Iran and Turan in the late sixteenth and seventeenth century established exceptionally favorable conditions for trade throughout the entire region. It is not just that merchants would have been able to move about more quickly and with less danger, that is, with less expense than formerly, but it is also likely that the construction of caravansarai systems themselves expanded the regional and international market economy more widely. Akbar's son Jahangir (r. 1605–27), generally regarded as the least politically sagacious Mughul emperor, still revealed a sophisticated grasp of the socio-economic implications of caravansarais when he urged that more "sara'is . . . mosques and dig wells" should be built "which might stimulate population and people might settle down in those sara'is."[122] He understood that caravansarais were fundamental institutions of economic development in mercantile societies. Depending on their location caravansarais sometimes evolved into market centers. One that Shah 'Abbas supposedly had built at Khur at the edge of the desert on the caravan route between Isfahan and Mashad became

the market for the scattered small villages of the area, whose main occupations were silk weaving and carpet making and merchants stopped at Khur to buy these goods and sell requisites to the producers.[123]

A recent geographic study of Iranian caravansarais has schematized the entire process by which caravansarais that were built on major trade routes could even evolve into significant agricultural towns with their own covered bazars.[124] Such settlements would have been the most significant examples of how the Mughul and Safavid policy of caravansarai construction could simultaneously stimulate the agricultural, commercial and local manufacturing economy.

[122] Beveridge, ed. and Rogers, trans., *The Tuzuk-i-Jahangiri*, I, 8.
[123] Mehdi Keyvani, *Artisans and Guild Life in the Later Safavid Period* (Berlin: Klaus Schwarz, 1982), 235. It isn't entirely clear from Keyvani's reference – to Steel and Crowther's travels – how he reconstructs the process that he describes here, but he may be drawing upon his Ph.D. dissertation on Iranian caravansarais which is cited in his bibliography.
[124] Masoud Kheirabadi, *Iranian Cities, Formation and Development* (Austin, Tex.: University of Texas Press, 1991). Based upon Keyvani and Kheirabadi's stimulating suggestions it may be possible to suggest that the caravansarai should be given a special category in central place theory. It may be possible to assign caravansarais a niche in the hierarchy of markets such as is suggested by G. William Skinner, "Marketing and Social Structure in Rural China," *Journal of Asian Studies* XXIV (1964), 3–44. Suraiya Faroqhi has an important discussion of Ottoman caravans and trade routes in which she emphasizes the significance of the waqf institution. See her book, *Towns and Townsmen of Ottoman Anatolia*. She also discusses Skinner's thesis more specifically in her article "Seventeenth Century Periodic Markets in Various Anatolian *Sancaks*," *Journal of the Economic and Social History of the Orient* XXII (1979), 32–80. The significance of caravansarais as religious endowments in Islamic states can scarcely be overestimated, although they have rarely been discussed at length from this perspective. See, however, the article of Halil Inalcik, "The Hub of the City: the Bedestan of Istanbul," *International Journal of Turkish Studies* I/1 (1979–80), 1–17.

Intra-Asian trade

By constructing hundreds of bridges, caravansarais and securing critical trade routes, Akbar, Shah 'Abbas and, to a lesser degree, 'Abd Allah Khan II and his successors, undoubtedly contributed to an upsurge in regional commerce that was roughly commensurate with that which is commonly believed to have taken place within both Mughul India and Safavid Iran in the seventeenth century.[125] As Bert Fragner, one of the foremost scholars of the socio-economic history of Safavid Iran has written,

We should recall how enormously important for oriental foreign trade in all ages was the maintenance of the trade routes. Commercial development depended in a high degree upon the safety of the roads, the density of the communications network, the number of well appointed halting-places, watering places, bridges, etc. The degree of development enjoyed by the cities was related ultimately to these factors also. For the city was, above all, a place of trade and exchange.[126]

Most of the later monarchs of these states were as publicly solicitous of the prosperity of inter-state trade as they were for their own internal commercial prosperity. In view of the critical importance of the silk trade to Iran, the substantial revenue that Uzbek states and appanages received from the horse trade with Mughul India and the income that Mughul rulers received merely from minting charges and customs revenues, these monarchs' public posture obviously reflected a profound, self-interested commitment to this trade. When a Safavid official wrote to Mughul authorities in 1644 to say that no restrictions had ever been placed on the movement of caravans between their respective territories even when "mutual relations were strained" he was being disingenuous. Both governments restricted commerce when they felt that it might help to achieve specific military or political ends – usually the reconquest of Qandahar. Shah Jahan, for example, forbade ships to leave Surat for the main Iranian port of Bandar 'Abbas in 1640.[127] Nevertheless both dynasties and the Uzbek states as well were inevitably committed to unrestricted trade.

As has already been indicated no baseline of statistics exists for the sixteenth century, or any earlier period, that can be used to measure what ultimately has to remain an assumed increase in Mughul–Safavid, Mughul–Uzbek commerce. There are, though, numerous anecdotal reports that illustrate how deteriorating political conditions led to a decline in trade. In the 1750s, for example, English merchants in Iran carefully recorded how insecurity in the country had led to a gradual decline in prosperity and a consequent decline in demand. They said that Iranian merchants from the interior still came to trade at Bandar 'Abbas but now

[125] Raychaudhuri, "The State and the Economy: The Mughal Empire," CEHI, I, 185, and Fragner, "Social and Internal Economic Affairs," CHI, II, 537.

[126] Fragner, "Social and Internal Economic Affairs," CHI, VI, 525.

[127] William Foster, *The English Factories in India, 1637–1641* (Oxford: Clarendon Press, 1912), 242.

they bought cheaper goods.[128] If equally alert and knowledgeable merchants had been present to record the state of trade in Mughul India and Safavid Iran throughout Akbar and Shah 'Abbas' reigns they would undoubtedly have been able to document the incremental rise in commerce that accompanied the securing of each major mountain pass and the construction of every new series of caravansarais.

One aspect of intra-Asian trade in this region can be at least partially documented, and that is the relative significance of Mughul trade with Iran and Turan within the context of Mughul foreign trade as a whole. The most precise data for this analysis are extant Mughul coin hoards that date from the century and a half between 1568 and 1703. The evidence of these coins contradicts the prevailing assumption that most Mughul silver coinage was generated by direct European imports through Surat or other major ports. During this period mints from the northwestern areas of the empire – Kashmir, Kabul, Lahore, Multan and Thatta – together issued the largest number of coins of all Mughul mints taken together, 36.7 percent.[129] Merchants who arrived from Iran and Turan would presumably have supplied most of the specie or bullion to the mints at Kabul, Lahore and Multan, while Thatta was a river port not only for trade with Bandar 'Abbas but for the Ottoman port of Basra and other Arabian Sea and Indian Ocean ports as well.

This figure seems surprisingly high in view of the traditional Eurocentric bias of commercial history of this period, but on closer examination it actually appears to be misleadingly low. First of all, no coins in these collections represent the Multan mint for the years 1598–1626, yet Multan was the principal departure point and terminus for caravans traveling to and from Qandahar and Iran.[130] These years also include those in which sea traffic was diverted overland due to naval skirmishes in the Persian Gulf between Dutch and English and Portuguese ships, culminating with the successful joint Anglo-Iranian expedition against Hurmuz in 1622.[131] Indian trade with Turan is itself likely to be underrepresented by these figures since most Indian cloth, sugar and indigo apparently were exchanged for Central Asian horses rather than generating an enormous currency surplus similar to that obtained from Iran. If this hypothesis is correct, few coins from Khiva, Bukhara or Balkh are likely to have been recoined as rupees in these northwestern mints.

Even if this numismatic evidence is itself limited it offers some definite idea of the scale of commerce that was conducted between the Mughul empire and the

[128] Chaudhuri, *Trading World*, 227.
[129] Aziza Hasan, "Mints of the Mughul Empire," in Satish Chandra, ed., *Essays in Medieval Indian Economic History*, 175.
[130] Hasan does not offer any suggestion that would explain why so few coins from the Multan mint were in the collections that she examined, but see also Deyell, "Akbar's Currency System and Monetary Integration," in Richards, *The Imperial Monetary System of Mughal India*, 13–67, where coins from the Multan mint are also poorly represented.
[131] Steel and Crowther, "Journey," 209. The authors estimated that when they traveled "twelve or fourteen thousand camel loads . . . pass over the mountains of Candahar into Persia."

contiguous Safavid and Uzbek states. Substantial trade was also carried on between these states from the preeminent Mughul port of Surat, as has been indicated by the English estimate that one million rupees' worth of Indian cotton textiles was shipped from Surat to Iran in 1661. Some of this cloth may have been shipped on to Turan via the caravan route through Kirman and Mashad, or westward to Ottoman cities. These sales would have generated substantial amounts of Iranian silver specie, much of which would presumably have been brought to the Surat mint. Thus, the combination of numismatic evidence and estimates of exports from Surat raises the possibility that more than half of Mughul India's cloth exports may have been made to its traditional markets in Iran, Turan and the Ottoman empire in the seventeenth century. This commerce is scarcely alluded to in modern historical scholarship, except as an ancillary aspect of the trade that was conducted between Europe and Asia, and consequently no attempt has ever been made to determine how it was financed and organized. Certainly no hint has ever been given that South Asian merchants themselves might have played a significant role in the commerce, apart from acting as brokers in major port and frontier cities for European, Iranian or Turkic merchants. Yet there is ample evidence in a number of pre-Mughul, Mughul and British period sources to indicate that merchants from Mughul territories constituted a numerous and influential diaspora throughout Iran and Turan, a presence that explains the speed with which they were later able to exploit the opportunities offered by the Russian conquests of Astrakhan in the mid-sixteenth century.

CHAPTER 3

The Indian diaspora in Iran and Turan

When spring-time flushes the desert grass,
Our kafilas wind through the Khyber Pass.
Lean are the camels but fat the frails,
Light are the purses but heavy the bales.
As the snowbound trade of the North comes down
To the market-square of Peshawur town.

Rudyard Kipling: "The Ballad of the King's Jest"

Panjabi Khattris, Pushtuns or Afghans and Marwaris were the principal merchant groups from Mughul territories who conducted business in Iran or Turan in the seventeenth and eighteenth century. Given the size, complexity and sophistication of the Indian economy they or other merchants from India's western and north-western provinces are likely to have visited or resided in marketing centers of these contiguous regions for centuries or even millennia prior to Akbar's reign. Inclusion of the Kabul region in many powerful Indian states from as early as the reign of the Mauryas of Magadha (324–183 BC) to the Hindu Shahi dynasty of the ninth and tenth centuries AD make such commercial migration even more likely.[1] Cities such as Balkh probably functioned as commercial outworks of these north Indian states, as is suggested by the report of the Arab geographer al-Maqdisi, who wrote in the twilight of Hindu Shahi rule that one of the city's gates was known as the *bab-i Hinduwan*, the gate of the Indians.[2] In records of the sixteenth to eighteenth centuries the largely allusive references to Indian mercantile activity outside of South Asia which are the commonplace of earlier sources give way to eyewitness accounts and documentary evidence. These data show that thousands of merchants from the Mughul empire resided semi-permanently in Iran and Turan where they exerted significant economic influence. They were, in essence, personifications of India's stature as a regional world economy.

---

[1] Deyell, *Living Without Silver*, 51–60, for Hindu Shahi currency and commerce.
[2] Barthold, *Historical Geography*, 12–13.

Trade routes

Merchants who traveled or shipped goods between Mughul India and Iran or Turan could choose among sea, riverine or overland routes. Most Europeans knew only the sea route from Surat, which for this reason has become the most widely known of all Mughul–Safavid trade routes, but the two alternatives were also regularly and widely used. Those who came from the Panjab or Sind could sail down the Indus in flat-bottomed boats to Lahori Bandar, aptly known as Lahore's port, since that city was the commercial center of the wealthy Panjab. Merchants could also travel overland from the Panjab or wind through one of the major mountain passes directly into Safavid territories or to Kabul and then across Hindu Kush passes to Balkh, Bukhara or Samarqand. These routes were complimentary rather than mutually exclusive. Not only did some individuals habitually use both land and water routes, but most merchants were capable of quickly shifting their trade from one to another when naval or ground warfare or political instability threatened the safety of their ships or caravans.

The bulk of Mughul India's exports to Safavid Iran were probably carried by water, either directly from Surat or down the Indus and onward by ship into the Gulf. This cannot be documented precisely, but sea and riverine routes were generally safer, usually cheaper and sometimes faster. The degree of this comparative advantage was reduced when Arab pirates in the Gulf interdicted shipping, as they did to a ship carrying the Russian emissary who was returning from the Mughul court in 1699.[3] Ships from Surat could make the passage to Bandar 'Abbas in only two to three weeks if they sailed with the northeast monsoon in the late fall or early winter, preferably between December and early March.[4] After arriving in the Gulf goods could be transshipped by caravan to Isfahan in a month or to Kirman in two and a half weeks. Kirman itself was not only a manufacturing center, but also served as an entrepôt on the caravan route from the Gulf to Mashad and onwards to Turan.[5] Return voyages to Surat could be made equally quickly if ships left the Gulf in late March or early April, although some merchants chose to sail to Iran and return overland to India in the spring.[6] If, then, Gujarati goods were being shipped from a manufacturing center

---

[3] Antonova, I, no. 258, 1716, 371–73. By far the best general discussion of the relative advantages of land and sea or riverine travel in the pre-modern period is that by S. D. Goitein, *A Mediterranean Society*, I, chapter 4, 273–352. See also A. M. Petrov, "Foreign Trade of Russia and Britain with Asia in the Seventeenth to Nineteenth Centuries," *Modern Asian Studies* XXI/4 (1987), 625–37. Petrov, though, exaggerates the ratio of sea to land trade because he relies on Moreland's outdated, excessively low estimates of overland trade. Both the origin and destination of merchandise naturally influenced the mode of transport to and from India. It would not have been economical in normal circumstances to have sent cotton goods that were manufactured in Lahore or Multan to Surat for shipment on to Iran when they could have been dispatched overland or via the Indus.

[4] Jean-Baptiste Tavernier, *Travels in India*, trans. and ed. by V. Ball (London: Macmillan, 1889), I, 4–5 and Foster, *English Factories, 1642–1645*, 87.

[5] Pottinger emphasizes Kirman's importance on the Gulf–Central Asian caravan route. *Travels in Beloochistan and Sinde* (London: Longman, 1816), 228–29.

[6] Ferrier, "An English View of Persian Trade," 203.

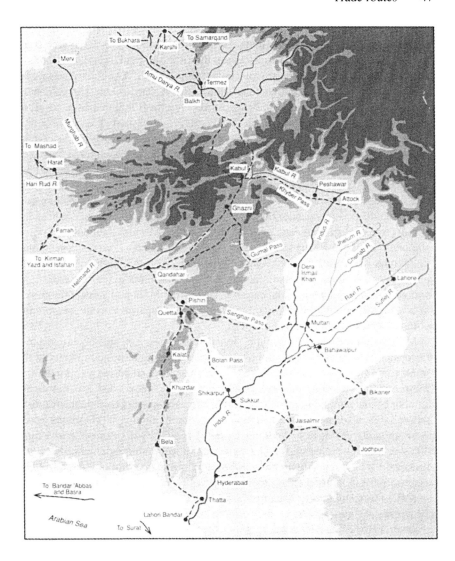

Sea level - 200 meters
200 - 1500 meters
1500 - 3,000 meters
Above 3,000 meters

Map 2 Northwest routes: India to Iran and Turan

such as Ahmedabad to Isfahan, the Safavid capital, the entire journey might take no more than two and a half to three months. This assumes that excessive snow would not block mountain passes between the Gulf and Iranian plateau.

Barge traffic down the Indus was considerably slower. Yet if merchants were shipping cotton cloth or indigo from Lahore or Multan to Iran it would have been faster to use this route or even to travel overland rather than to dispatch merchandise to Surat and then send it onwards by sea. Goods could be shipped down the Indus from Multan throughout the year, but the upper reaches of the Indus and the Ravi between Multan and Lahore were only navigable between March and October, and it took fully-loaded vessels three months to sail the entire distance from Lahore to Lahori Bandar.[7] Merchandise also reached that Arabian Sea port overland from Jaisalmir, the fortress-city entrepôt in the westernmost Rajasthan desert.[8] A trip from Lahore to Isfahan via the Indus and the Arabian Sea could, therefore, take four and a half to five months. Many of the goods that were shipped via this route were undoubtedly destined for Isfahan, Tabriz or even Basra in Ottoman dominions,[9] for if they were being sent to Harat or Mashad it probably would have been more economical to send them directly overland. As caravans regularly traversed the entire distance from Multan to Isfahan the choice of a route between the Panjab and Iran may have depended on the season and political factors more than anything else.

Maritime trade between Mughul India and Iran is so well documented in European sources that it does not require any additional discussion here, but the same cannot be said for the overland routes that connected the two kingdoms. These remain inadequately described and poorly understood. A significant amount of trade normally passed through these northwestern passes, at least three thousand camel loads a year in the early sixteenth century.[10] This represented approximately 750 tons of goods per year if even a "weak" camel could carry 500 pounds.[11] Overland trade had a significant impact on Iranian markets, as was illustrated by the report that when a thousand camels carrying cloth and indigo reached Isfahan in 1665 local prices fell by 15 percent.[12] When the narrow Gulf sea lanes were unusually dangerous overland trade might increase as much as 300 percent a year, as Steel and Crowther reported to have occurred for this reason in 1616.[13] The interchangeability of sea and land routes was again made

[7] "Henry Bornford's Account of his Journey from Agra to Tatta," in Foster, ed., *English Factories, 1637–41*, 137. Along with Bornford's invaluable account see also D. H. A. Kolff and H. W. Van Santen, eds., *De Geschriften van Francisco Pelsaert over Mughal Indië, 1627 Kroniek en Remonstrantie* (s'Gravenhage, Netherlands: Martinus Nijhoff, 1979), 276–79, "De Provincies Ten Noorden en Ten Westen Van Agra." Pelsaert gives an excellent summary of the river and overland trade routes in the Panjab and Sind and of the goods carried in each area.
[8] "Henry Bornford's Account," 137–38.
[9] *Ibid.*, 135.
[10] Steel and Crowther, "Journey," 209.
[11] F. C. Danvers and William Foster, eds., *Letters Received by the East India Company from its Servants in the East*, 6 vols. (London: Sampson, Low & Marston, 1901), V, 1617, 237.
[12] Foster, ed., *English Factories, 1655–1660*, 128.
[13] Steel and Crowther, "Journey," 209.

obvious a half-century later when Iranian officials told the English that if a commercial dispute between them prompted English ships to interdict Iranian sea-borne commerce their economic interests would not be seriously damaged. If that happened, they pointedly observed, "we shall have supply enough way of Candahar."[14] On occasions when the opposite was true, when Mughul–Safavid warfare at Qandahar stopped caravan traffic, merchants quickly adjusted and began shipping their goods by sea. A very general indication of the volume of goods that this perennial conflict could cause to be diverted from overland to sea trade was indicated by the pressure that it sometimes put on shipping resources at Surat. In 1639, for example, English East India company factors reported that as a result of Mughul–Safavid warfare around the city "fraught goods . . . so abound in Surat that here are not vessells enough to transport them."[15]

Most overland trade between Mughul and Safavid territories was funnelled through one of three passes; from the south to the north these were: the Bolan, the Sanghar and the Gumal. As trade routes they shared two characteristics: they were dangerous and trade through them, like both the sea and the Indus routes, was seasonal. Tribal attacks posed the greatest and most constant threat. Baluchis and Afghans dominated the Bolan area while Afghans controlled most of the territory on both the eastern and western sides of the more northerly passes. Mughul and/or Safavid officials controlled the eastern and western approaches to the passes throughout most of the seventeenth century, but their authority ebbed quickly in the early decades of the eighteenth century.[16] The seasonal nature of the traffic was partly due simply to the extremes of winter and summer weather. Merchants usually avoided travel in the winter because of severe cold or heavy snow, and early spring torrents could obliterate caravans that tried to traverse the narrow passes too early in the season. Searing summer heat and lack of water in the largely seasonal rivers and streams made travel in mid-summer not only undesirable but virtually impossible for large camel caravans. Even during the monsoon season in August the riverbed of the Bolan Pass usually remained completely dry. However, most merchants would not in any case normally have been able to ship large amounts of merchandise in mid-summer, because most of the transport camels were owned by Afghan nomads who would take goods through the passes to the west on their spring migration and return eastward to Mughul territories in the fall. Not enough camels or tribal protectors would have been available at other times.

Merchants regularly used all of these passes if they were sending goods from Mughul India to Iran in the seventeenth century, and Mughul troops also used the Bolan and Sanghar passes for military expeditions sent to retake Qandahar from the Safavids. The Bolan, the best known of these three passes, was historically a

---

[14] Foster, ed., *English Factories, 1655–1660*, 128.
[15] *Ibid., 1637–1641*, 211.
[16] Islam, *Calendar of Indo-Persian Relations*, I, 471–74, illustrates how conditions deteriorated in the area of the eastern approaches to the Bolan Pass in the early eighteenth century.

Plate 2   Western entrance to the Bolan Pass

passageway that linked Sind with the eastern Iranian plateau.[17] While the ascent to the summit of the pass climbs to more than 5,000 feet from its eastern terminus at Dadhar, near Sibi, it was rarely closed by snow anywhere along its nearly 80-mile length, but extreme cold usually discouraged even horse traders from using it between November and early March.[18] It was wide enough for Dara Shikoh, Shah Jahan's eldest son, to have been able to dispatch his heavy artillery through in 1653 when he commanded the last Mughul army that attempted to retake Qandahar.[19] Darak Shikoh sent his main field army through the more northerly Sanghar Pass, a decision that was dictated by the fact that it rather than the Bolan was the most direct route between Multan, the Mughul provincial capital of the southern Panjab, and Qandahar.

In the twentieth century the Sanghar was the least well known of these three passes, but it may have been the most important commercial and military route between northwestern India and Iran in the seventeenth century. With its eastern entrance located northwest of Multan where the Sanghar river debouches into the Derajat plain, the Sanghar Pass blended together with the Sakhi Sarwar Pass just to its south and offered armies and merchants the shortest and most direct caravan route between Multan and Qandahar.[20] As these two cities were the most important emporia of the southern Panjab and the eastern Iranian plateau respectively, commercial traffic had apparently traversed this pass for centuries. Arab writers knew that Indian caravans for Iran assembled in Multan,[21] and they

---

[17] Jean-François Jarrige and Richard R. Meadow, "The Antecedants of Civilization in the Indus Valley," *Scientific American* CCXLIII/2 (August 1980), 122–33.

[18] Edward Thornton, *A Gazetteer of the Countries Adjacent to India* ... (London: W. H. Allen, 1844), I, 109–12 for a description of the Bolan Pass. Henry Pottinger described how winter cold in the Bolan Pass kept horse merchants away until spring. *Travels*, 41.

[19] Henry George Raverty, *Notes on Afghanistan and Baluchistan*, repr. (Quetta: Nisa Traders, 1982), I, 22–24.

[20] *Ibid.*, I, 8. Steel and Crowther provided compelling eyewitness testimony about the importance of this route in 1615, for they accompanied caravans that went from Lahore via Multan to Qandahar rather than traveling through the Khyber.

Pelsaert reported on the importance of the Multan–Qandahar route in 1627. Kolff and Van Santen, *De Geschriften*, 278. Note, however, that Tavernier says in his travels, published in 1676, that "from Kandahar to Agra ... there are only two routes via Kabul or Multan respectively. The latter is shorter than the other by ten days, but the caravan scarcely ever takes it because from Kandahar to Multan it is desert country almost all the way, and because one must march for three or four days without meeting water": Tavernier, *Travels in India*, ed. by William Crooke (Oxford: Oxford University Press, 2nd ed., 1925), I, 73. Yet a page later Tavernier also says that "Multan is the place from whence all the Banians migrate who come to trade in Persia . . . " The latter comment suggests that caravan traffic between Multan and Qandahar continued. *If* Tavernier was correct in stating, or reporting the comments of informants, that Indo-Iranian caravan traffic primarily moved through the Khyber in the late seventeenth century, the cause of this historic shift away from the Sanghar route may have been the result of the increased importance of Lahore relative to Multan in the late Mughul period. The lack of water along sections of the Multan–Qandahar route was not, after all, a new development. See also C. R. Markham, "The Mountain Passes on the Afghan Frontier of British India," *Proceedings of the Royal Geographical Society*, n.d., I (1879), 55. Markham's article is probably the best general discussion of the northwestern passes published in the nineteenth century.

[21] Raverty, *Notes*, II, 547–48.

probably traveled through the Sanghar. Steel and Crowther joined such a caravan in the city and then journeyed through the pass and on to Qandahar in May, June and July, 1615.

They traversed the steep, broken terrain of the pass and then completed the trip between the two cities in just over five weeks, constantly threatened by Afghan tribesmen. On the route their caravan passed three Mughul garrisons in the mountainous terrain between the pass and Qandahar. These forts were a good indication of the importance that the Mughuls attached to this route; they were also evidence of the security afforded to merchants in even the remotest regions of the empire.[22] When they arrived in Qandahar their caravan broke into smaller groups because, they said, provisions were so scarce in Iran,[23] but their willingness to travel in Iran unprotected by large caravans was also indicative of the relative security of Iranian roads. Steel and Crowther were not afterwards molested or threatened in Iran, apart from having to pay customs duties at Farrah, during the further two months that it took them to reach Isfahan.[24] The greatest danger in Iran came later in the century when provincial officials evidently felt that they could take advantage of an increasingly moribund central government, for in 1673 the governor of Qandahar conspired to rob the Indian caravan that was said to be worth "several millions."[25]

North of the Sangar was the Gumal Pass. It too was used for Iranian trade, but it was more important for merchants who traveled between Hindustan, "Kabulistan" and Turan. Like the Bolan and the Sanghar passes it was also named for the principal river that carved a pathway through the Sulaiman range to the Indus plain. Travelers entered the eastern end of the Gumal Pass west-northwest of Dera Ismail Khan and first followed the Gumal and Kundar rivers southwest through the Sulaiman range at which point they would turn northwest along the Gumal in the direction of Ghazni. Like the other two passes to the south the actual Gumal Pass was part of a much longer route across the mountains. In the case of the Gumal it was a difficult, 120-mile-long caravan path from the Derajat plains to northeastern Afghanistan. Babur was warned against following the Gumal back to Kabul in 1510 because of the danger from high water in the river and "uncertainty on the Gumal road," the latter comment an obvious allusion to the threat of Afghan attacks.[26]

The commercial viability of this route in the Mughal period and later was largely the consequence of its use as the principal migratory path for a number of Afghan nomadic clans and tribes known collectively as *powindahs*.[27] They traded during their migratory cycle that took them from their summer pasturage in the

[22] Steel and Crowther, "Journey," 210–11.
[23] *Ibid.*, 213.
[24] *Ibid.*, 213–16.
[25] Chardin, *Travels in Persia*, 73. The man was, however, arrested!
[26] Beveridge, *The Babur-nama in English*, 235.
[27] Raverty, *Notes*, II, 483–504, and J. A. Robinson, *Notes on the Nomad Tribes of Eastern Afghanistan*, repr. (Quetta: Nisa Traders, 1980).

highlands west of the Sulaiman range to the Indus plain in the fall, where they generally remained with their animals until they could retrace their steps back across the mountains in the spring. This route may have acquired special significance during periods when governments in India, Afghanistan and Iran were incapable of maintaining control of alternative routes.[28] The most important tribes that utilized the pass were the Luharni or Nuharni. They were armed and capable of fighting their way through the mountains in face of constant harassment by the Waziri Afghans, who dominated most of the territory along the length of the Gumal river.[29] A trip from Dera Ismail Khan through the Gumal to Ghazni could take up to a month. Just before reaching Ghazni, though, powindahs and merchants who traveled under their protection would turn off southwest towards Qandahar or northeast towards Kabul.

In the Mughul period many Luharnis traded beyond Kabul to Bukhara or Samarqand, but in the relatively stable seventeenth century most individual merchants who had to travel between India and Turan probably chose to use the Khyber pass. Despite its later fame the Khyber had not always been the preferred route between northwestern India and Turan.[30] While relatively short, well-watered and gradual in ascent it was also, in the Mughul emperor Jahangir's words, *marpich*, or serpentine,[31] and the more infamous passages through its narrow defiles were less than 100 feet wide. Afghan uprisings often blocked the pass even at the height of Mughul power.[32] By widening the road, building caravansarais and co-opting, however provisionally, Afghan chiefs to act as Mughul officials and guard the pass, Akbar and his successors made the Khyber the safest and preferred route between Hindustan, Kabul and Turan.[33] Shah Jahan, the great Mughul builder of the mid-seventeenth century, supplemented Akbar's road improvements and security system by having bridges built at either end of the pass, work that may have been supervised by his well-known engineer, 'Ali Mardan Khan.[34]

The route through this serpentine pass began just west of Peshawar, a city where 'Ali Mardan Khan constructed a large caravansarai in the heart of the city behind the Mughul fortress, and wound its way northwest to the Jalalabad plain, a distance of slightly more than 30 miles. The summit of the pass rose to only

[28] This likelihood is partly suggested by Raverty's comments, *Notes*, II, 501.
[29] For a personal narrative of the Luharni caravan through the Gumal see G. T. Vigne, *A Personal Narrative of a Visit to Ghuzni, Kabul and Afghanistan*, repr. (Lahore: Sang-e-Meel Publications, 1982), 67–104.
[30] AA, II, 406.
[31] Beveridge, ed. and Rogers, trans., *The Tuzuk-i-Jahangiri*, I, 102.
[32] Markham, "Mountain Passes," 43–44. For examples see Beveridge, ed. and Rogers, trans., *The Tuzuk-i-Jahangiri*, I, 321, and Antonova, I, no. 126, 1676, 220–21; no. 128, 1676, 222; and no. 130, 1677, 223. A Russian mission was forbidden to proceed beyond Kabul because of Mughul–Afghan wars.
[33] Abu'l Fadl does not say that the Khyber was used for Iranian trade at this time, but see Tavernier's comments cited above in n. 20.
[34] Habib, *An Atlas of the Mughal Empire*, sheet 1A–B, 3. Habib merely says that the bridges were built in Shah Jahan's reign.

3,373 feet but it was usually blocked by snow in the winter months. In April–May 1607, Jahangir moved unhurriedly through the Khyber in royal procession, passing from Peshawar to Jalalabad in about a week. Afghans holding Mughul appointments met him at both cities.[35] The steepest ascent in the entire trip from Peshawar to Kabul occurred not in the pass itself but along the Kabul river between Jalalabad and Jundmak, 28 miles to the east and 4,500 feet above sea level. This stage of the journey also brought travelers from the warm climate of Jalalabad, famous for its pomegranates and other fruits, to the continental weather of the Kabul region, 6,000 feet above sea level.

Merchants and other travelers who then journeyed on from Kabul to northern Afghanistan and Turan had to make their trips between mid-April and mid-November because in winter snow blocked the lofty heights of the Hindu Kush passes, three of which exceeded 10,000 feet.[36] In consequence round-trip journeys had to be carefully planned. Babur reported that seven possible roads connected Kabul with Balkh and Qunduz in Badakshan,[37] a distance of 300 miles that represented the first segment of the two-stage trip to Bukhara and Samarqand. The most direct route ran almost due north from Kabul through Charikar and Parwan, south of the mountains, to Khinjan, just north of the Hindu Kush and then on to Balkh.[38] In the seventeenth century merchants reported that camels took slightly more than three weeks to make this part of the trip, although at least another two weeks would be added if they went "around the hills." This may have been a reference to the only slightly less daunting route that Alexander Burnes took in 1837,[39] or perhaps an allusion to the much longer route via Harat and Mashad which would certainly have taken much more than an additional two weeks. On the second stage of the journey, from Balkh to Bukhara, the caravan path was a relatively easy, largely level track, although a large camel caravan could be delayed for several days by the ferry at the Oxus river crossing. Attacks by Turkmen tribes represented the greatest dangers that merchants faced as they crossed the desert, although extreme heat was also a problem, forcing them to travel at night in order to maintain the 25 to 30 mile per day pace that healthy animals could usually manage in this terrain. If caravans were lucky they could cover the distance from Balkh to Bukhara in an additional two weeks. Thus if a merchant left Lahore in later February he could hope to reach Bukhara or nearby Samarqand in early June.[40]

Bukhara, the principal emporium of western Turan in the Uzbek period, was the destination of most caravans from Mughul territories, but not all merchants chose

[35] Beveridge, ed. and Rogers, trans., *The Tuzuk-i-Jahangiri*, I, 101–6. Russian officials were told that it took six days to cover this distance by camel, so Jahangir's trip was apparently typical in duration. Antonova, I, no. 32, 1646, 81.

[36] Burnes, *Travels into Bokhara*, II, 150–71, for a description of the Bamian route in early May.

[37] Beveridge, *The Babur-nama in English*, 204–6.

[38] Antonova, I, no. 32, 1646, 88 and no. 91, 1670, 168.

[39] See above, n. 36.

[40] Antonova, I, no. 91, 1670, 168–70, for a description of the time needed to make the journey from Turan to India.

to travel or to dispatch their goods via the northern Afghan route. Others traveled to Turan from Mashad in Iranian Khurasan, which they might have reached either via Bandar 'Abbas and Kirman or from one of the northwest Indian passes and Qandahar. As Steel and Crowther discovered, the 360-mile road from Qandahar to Mashad by way of Harat was reasonably safe; it was interrupted mainly by a few streams whose spring floods might delay caravans for several days.[41] As in the case of the northern Afghan route, caravans faced the greatest dangers from Turkmen attacks in the desert and steppe country between Mashad and Bukhara. A tragic case in point was the report which Anthony Jenkinson heard in Bukhara in 1558 that a caravan, "which had come out of *India* and *Persia*," had been "destroyed" while still ten days journey from Bukhara.[42]

Multan and the Multanis

Whatever route they chose most of the merchants from Mughul India who conducted business in Iran, Turan or Russia in the seventeenth century migrated to those areas from Multan. In Iran and Turan especially such merchants were often identified specifically as Multanis. This was a name or *nisba* which in its most particular usage indicated that these men were either natives or residents of Multan, although sometimes it appears to have been used in a broader sense to refer to emigré traders from throughout the Panjab who had merely traveled to Safavid, Uzbek or Russian territory via the city.[43] The prevalence of Multanis in the Indian diaspora indicates that Multan was a major commercial center in this period, even though its importance has been almost entirely overlooked in the modern historiography of the Mughul empire. As is true of so many other aspects of early modern commercial history, this neglect seems to be largely due to scholars' Eurocentric bias, in this case to their preoccupation with Surat's well-known role as the Mughul empire's premier port for European and Indian Ocean commerce. Surat's volume of trade with both Europe and Asia undoubtedly did exceed that of any other single Mughul city. It did not, though, exercise the preeminent economic influence that has been attributed to "capitalist cities" that were successively centers of the European world economy, Venice, Amsterdam and London.[44] At its height the Mughul empire had a nearly subcontinental-sized economy that included several major urban commercial centers which exerted regional economic influence. Multan was one of these and had been a major commercial and political center throughout Indo-Muslim history.

[41] Thornton, *A Gazetteer*, Appendix, 293–304, "Route from Kandahar to Herat, performed in 1839."

[42] Jenkinson, *Early Voyages and Travels*, II, 93. Jenkinson's wording, that the caravan came "out of *India* and *Persia*," suggests that a caravan from India using the Qandahar–Mashad route had joined with an Iranian caravan somewhere in Khurasan.

[43] *Nisba* from the Arabic verb *Nasaba*, to relate, to link, to trace, i.e. ancestry, is often suffixed to names in Islamic societies to indicate origin, residence, etc. Thus, Multani, Isfahani, Bukhari, etc.

[44] Fernand Braudel, *Perspective of the World*, 27–35. Braudel implies that Surat was the South Asian equivalent of dominant cities in the European world economy or of Nanjing and later Beijing in China, but he does not really attempt to analyze the South Asian case.

The capital of Arab–Muslim Sind for three centuries after the initial Arab conquest in 714 AD, Multan was later to be a major provincial capital of successive north Indian Muslim states as well as a mint town and provincial capital of the Mughul empire.[45] The city's importance was partly due to the fact that it was a textile manufacturing center. It was situated in an important cotton-growing region of the southern Panjab and northern Sind, and local weavers produced large quantities of cotton textiles that were its most important exports.[46] Artisans in the city also wove several varieties of silk cloth from raw silk that was imported in large quantities from Bukhara and its neighboring region.[47] The amount and value of these textile manufactures may have been quite modest when compared with Lahore's output, not to speak of the production of Gujarat and Bengal in any given year, but Multan's strategic position elevated it above the level of an otherwise modest provincial manufacturing town to that of a major regional commercial city.

Located at the crossroads of the overland and riverine/sea routes that connected northwestern India with Afghanistan, Iran and the Arabian Sea, Multan was the principal entrepôt of this area during the Sultanate period (1206–1526), and it retained much of its importance even after Akbar and his successors had secured the Khyber Pass. The fact that in 1615 Steel and Crowther and other merchants from Lahore traveled from Lahore to Qandahar via Multan is one indication of its continued significance in the seventeenth century. Not only was the city still functioning as the principal dispersal point for merchants from the entire Panjab area who traveled to Safavid Iran, but it is likely that some of the substantial amounts of goods that were shipped overland to Iran from Sind each year were also sent via this route,[48] as Multan functioned as the commercial center of the northern Sind as well as the southern Panjab.

Multanis are first mentioned as important north Indian merchants by the Sultanate historian, Zia al-Din Barani. Writing in the late fourteenth century, Barani said that Multanis controlled a significant portion of Muslim India's long-distance trade.[49] Barani's remarks are generally consistent with the prominence

---

[45] For the early history of Multan see Derryl N. Maclean, *Religion and Society in Arab Sind* (Leiden: E. J. Brill, 1989); Ahmad Nabi Khan, *Multan, History and Architecture* (Islamabad: Institute of Islamic History, Islamic University, 1983) and H. T. Lambrick, *Sind* (Hyderabad, Pakistan: Sindh Adabi Board, 1964), 1.

[46] Humaira Dasti, "Multan as a Centre of Trade and Commerce During the Mughal Period," *Quarterly Journal of the Pakistan Historical Society* XXXVII/3 (July 1990), 247–56. See also Habib, *An Atlas of the Mughal Empire*, 4b, "Punjab, Economic."

[47] *Ibid.*, 251 and Vigne, *Personal Narrative*, 21–22. Vigne reported that "Several hundred maunds of raw silk are brought to Multan every year by the Lohanis, chiefly from Bokhara and Turkistan: these are manufactured in one hundred and fifty workshops."

[48] Willem Floor, "The Dutch East India Company's Trade with Sind in the 17th and 18th Centuries," *Moyen Orient and Ocean Indien XVIe–XIXe s.* III (1986), 112. According to the Dutch, 680,340 Dutch florins' worth of goods were sent overland to Iran each year from Sind.

[49] See Irfan Habib's careful discussion of Barani's text in "Non-agricultural Production and Urban Economy," CEHI, I, 85. Habib is not able to identify these Multanis more specifically.

accorded Multanis in several later sources, particularly those that relate to Safavid Iran. The Russian merchant, F. A. Kotov, identified all the Mughul-Indian merchants whom he saw in Isfahan in 1623, both Hindus and Muslims, as Multanis,[50] and more than fifty years later in 1676 the Frenchman, Jean-Baptiste Tavernier, remarked that the "banians," that is Hindu or Jain merchants, who did business in Iran came from Multan.[51] Less than a decade later, in 1684–85, the German physician, Engelbert Kaempfer, said that 10,000 Multanis resided in Isfahan.[52] Eight Multani merchant families were still living in the carpet manufacturing center, Kashan, in 1723, a year after the collapse of the Safavid dynasty.[53] Apart from this eyewitness testimony, the most compelling evidence that the Indian trade diaspora in Iran was dominated by Multanis occurs in the 1747 Russian census of the Astrakhan Indian community, which showed that nearly all of these merchants came from Multan or nearby villages. This information is so important because many of these men are likely to have migrated to Astrakhan from northern Iranian commercial centers in the first instance.[54] The census clearly shows that many of them traded for or with relatives in Azerbaijan or Gilan provinces who were, therefore, almost certainly Multanis themselves.

The equation between Mughul-Indian merchants and Multanis is much less certain for Turan, because few European merchants lived in Central Asian cities for any length of time in the seventeenth century. There was, that is, no Chardin for seventeenth-century Turan. Records definitely show that some Muslim Multanis were active in the textile trade in Samarqand and Bukhara in the sixteenth and the seventeenth century.[55] Hindus are also likely to have lived among them at this time, and to have made up a substantial part of the population of approximately 300 "Indian" merchants who lived in Bukhara in 1736. This information was furnished to the Russian government by an Astrakhan Indian merchant who had visited the city a short time earlier.[56] Certainly, Burnes and other nineteenth-century European observers knew that

[50] F. A. Kotov, *Khozhdenia kuptsa Fedota Kotova v Persiiu* [The Tour of the Merchant Fedot Kotov in Persia] (Moscow: Eastern Literature, 1958), 91.
[51] William Crooke, ed. and V. Ball, trans., *Travels in India by Jean Baptiste Tavernier* (Oxford: Oxford University Press, 2nd ed., 1945), I, 74.
[52] Engelbert Kaempfer, *Am Hofe des persischen Grosskönigs 1684–1685* (Tübingen, Basel: Walter Hinz, 1977), 204.
[53] Vera Basch Moreen, *Iranian Jewry*, 35.
[54] Antonova, II, no. 132, 1747, 265–69.
[55] Multani merchants in Samarqand are discussed by Mukimova, *Social Differentiation*, 53–68. Evidence of Multani merchants residing in Bukhara is provided by Golikova, *Essays*, 171, where the author mentions six Multani merchants who lived with Bukharans in Samarqand. The exact date of their residence is unclear but it was probably in the late seventeenth or early eighteenth century. See also N. B. Baikova, *Rol' Srednei Azii v Russko-Indiiskikh Torgovykh Sviaziakh* [The Role of Central Asia in Russian–Indian Trade Connections] (Tashkent: Nauka, 1964), 90, where the Indian colony in Bukhara is mentioned in the first half of the seventeenth century.
[56] Antonova, II, no. 74, 1736, 139.

many influential Hindu merchants and bankers then lived in Bukhara and Samarqand.[57]

The caste or ethnic identity of Hindu and Muslim Multani merchants is rarely indicated in seventeenth or eighteenth-century sources. Europeans of this period never made such precise identifications of Mughul Indian merchants, and much of the other evidence is circumstantial, such as the concentration of particular populations in and around Multan. However, a strong likelihood exists that nearly all of the Hindus who carried this nisba in Iran, Turan or Russia were Panjabi Khattris and that most of the Muslims were Afghans or Pushtuns. This identification may seem questionable in the Hindu case, for many Europeans in Iran did not identify Hindu merchants as Multanis, but referred to them, as Chardin commonly did, as "banias" or "banians." Indians themselves would never have classified Khattris as banians, for members of this caste believed themselves to be descended from the Aryan warrior class, the Kshatriya, and therefore claimed a higher ritual rank than the many commercial castes whom Indians commonly included in the general bania category.[58] However, most Europeans were not well informed about the ritual subtleties of Indian caste relationships, and outside of India especially they usually used the term bania as an occupational category for all Hindu merchants and for Jains as well. That is, the occupational category bania and the geographic designation Multani in most cases referred to the same group of merchants. Tavernier exemplified this usage when he said that banias migrated from Iran to Multan!

Only a few explicit examples are known from seventeenth- and eighteenth-century sources where the Multani nisba is unmistakably linked to a Khattri name. The earliest dates to the 1670s, and is found in the Astrakhan customs and judicial records. In particular a 1673 document describes a complicated dispute between the Iranian ambassador to Russia and a group of Indian merchants from Multan, all of whom have, even though the opaque lens of Russian spelling, recognizably Hindu names. One of these men is fully identified, including his subcaste name, as Banda Kapur Chand.[59] Kapurs were and are a subcaste of the large Khattri-caste group that was one of the wealthiest and most influential castes in the Panjab and northwestern India throughout the Mughul and British

---

[57] Apart from Burnes, see also the very late but well-informed evidence of the American diplomat, Eugene Schuyler, *Turkistan, Notes of a Journey in Russian Turkistan, Kokand, Bukhara and Khuldja*, ed. by Geoffrey Wheeler, abridged by K. E. West (London: Routledge & Kegan Paul, 1966), Hindus in Tashkent, 107, Hindus, Jews and Afghans in Samarqand, 134, Hindus, Jews and Afghans in Kokand, 204, Hindus in Bukhara, 255.

[58] For a definition and discussion of the term banian see especially Lakshmi Subramanian, "The Eighteenth Century Social Order in Surat: A Reply and Excursus on the Riots of 1788 and 1795," *Modern Asian Studies* XXV/2 (1991), 321–65, and Rajat Kanta Ray, "The *Bazar*: Indigenous Sector of the Indian Economy," in Dwijendra Tripathi, ed., *Business Communities of India* (New Delhi: Manohar, 1984), 241–67. Europeans in Iran may well have encountered genuine banian castes in Hurmuz or Bandar 'Abbas and then used the term generally for all of the Hindu and Jain merchants whom they later met in the interior of Iran.

[59] Antonova, I, no. 105, 4, 1673, 185.

periods.[60] More than 200 years later Kapurs were known to be one of the Khattri subcastes that resided in Multan.[61] Multani Khattris represented a regional grouping of members of a caste that was, at the date of British census reports, concentrated in the central and northwestern Panjab.[62]

Khattri merchants undoubtedly made their headquarters in Multan because of its dual importance as a manufacturing center and commercial entrepôt. It is easy to imagine how they might have come to use the city as their principal exporting center and then incrementally expanded their trading networks from there into Iran, increasing their business activity and concentrating it in Isfahan during the relatively secure and prosperous seventeenth century. The English East India company agent, George Forster, probably encountered the Khattri remnant of the Multani diaspora when he met "Hindoo merchants, chiefly of Moultan" in Qandahar, Harat and the southwestern Caspian port of Baku in 1798.[63] Just ten years later when the British envoy to Afghanistan, Mountstuart Elphinstone, visited Kabul, he learned that Khattris could be found throughout Afghanistan and as far west as Astrakhan functioning as "bankers, merchants, goldsmiths and sellers of grain."[64]

There were, however, a small number of Hindu and Jain merchants who were not Multanis, but were in fact genuine banias in the Indian sense of the term. They also traded in Iran, newly independent Afghanistan and southern Russia in the eighteenth century, although there is no evidence to show that they were active in these areas earlier. These were Marwaris, who were always clearly identified in Russian records by this particular nisba as natives or residents of the Marwar areas of Rajasthan. They are first mentioned in Astrakhan customs and judicial documents of the 1720s and 1730s. One "Marwar Bara(ev)" figures prominently in these records. As a "bara" he appears to have been the eldest or most important local representative of a far-flung commercial network which roughly paralleled that of the Khattris, although it appears to have been considerably less extensive.[65]

---

[60] Fray Sebastien Manrique, *Travels of Fray Sebastien Manrique, 1629–1643* (Oxford: Hakluyt Society, 1947), II, 156, and H. A. Rose, *A Glossary of the Tribes of the Punjab and the North-West Frontier* (Based on the Census Report for the Punjab, 1883 by the late Sir Denzil Ibbetson, K.C.S.I. and the Census for the Punjab, 1892 by the Hon. M. E. D. Maclagan, C.S.I.) (Delhi: Punjab National Press, 1970), II, 506.

[61] See E. D. Maclagan, *Gazetteer of the Multan District 1901–1902* (Lahore: Civil and Military Gazette Press, 1902), 127. "The Khatris are mainly confined to the town of Multan, and very few own any land. They are largely immigrants from the Punjab proper . . . the Khatris of this district are chiefly Mirhotras, Khannas and Kapurs . . . "

[62] J. S. Grewal, "Business Communities of Punjab," in Tripathi, ed., *Business Communities of India*, 216–18, and Rose, *Glossary of Tribes*, 507–8.

[63] George Forster, *A Journey from Bengal to England through the Northern Part of India, Kashmire, Afghanistan, and Persia, and into Russia, by the Caspian Sea* (London: R. Faulder, 1798), II, 103.

[64] Mountstuart Elphinstone, *An Account of the Kingdom of Caubul and its Dependencies in Persia, Tartary and India*, repr. (Graz, Austria: Akademische Druck- u. Verlagsanstatt, 1969), 317.

[65] Surendra Gopal summarizes what is known of this man's career, including his eventual conversion to the Russian orthodox church, in his Introduction to his translation of a selection of the *Russian-Indian Relations* documents. See his *Indians in Russia in the 17th and 18th Centuries* (New Delhi: Indian Council of Historical Research, 1988), 7–8.

Several other Marwaris are also mentioned in these early eighteenth-century sources, but because Marwari names do not appear in earlier documents all of them may have been relatively late arrivals in the city and in Iran as well. The Marwaris in Astrakhan included several who traded with their relations in Tabriz, a commercial pattern that was also common among Khattris.[66] George Forster also confirmed the persistence of this Marwari trading network in the later eighteenth century when he reported meeting Marwaris in Qandahar and Tirshiz, a town near Mashad. In Qandahar Forster met Hindus from Multan and Rajasthan, and in Tirshiz he was told that about 100 Hindu families "from Moultan and Jessilmere" lived in the city.[67] Jaisalmir was the westernmost Rajasthani entrepôt, and the massive Jain temple located near the summit of the fortress-city is a testament to the former prosperity of the Marwari Jain caste, the Oswals.

The Marwari nisba was and is used as a collective designation for Hindu and Jain commercial castes such as the Hindu Agarwals and the Jain Oswals who originated in Marwar. These castes and others evidently began their commercial ascent and migration from their home districts by associating themselves with Rajput armies that assisted Mughul expansion in eastern India in the late sixteenth and early seventeenth century.[68] Marwari accumulation of large capital resources has been attributed more particularly to their role in furnishing credit for Mughul land revenue collections, leading to their expansion as a major commercial and financial caste throughout northern and northeastern India by the late seventeenth and early eighteenth century. The major thrust of Marwari migration out of Rajasthan was into the densely populated Gangetic heartland.[69] However, some of them evidently made their way westward along the well-known caravan routes from Jaisalmir or nearby Bikaner to the Indus at Bahawalpur or Sukkur where they could have joined caravans going through the Bolan or Sanghar passes. Others may have made the short trip to Lahori Bandar and sailed into the Gulf. If any Marwaris were in fact among the many banians who worked in Bandar 'Abbas throughout the seventeenth century, they are just as likely to have sailed there

---

[66] Antonova, II, no. 48, 1725, 75. The Marwari mentioned in this particular document is "Marwari Rajaram(ov)."

[67] Forster, *A Journey from Bengal to England*, I, 166.

[68] G. D. Sharma, "The Marwaris: Economic Foundations of an Indian Capitalist Class," in Tripathi, ed., *Business Communities of India*, 186. This association brings to mind the association of the rise of Florentine families with their collections of papal revenue. In both cases merchants were apparently able to generate substantial capital by acting as agents for wealthy administrative systems. See Gene Brucker, *Renaissance Florence* (Berkeley: University of California Press, 2nd ed., 1983), 53–55. See also the important early account by (Lt.) A. H. E. Boileau, *Personal Narrative of a Tour Through the Western States of Rajwara in 1835 . . .* (Calcutta: Baptist Mission Press, 1837), for descriptions of influential Marwari merchants. Boileau's account is especially interesting for its evidence of how Marwari merchants contributed to state building among the Rajputs by acting as their financial advisors or ministers.

[69] Thomas Timberg, *The Marwaris* (New Delhi: Vikas, 1978).

from Surat, where a number of Marwari businessmen always lived during the Mughul period.[70]

The Muslim Multani merchants whom Kotov reported to be working in Isfahan in 1623 are most likely to have been Afghans, although they are not so identified. During Mughul rule Afghans, members of Pushtun-speaking tribes, played a major role in both Indo-Iranian and Indo-Turanian trade. They had probably done so for centuries prior to Mughul rule, since they occupied the territory athwart the principal overland routes that connected Mughul India with Safavid and Uzbek territories. At least the historian Muhammad Qasim Ferishta (c. 1570–1611), an Iranian who settled in the Deccan sultanate of Bijapur, said of them, "It is related that in early times the tribe of Afghans, forming themselves into a commercial community, carried on trade between Persia and Hindoostan."[71] In his autobiographical memoir, the *Babur-nama*, the first Mughul emperor reported that virtually all of this overland commerce flowed through two predominantly Afghan cities, Kabul and Qandahar.

There are two trade-marts on the land route between Hindustan and Khurasan [Iran]; one is Kabul, the other, Qandahar. To Kabul come caravans from Kashgar, Ferghana, Turkistan, Samarqand, Bukhara, Balkh, Hisar, and Badakshan. To Qandahar they come from Khurasan. Kabul is an excellent trading center; if merchants went to Khita [north China] or Rum [Anatolia] they might make no higher profit. Down to Kabul every year come 7, 8 or 10,000 horses and up to it, from Hindustan, come every year caravans of 10, 15 or 20,000 heads-of-houses, bringing slaves (barda), white cloth, sugar-candy, refined and common sugars and aromatic roots. Many a trader is not content with a profit of 30 or 40 in 10. In Kabul can be had the products of Khurasan, Rum, Iraq and Chin [China] while it is Hindustan's own market.[72]

The 20,000 "heads-of-houses" who, Babur reports, came from Hindustan to Kabul each year, he describes in his original Chaghatai text as "tribesmen." These were almost certainly Afghan powindahs.[73] Babur himself mentions the name of a prominent powindah merchant when he narrates how he and his followers descended from Kabul to the Derajat plain in 1505 to pillage resources to support the thread-bare Timurid state that he had established in Kabul in the previous year. Between the Indus and the Sulaiman range he and his men attacked a small Afghan caravan from which they took white cloth, horses and sugar, all staple items in the commerce between Mughul India, Iran and Turan. During the

---

[70] Among the many references to the large "banian" community in Bandar 'Abbas, see Jean-Baptiste Tavernier, *Voyages en Perse*, repr. (Paris: Editions Carrefour, 1930), especially the map on 328–29 illustrating the location of "l'arbe des Banianes."

[71] Muhammad Qasim Ferishta, *History of the Rise of the Mahomedan Power in India*, trans. by John Briggs, repr. (Calcutta: Editions Indian, 1966), I, 317.

[72] Beveridge, *The Babur-nama in English*, 202.

[73] The word that Beveridge translates as "heads-of-houses" is "oymuq" in the Turki text. Annette S. Beveridge, *The Babar-nama*, repr. (London: Luzac, 1971), fol. 129. Jean-Louis Bacqué-Grammont translates the word as "caravaniers." *Le Livre de Babur* (Paris: Imprimerie Nationale, 1985), 132. For Afghan trading see also H. C. Verma, *Medieval Routes to India* (Calcutta: Naya Prakash, 1978), 236–37.

skirmish that followed they killed a wealthy merchant named Khwaja Khizr Luhani.[74] This man's name is extremely significant, because Luharnis are known from nineteenth and twentieth-century sources to have been one of the principal powindah tribes that traded between India, Kabul, Iran and Turan.

The Luharnis were one of several eastern Afghan tribes who may have been expelled from earlier western Afghan homelands in the fifteenth century, settling then near Ghazni, although according to their own traditions they had traded between India and Kabul at least since the tenth century.[75] G. T. Vigne, who accompanied a Luharni caravan through the Gumal Pass in 1836, alludes to Babur's reference to this tribe, and says that "They traded then as now and their merchandise was of the same description."[76] According to Vigne, the first traveler who is known to have left an eyewitness account of the Luharni migrations, their annual trek took them from the steaming Derajat plains in April and May to their summer highland pastures west of the Sulaiman range, or in their terms, "Khurasan."[77] From there Luharni merchants traveled on to Iran, Kabul or Turan.

Luharnis and other powindah tribes were "natural" merchants, since like other pastoral nomads their specialized economy and migratory life precluded them from manufacturing most products apart from a limited range of carpets and flat weave products. Some powindahs traded within a limited area defined by their migratory range on either side of the Sulaiman range, exchanging animals or animal products for inexpensive cloth and other basic necessities that they required in their daily lives. Others, the Luharni in particular, extended their basic migratory cycle northward to Kabul, Balkh, Bukhara and Samarqand and south-eastwards as far as Bengal. It is difficult to determine why any particular tribe or clan expanded their trading activities to the extent that they largely abandoned their former pastoral economy and continued only to accompany their tribal confederation on its annual migrations. In the case of the Luharni, having their pasturage grounds near a critical mountain pass may have been a contributing factor. Luharnis may also have begun trading as far eastwards as Bengal, because many of their tribesmen became familiar with the region during the reign of Afghan dynasties in northern India in the fifteenth and sixteenth century. Thousands of Luharnis fought for the Afghan Lodi state that Babur overturned in 1526. Abu'l Fadl estimated that the Luharnis alone had 50,000 horsemen in India when Babur's army defeated the Lodis and pushed their combined forces into

---

[74] Beveridge, *The Babur-nama in English*, 235.
[75] G. Morganstierne argues that a large-scale eastward expansion of Afghan tribes occurred in the Sultanate period. He specifically attributes the Luharnis' presence in eastern Afghanistan and western South Asia to the expulsion of this tribe from its previous western Afghan homelands. "Afghan," *Encyclopaedia of Islam*, new ed., I, 218. Vigne quotes from the Luharnis' own claims: *Personal Narrative*, 54.
[76] *Ibid.*, 69.
[77] It is useful to remember this local usage in which "Khurasan" meant the eastern Iranian plateau extending to the western edge of the Sulaiman mountains and not the more usual restricted geographical and political usage which refers to northeastern Iran and northwestern Afghanistan.

Bihar and Bengal where one Luharni chief, Darya Khan, briefly ruled.[78] When Mughul forces eventually gained military control of these provinces in the early seventeenth century, Luharnis were scattered across the Mughul empire from Ghazni to Bengal. They were particularly well entrenched in eastern India where, in fact, Babur had given them imperial land grants in the early sixteenth century.[79]

Apart from Babur's reliable, eyewitness account of Kabul and adjacent regions during his more than 20-year rule from the Afghan capital, there are relatively few references to Luharni, powindah or even Afghan involvement in overland trade in the Mughul-period sources. Luharnis are mentioned selling horses in 1599 and supplying grain to Dara Shikoh's army before Qandahar in 1653.[80] Yet other Indian merchants who are identified only as Muslims are likely to have been Afghans, powindahs and possibly Luharnis as well. This was especially likely where Central Asian trade was concerned. A group of textile merchants and craftsmen who operated in Samarqand in 1589–90 were probably Afghans, although they are identified in a collection of promissory notes only as Muslims and Multanis, with the exception of a Hindu from Lahore who worked for them. The dominant figure in this group was an individual named Darya Khan Multani, a substantial merchant-capitalist who employed other Muslim Multanis and the Hindu as bleachers, dyers and printers of cloth.[81]

Several considerations suggest that Darya Khan and many of his associates were Afghans. First, not only were Afghans heavily involved in Indian–Central Asian commerce, but they were thickly settled in and around Multan.[82] Second, Afghans were the only Indo-Muslim merchants whose names are mentioned repeatedly in other promissory notes from Samarqand in Darya Khan Multani's time, and they were also the only community whose presence in Turan has been memorialized by having a suburb named after them in Bukhara.[83] Third, Darya Khan was a relatively common Afghan name that this particular merchant shared with Darya Khan Luharni, the Lodi commander and ruler in eastern India. The Afghan presence in Isfahan is much more conjectural. Nonetheless, Afghan dominance of the land routes between Mughul and Safavid territories and their virtual monopoly in transport animals in Multan, Kabul, Qandahar and Harat makes it likely that at least some of the Multani Muslims whom Kotov mentioned were Afghans. Afghans must frequently have arrived in the Safavid capital with Indian caravans from Multan or Qandahar. However, in contrast to their prominence in Turan, Afghan merchants do not appear to have been active in large numbers west of Harat. Thus it is quite likely that some of the Muslim Multanis

[78] Beveridge, trans., AN, I, 251.
[79] Rita, Joshi, *The Afghan Nobility and the Mughals, 1526–1707* (New Delhi: Vikas Publishing House, 1985), 49.
[80] AN, III, 1160, and Raverty, *Notes*, II, 488–89.
[81] See above, n. 55.
[82] See Ferishta's discussion of Lodi Afghan control of Multan during the Tughluq period of sultanate history (1320–1412). Briggs, trans., *Rise of Mahomedan Power*, I, 317.
[83] O. A. Sukhareva, *Kvartal'naia Obschina Pozdnefeodal'nogo Goroda Bukhary* [Neighborhood Communities of the Late-feudal City of Bukhara] (Moscow: Nauka, 1976), 218–19.

in Isfahan were other Indian-born Muslims or even Iranians who used Multan as their commercial headquarters.[84]

Mediatory trade

Afghan powindahs played an important role in the overland trade between Mughul India and Safavid Iran and Uzbek Turan, but brief textual allusions to their activities do not explain the nature of their relationship with Khattris or other merchants from sedentary South Asian societies. In lieu of more elaborate evidence than is contained in sources for the period, the concept of "mediatory trade" advanced by the Russian anthropologist A. M. Khazanov offers one hypothesis for interpreting this relationship. Khazanov invokes the phrase to describe commercial relations between desert and steppe pastoral nomads and sedentary merchants. Referring to nomads Khazanov writes:

It was not only their geographical location, mobility, and ownership of transport animals that was to the advantage of nomads, but also their attitude toward traveling, migration and movement beyond the boundaries of territories they traditionally occupied. It was not by chance that all the great overland routes of antiquity and the Middle Ages were pioneered by nomads or with their participation.[85]

Khazanov regards Afghan powindahs as the classic example of mediatory trade in the Middle East and Central Asia. "Already in the thirteenth and fourteenth centuries," he writes, "they supplied transit trade on the routes linking India with Persia and Middle Asia [Turan]. They were able to do so because their caravan routes coincided with the routes of their pastoral migrations."[86]

The idea of mediatory trade is a useful one for conceptualizing how major agrarian and urban cultures were commercially linked with each other across intervening desert and steppe regions, but it also begs many questions about economic relationships between Afghan powindahs and Khattri and Marwari merchants in the commerce between Mughul India and the neighboring Safavid and Uzbek territories. Khazanov actually derives his concept primarily from the powindah case, but he implies that Afghans merely provided the animals and the indispensable experience of annual migrations between major urban areas. That is, in the traditional but often quite meaningful stereotype of pastoral nomads, Afghan powindahs quite literally worked as the pilots of desert and mountain ships, and navigated between the Scylla and Charybdis of human and natural

[84] A. K. S. Lambton gives an example of an Iranian Multani during the British period: "The Case of Hajji 'Abd al-Karim," in C. E. Bosworth, ed., *Iran and Islam* (Edinburgh: Edinburgh University Press, 1971), 331–60.

[85] A. M. Khazanov, *Nomads and the Outside World*, trans. by Julia Crookenden (Cambridge: Cambridge University Press, 1984), 209.

[86] *Ibid.*, 212. Within India "Hundiwallahs" may be said to have also fulfilled this mediatory function. See C. A. Bayly, *Rulers, Townsmen and Bazaars* (Cambridge: Cambridge University Press, 1983), 150. Baluchis did also but not always reliably, as British factors discovered. William Foster, *The English Factories in India, 1618–1621* (Oxford: Clarendon Press, 1906), 347.

dangers, extortion and robbery on the one hand and winter snows, spring floods and summer heat on the other. Yet as Babur's experience suggests some Luharnis took a far more active part in overland commerce than merely acting as shipping agents. The man that he and his followers plundered and killed, Khwaja Khizr Luhani, appears to have been a substantial merchant and not merely a nomad who transported goods across the mountains for a modest fee. Khwaja Khizr would probably more reasonably be characterized as a powindah merchant who occupied the middle range of a relatively broad spectrum of mediatory traders.

Powindahs who merely supplied animals and expertise for a fee would have occupied one end of such a spectrum, while others who had completely abandoned nomadic life to become full-time businessmen stood at the opposite end. Darya Khan Multani of Samarqand may have been one of the latter types of powindahs, but if that characterization is hypothetical there are a number of well-documented examples in post-Mughal sources that illustrate the type. The early nineteenth-century English traveler, Henry Pottinger, offered an encapsulated description of sedentarized powindah merchants when he described members of the Babi tribe whom he met in Khilat, near Quetta, in 1810. "Great merchants" of the tribe had settled permanently in the city. "They are," Pottinger wrote:

an industrious, pastoral set of people, the majority of whom dwell in the dominions of the king of Kabool, and in the Douranee country, where they pasture their flocks and reside in tents; some of them are also great merchants, and to follow their commercial avocations they quit their native wilds and settled in cities or towns.[87]

Such men might have been mediatory traders in the most complete sense; they may have both financed commerce and arranged for their still-nomadic kinsmen to ship their goods.

Sedentary merchants, whether Khattris, Marwaris or other Afghans, had to use powindahs to move their goods across the mountains to Iran or Turan. In cases where the Afghans were merely shipping agents they may have simply been hired for a set fee, but where they were also involved marketing goods their agreements were probably expressed as variants of the well-known commenda contracts. These contracts, which merchants used for centuries throughout the Middle East and Europe, can be regarded as one of the most important legal instruments of mediatory trade. In essence, they defined the division of profits between merchants who supplied most of the capital or goods for long-distance trade and tribesmen who possessed pack animals, expert knowledge of the routes and had experience in coping with the risks of long-distance travel.[88] It is easy to imagine Khwaja Khizr Luhani and others like him acting in this capacity. Unfortunately, no record of such a contract is known to have survived from the Mughul period, but hints of commenda-like arrangements occur in nineteenth and twentieth century studies of powindah tribes. A very late example is an 1882–83 agreement

[87] Pottinger, *Travels*, 79.
[88] Udovitch, *Partnership and Profit*, 172.

between a Panjabi merchant of the Arora caste and a group of powindahs that
prompted the merchant to open a branch office in Calcutta to supply the tribesmen
with capital.[89] The likelihood that merchants and powindahs concluded
commenda agreements at an earlier period as well is heightened by the numerous,
well-preserved commenda contracts that Indian merchants in Astrakhan
concluded with Turks, Armenians and Russians in the seventeenth and eighteenth
century.[90]

In the broader framework of long-distance commerce, commenda contracts
were similar in certain respects to shipping agreements between sedentary
merchants and shipowners and captains who operated from Lahori Bandar or the
great port of Surat. When English East India Company factors in Iran recognized
that Indians controlled most of the trade between Mughul India and Iran they
suggested to their colleagues in Surat in 1617 that the English should become
mediatory traders by convincing Indians to abandon overland commerce for the
sea route. They wrote:

> We . . . desire that you advise speedily throughout all factories in India, and to treat and
> persuade with such Bannian and Moor merchants who usually trade from thence overland
> into Persia, that they with their goods and carriages do yearly on our shipping embark at
> Surat for this place [Isfahan].[91]

English and other shippers also shared powindahs' functions as mediatory traders
in another sense. They provided transport for merchants who wished to travel or
settle in Iranian or Central Asian commercial centers, although if Tavernier's
testimony was accurate then the "banias," that is the Khattris who migrated from
Mughul territories to Iran, did so via Multan. Individual merchants who traveled
to urban centers in Iran or Turan would have crossed the mountains under
powindah protection, an arrangement that Alexander Burnes described in the early
nineteenth century. In his account of the Luharnis' spring migration he remarks
that Hindu merchants who were traveling through the Gumal always accompanied
the third group of tribesmen who traversed the pass.[92] These Hindus may have
been heading for Kabul or Bukhara, but others would have accompanied caravans
through the Bolan and Sanghar, as Steel and Crowther and unnamed Lahori
merchants did in 1617.

The Multanis of Isfahan

As the discussion of Multanis has suggested, the Mughul–Indian trade diaspora
numbered in the thousands in Safavid Iran and in the hundreds in Uzbek Turan.
Safavid Iran was the focal point of expatriate Indian mercantile activity in the
Mughul–Safavid period. In 1647 an Astrakhan Indian merchant, who regularly

[89] Robinson, *Nomad Tribes of Eastern Afghanistan*, 26.
[90] See below, chapter 4, for details of these agreements.
[91] Danvers and Foster, eds., *Letters Received*, V, 1617, 232–33.
[92] Alexander Burnes, *Cabool, Being a Personal Narrative* . . . (London: John Murray, 1842), 79.

traded between Isfahan, Astrakhan and Moscow and knew Iran well, estimated that there were then "10,000 Indians who live in Iran without leaving."[93] Chardin believed that there were 10,000 Indians just in Isfahan in the 1670s, and this figure agrees with Kaempfer's figure for the number of Multanis in the city about a decade later. These numbers are corroborated in general terms by an account of the large numbers of Indian textile merchants who sold goods in the Isfahan bazar.[94] The figure 10,000 occurs far too often to be more than a formulaic number, but its repeated citation can at least be taken to indicate the substantial numbers and perceived economic influence of Indian merchants in Safavid territories. The Indian's observation that they stayed in Iran "without leaving" is also a trenchant reminder that these men were not transitory peddlers, but that they represented instead a well-entrenched emigré population.

The Indian merchant community that conducted business in Iran or Turan during the seventeenth century probably grew up through an incremental migration of relatives who represented the family firm, the basic business unit of most pre-modern societies. This was the process that brought most Marwaris from their desiccated homelands in Rajasthan to the prosperous Gangetic heartland in the seventeenth, eighteenth and nineteenth centuries.[95] It is particularly easy to imagine how Khattris could have been migrating from the nearby Panjab, perhaps since Barani's day, on yearly caravans through the Sanghar and Gumal passes. The increased commercialization of the Panjab during Mughul rule may itself have stimulated Khattris to expand their trade.[96] The large community of Indian merchants that nearly every European visitor with commercial interests noticed in Isfahan probably grew up especially quickly after Shah 'Abbas shifted his capital to that city, and simultaneously constructed an improved commercial infrastructure throughout Iran. Many of the newly arrived Indian merchants might also have first come from commercial bases in the Safavid's eastern and predominantly Afghan cities of Harat and Qandahar, for in the early nineteenth century at least members of this caste especially provided essential commercial and financial services in Afghan cities, towns and villages which were characterized by a relatively slight degree of occupational differentiation. Thus even as late as 1845 broken copper and brass vessels had to be shipped from the important emporium of Qandahar to be repaired in Shikarpur, where trained artisans could be found to do the work.[97]

---

[93] Antonova, I, no. 33, 1647, 85.

[94] Gauber and Wirth, *Der Bazar von Isfahan*, quoted by Edmund Herzig, "Armenian Merchants," 144. I am indebted to Professor Herzig for bringing this source to my attention.

[95] Timberg, *The Marwaris*, see especially Section B, 4 "Marwari Merchant Migration," 85–124.

[96] See Chetan Singh, *Region and Empire, Panjab in the Seventeenth Century* (Delhi: Oxford University Press, 1991), chapters 5 and 6.

[97] In 1930 it was reported of Attock district that Hindus composed only 8.5% of the district, but that "Khatris, Aroras and Brahmans . . . divide between them almost the whole trade and money-lending business of the district." Punjab Government, *Attock District*, Vol. 29a of Punjab District Gazetteers 1930 (Lahore: Government Printing Office, 1932). Postans, "Miscellaneous Information," 97.

Plate 3 Bazar flanking the entrance to the *masjid-i-jami'*, Isfahan

A rare, first-hand account of incremental migration based on kinship ties was supplied by an Indian whose name is given in Russian documents as "Sutur" and several similar variant spellings.[98] In a series of petitions that he had addressed to the tsar about various commercial disputes, he said that he had gone to Astrakhan in the 1620s "from India," although he may have meant no more by that phrase than that he was an Indian, for based upon other passages of his petitions it seems likely that he had originally traveled to Astrakhan from northern Iran where so many other Indians conducted business in the seventeenth century.[99] According to Sutur he had experienced such favorable treatment in Russia that he had written to his brother to encourage him to trade in Astrakhan, and in consequence his brother and twenty-five other Indian merchants had traveled to the city in 1646 with thousands of roubles of Indian merchandise.[100] His brother apparently stayed on to do business, but in Iran rather than in Astrakhan, for a few years later Sutur mentioned that two of his brothers worked in northern Iranian cities. This was a typical pattern of Indian firms in the seventeenth and eighteenth century when many Indians in Astrakhan had relatives in Iran with whom they jointly carried on trade.

Once settled in Iran and Turan – and later in Russia – Indian merchants joined members of a diaspora that wielded substantial economic power in those areas. Identifying the full range and nature of these merchants' influence resembles the archaeological reconstruction of a lost civilization; inferences have to be drawn from small, widely dispersed fragments of evidence. This is much easier to accomplish for Safavid Iran than for Uzbek Turan, because of the presence of such well-informed European observers as Jean Chardin. Even then only the outlines rather than the details of their occupations and business organizations are evident. In seventeenth-century Iran Indian merchants appear to have exerted a pervasive economic influence in the country; dominating the foreign trade between India and Iran, operating as influential merchants within Iran and supplying capital to a chronically capital-starved Iranian economy.

It is in this latter role as moneylenders and financiers that Indian merchants in Iran have most commonly been represented in Safavid historiography. Indeed, with only one or two exceptions Iranian historians have ignored Mughul, British, Dutch and Russian data on Indian merchants in Iran and have been content to portray them exclusively and stereotypically as a community of usurers who distorted "normal" economic relationships and unfairly drained scarce capital resources from the country. Derived from one or two well-known seventeenth-century sources this characterization has the validity of most stereotypes; it is based upon a kernel of truth but otherwise fundamentally misrepresents the complexity of the actual situation.

---

[98] Baikova, *Rol' Srednei Azii v Russko-Indiiskikh Torgovykh Sviaziakh*, 142 n. 62, discusses the possible spellings of this man's name.

[99] Antonova, I, no. 34, 1647, p. 85. For example, he discusses business conditions in Iran at great length and had extensive business contacts in Isfahan.

[100] *Ibid.*, 85.

The prevalent idea that Indians in Iran were solely or predominantly money-lenders derives primarily from Jean Chardin's late seventeenth-century description of Indians in Isfahan as usurers who drained Iran's gold and silver reserves by repatriating their ill-gotten gains to India. Chardin's comments have been most commonly quoted in Vladimir Minorsky's influential precis that Minorsky included in the Introduction to his translation and commentary of the Safavid administrative manual, *The Tadhkirat al-Muluk*:

A nefarious influence on credit and the money market was exercised by a multitude of Indian usurers (in Isfahan alone there were over 10,000 banyans!). 'Abbas I prevented them from settling in Persia, but Shah Safi was bribed by their presents with the results described by Chardin . . . Ces Indiens, comme de vraies sangsues, tirent tout l'or et tout l'argent du pays et l'envoient dans le leur, de manière que l'an 1677 que je partis de la Perse on n'y voyait persques plus de bon argent; ces usuriers l'avaient fait entièrement disparaître.[101]

It is ironic that Chardin of all seventeenth-century observers should be used to characterize Indian businessmen in Iran in this one-sided manner, for taken as a whole his multi-volume treatise offers the most sophisticated, multi-faceted analysis of Indian economic activity in the Safavid era that has ever been published. It even comes complete with a socio-economic explanation that tries to account for the Indians' relative success vis-à-vis their Iranian counterparts.

Chardin probably knew both Isfahan and members of its Indian mercantile community better than any other European of the period, so there is little reason to question his assertion that they derived great profits from money-lending, or that these sums were then repatriated to India. It is simply that his comments about these Indians' usury have to be reconciled – with his important evaluation of Indian merchants' overall role in foreign trade, with observations of well-informed Europeans and with an elementary knowledge of general pre-modern commercial practice. Speaking of the roles of various non-Iranian merchant communities in Safavid Iran's foreign trade Chardin wrote:

Wherefore in *Turky*, the Christians [Armenians] and *Jews* carry on the main foreign trade; And in Persia the *Christians* and the Indian Gentiles [Hindus and Jains]. As to the *Persians* they trade with their own Countrymen, one Province with another, and most of them Trade with the *Indians*. The Armenians alone manage the whole of European Trade . . . [102]

By implication Indian merchants dominated Indian–Iranian foreign commerce. This was consistent in very general terms with Barani's remark about Multani influence over long-distance trade, and it was corroborated by merchants of both the Dutch and English East India companies who knew very well, as one English

---

[101] Minorsky, ed. and trans., *Tadhkirat al-Muluk*, 19.
[102] Chardin, *Travels in Persia*, 280–81.

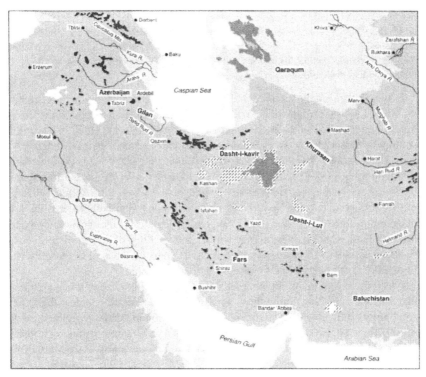

Sea level · 200 meters
200 · 1.500 meters
1.500 · 3.000 meters
Above 3.000 meters
Desert

Map 3 Iran

factor wrote in 1662, that "the merchants engaged in the trade [from Surat] to Gombroon [Bandar 'Abbas] were mostly Indians."[103]

What this could mean in everyday marketing terms in Iran was described nearly a half-century earlier by the English factor who served in Isfahan in the second decade of the seventeenth century, Edward Pettus. Pettus related how Indian merchants repatriated Iranian specie that they had acquired from textile sales, and he made it clear that not only were they shipping goods to Iran, but they were aggressively marketing them in the streets of the capital. Typically describing Indians in general occupational terms as banians he observed, with the irritation of a competitor,

---

[103] William Foster, ed., *The English Factories in India, 1661–1664* (Oxford: Clarendon Press, 1900), 214. The conclusion about Dutch sources is based upon a conversation with Dr. Willem Floor, 26 November 1991, who has extensive knowledge of such sources for this period.

the bannians, the Cheif [sic] Marchantes whoe vende Linene of India, of all sorts and prices, which this Countrye cannot bee without, except the people should goe naked ... they vende most of the linene they bring to Spahan after a most base pedlinge, and unmarchante like manner, retaleinge them by the whole, halfe and quarter Coved, carrying it up and down on their shoulders [in] the Bazar.[104]

It is surprisingly easy to reconcile Chardin's implied assertion that Indians dominated Iran's foreign trade with South Asia with his remark about Indian usury, although it cannot be done strictly from Iranian evidence. The simple solution is suggested by the exceptionally well-documented business practices of Astrakhan Indian merchants, and indeed the practices of most merchants throughout early modern Eurasia. That is, Indian usurers in most instances are likely to have been exactly these same merchants who were generating such large profits through sales of textiles, indigo and other Indian staples that were regularly marketed in Iran. One of the most conspicuous features of the business practices of the Multani Khattris of Astrakhan was the indivisibility of their commercial and financial activities. In years for which accurate statistics exist all of these Indians in Astrakhan who lent money were also active merchants.[105]

Given the much greater Indian merchant population in Isfahan it is quite likely that members of the community specialized to a greater degree than their compatriots were able to do in the more restricted commercial environment of the Muscovite state. Some may have exclusively concentrated on trade or money-lending or even on foreign exchange transactions. Nonetheless, the pattern of the Astrakhan Indian merchants' commercial behavior was absolutely typical of early modern merchants in general, such as those from the Tuscan cities of Florence and Siena where "great merchants" have been described as those "primarily engaged in the business of exchange and in the import and export of cloth."[106] Astrakhan Indians also pursued the same combination of financial and commercial activities. Many Indians who lent funds in Isfahan – and throughout Iran – are likely to have fallen into this category of "great merchants," those whose textile sales had generated the same kind of profits as were reaped by their countrymen in Ottoman Aleppo in the 1620s,[107] and these profits are likely to have generated most of the funds for their loans. Such businessmen were probably similar to those whom the Iranians labeled as *tujjar*. Both these Indians and Iranian tujjar probably resembled

---

[104] Ferrier, "An English View of Persian Trade," 192.

[105] See below, chapter 4, where the Astrakhan documents show that most loans were made to help finance commercial ventures.

[106] Gino Luzzatto, "Small and Great Merchants in the Italian Cities of the Renaissance," in Frederic C. Lane, ed., *Enterprise and Secular Change* (Homewood, Ill.: Richard Darwin, 1953), 48. The Italian and Iranian definition of the "merchant" as one who engages in foreign trade is virtually identical. See also M. N. Pearson, "Brokers in Western Indian Port Cities, their Role in Servicing Foreign Merchants," *Modern Asian Studies* XXII/3 (1988), 457, where Pearson emphasizes the multiplicity of brokers' business pursuits.

[107] Bruce Masters cites an example of Indian and other merchants trading in Indian goods who repatriated their profits in bullion from Aleppo in 1621. *The Origins of Western Economic Dominance in the Middle East* (New York: N.Y. University Press, 1988), 147.

the "mercantile speculators" that Pottinger referred to when he used this phrase to characterize 400–500 Hindu merchants from Multan and Shikarpur whom he met in the Baluchistan city of Khilat in 1810.[108] Pettus himself probably thought of Indians in these respectable, substantial terms when he criticized them for their "unmarchantelike" behavior.

Profits from cloth sales probably represented the major percentage of Iranian silver that Indians remitted to India, although this is impossible to prove statistically. Chardin himself, though, also believed that the success of Indian merchants in Safavid Iran stemmed from a competitive advantage that they enjoyed over Iranian merchants. In his opinion the advantage was due to cultural differences that helped Indians to generate profits from financial transactions apart from their cloth sales. He argued in particular that Iranians simply had "not a Genius naturally bent on Traffick,"[109] even though trade was a lucrative and prestigious profession in Iran and "some *Persian* Traders . . . have Deputies in all Parts of the World."[110] According to Chardin Islamic law that forbade usury severely hampered "The Mahometan improvement of Trade," although he also knew that "Parties have a way of eluding the Law just as they please."[111] Chardin believed it to be symptomatic of the prescription on usury that Iranian merchants used their profits to buy houses, bazars and caravansarais, because they could not envisage, or did not feel comfortable, employing their money more profitably.[112]

Chardin saw shades of difference rather than stark contrasts between the attitudes and practices of Iranian and Indian merchants, but even slight differences may help to explain the Indians' business success, not so much in their ability to market coveted Indian cloth as in financial and monetary affairs. As Chardin himself pointed out, Muslims, whether Iranians or others, were not reluctant to charge interest at usurious rates. Some men were more concerned than others to conceal this aspect of their affairs, since the practice of *riba*, or usury, contravened Islamic law but also threatened the position of urban guilds.[113] They often did so simply by omitting any mention of interest from contracts or through the practice of disguising interest as part of the total price of the goods or funds. In late sixteenth-century Samarqand such agreements were known as *bijayiz*, impermissible or illegal contracts;[114] 300 years later in Turan similar evasions were known by the names of particular cities where a particular technique

---

[108] Willem M. Floor discusses "tujjar" and the Iranian merchant class in Qajar Iran, *Zeitschrift der Deutschen Morgenländischen Gesellschaft*, CXXVI/1 (1976), 101–35, and Pottinger, *Travels*, 78.
[109] Chardin, *Travels in Persia*, 195.
[110] *Ibid.*, 282.
[111] *Ibid.*, 281.
[112] *Ibid.*, 195. Suraiya Faroqhi makes a similar point about the investment pattern of Ottoman officials, who, while they were not professional merchants, often invested in this way. *Towns and Townsmen*, 46.
[113] Inalcik, "Capital Formation in the Ottoman Empire," 104–7.
[114] R. R. Fitrat and B. S. Sergeev, trans. and ed., *Kaziiskie Dokumenty XVI Veke* (Tashkent: Uzbek SSR Committee of Sciences, 1935), 68. See also Subhi Y. Labib, "Capitalism in Medieval Islam," *Journal of Economic History* XXIX/1 (March 1969), 88 and 90, and Halil Inalcik, "Capital Formation in the Ottoman Empire," in *Ibid.*, 101, 109 and 139–40.

originated as the "Bukharan path," the "Samarqand path," or the "Tashkent path."[115] Yet even if Muslims consistently transgressed against customs and religious practices regulating riba, social disapproval of the practice may have had the effect that Chardin suggested. That may have not been true of the well-known Karimi merchants of Egypt, but it may well have been significant in the Iranian case.[116] Unfortunately, so little is known about the business culture of the Iranian merchant class in the Safavid period that it is impossible to evaluate the accuracy of Chardin's anecdotal observation for any region, city or village.

What was undeniably true in the Iranian case was that Khattris and Marwaris were not liable to be criticized within their own communities for engaging in financial practices that could have earned their Muslim counterparts public censure. Quite the opposite, the banking and moneylending practices of Hindu and Jain mercantile castes were not only socially sanctioned but, particularly in the case of Marwaris, were positively reinforced by a type of commercial devotionalism. The tools of their trade, account books, pens and ink, came to symbolize deities in the expansive Hindu/Jain pantheon.[117] In later times at least merchant family members sometimes approached these implements ritually as incarnations of family gods. Few Weberian Protestants, much less Middle Eastern Muslims, would have unblushingly made the same explicit equation between their commercial and spiritual lives, and it is important to recognize that for Hindu and Jain castes this explicit sanctification of their profession was only the most visible sign of their affirmation of a social ethic and economic discipline that encouraged investment and discouraged conspicuous consumption.[118] As a Huguenot Chardin may have been inclined to appreciate and possibly exaggerate the contrast between the ethos of Hindu, Jain and Armenian merchants and indigenous Iranian traders. It was a commonplace, though, for Europeans of his day to comment on the remarkable discipline and commercial and financial acumen of these Indian castes.

The ability of Indians to accumulate capital from trade and moneylending gave them a similar position in Iranian society to that which a smaller number of their compatriots occupied in late seventeenth- and eighteenth-century Astrakhan. They became bankers in a society that possessed no formal institutions that accumulated capital and extended credit. Indians in most of Iran's major cities are known to have lent money to Iranian merchants;[119] in Astrakhan it is virtually

[115] Eugene Schuyler, *Turkistan*, 107. To some extent these practices may reflect Hanafite law, which allows interest terms simply to be removed from contracts. See Nicholas J. Coulson, *A History of Islamic Law*. repr. (Edinburgh: Edinburgh University Press, 1991), 100.
[116] Labib, "Capitalism in Medieval Islam," 83–84.
[117] For twentieth-century Marwari practices see D. K. Taknet, *Industrial Entrepreneurship of the Shekawati Marwaris* (Jaipur: D. K. Taknet, 1986), 163. See also the photographs in Taknet's book. Bayly has an important discussion of the socio-religious significance of the account book in north Indian merchant households during the late eighteenth and early nineteenth century. *Rulers, Townsmen and Bazaars*, 375–80.
[118] *Ibid.*, for a subtle discussion of the "merchant family."
[119] Keyvani, *Artisans and Guild Life*, 230.

certain that most loans were given for this purpose. Indian merchants in Iran undoubtedly repatriated profits from these transactions as Chardin indicated, thus adding currency generated by this invisible export of financial expertise to the stream of silver that they also remitted to India from the sales of cotton cloth, indigo and other products. To suggest that this was a conspiratorial activity that originated when Indian moneylenders bribed Shah Safi to allow them to settle in Iran, an apocryphal story related by Chardin, not only fundamentally misrepresents the comprehensive nature of Indian mercantile activities in Safavid territories, it also fails to appreciate the Indians' role as providers of funds in that capital-starved country. In this connection Pottinger's story about the stature of Indian merchants in Harat in 1810 is likely to have been germane for the later Safavid period as well. Pottinger reported that this community of approximately 600 Hindus was respected and protected because they "alone possess capital."[120] Capital was probably in shorter supply in Harat in 1810 than it was in late seventeenth-century Isfahan, but the difference was probably only a relative one when it came to the position of Indian merchants. Informed observers such as Pettus constantly alluded to the shortage of funds even in Shah 'Abbas' time. The shortage was not caused primarily by devious Indian moneylenders but by Iran's structurally weak position in the international commerce of the early modern period.

Technology transfers

It is likely that Indian merchants in Turan occupied a similar position in the local economy to those in Iran, except that Afghans were also prominent in Balkh, Bukhara and Samarqand, whereas they do not appear to have been especially influential in Isfahan or in other cities west of Harat. While there is little information on Indian mercantile affairs in Turan, the business activities of Darya Khan Multani illumine another largely unappreciated dimension of the Indian diaspora. From the promissory notes in which his name is given as the creditor, Darya Khan appears to have been engaged in a number of related business activities. Referred to in these documents as *janab* or master, Darya Khan was owed money, carded wool and finished cloth by eight different individuals: a Hindu cotton textile printer and seven others, all Muslims who carried the Multani nisba, three of whom were designated as *ustads*, masters or teachers.[121] The latter title was frequently used to designate senior artisans or master craftsmen. The notes seem to indicate that Darya Khan had organized his firm around a system of cash advances or possibly a combination of advances and a putting-out arrangement in which he advanced funds or raw materials to his semi-autonomous craftsmen in exchange for cloth or wool that they then manufactured. By paying these men on a piece-work basis rather than hiring them as employees he

---

[120] Pottinger, *Travels*, 415.
[121] Mukimova, *Social Differentiation*, 53–68.

presumably kept his costs as low as possible. Typical of these documents is one that was dated 19 Zul qaʻda, 998, which reads:

Done correctly, according to the law, the declaration of Ustad Rajab Hazar Multani being in sound mind, [declares] the following. I am indebted and must pay to Darya Khan, son of Sheikh Saʻdi, the sum of twenty-eight new, unalloyed, circulating pure silver tanghas and also seven pieces of cloth *purband* twenty gaz and one gaz wide. All this according to the demand of the above mentioned, in favor of whom I make this declaration, I will pay in full.[122]

> Testified to this: Witness to this:
> Mulla Abd al-Rahim,   Hafiz Mahmud
>   Muhtasib

In some of the other documents the debtor was supposed to "pay" certain types of cloth to Darya Khan after a specified number of months, undoubtedly the time it would take to prepare the cloth.

These notes record only debts and terms of repayment – including the use of an Indian slave as collateral – in which silver tankas are always cited as the currency of the debt. While they do not delineate the full nature of Darya Khan's business affairs they do reveal the existence of a phenomenon that has occurred in both pre-modern and modern diasporas, the transfer of technology or production techniques to the location of a long-established export market where local raw materials are employed in production. The Hindu cloth printer and the Multani ustads were presumably brought to Samarqand because they were proficient in the superior Indian textile technology that gave Indians their competitive advantage in both Iran and Turan. By bringing these men to Samarqand Darya Khan presumably also reduced costs – and the dangers of periodic caravan trips over the Hindu Kush. His firm appears to have represented the same phenomenon as the establishment of Dutch factories in seventeenth-century Russia or Japanese automobile plants in late twentieth-century United States, although more would have to be known about his activities to characterize them with absolute certainty.

Other Darya Khans, whether Afghans, Khattris or Marwaris, probably lived in Iranian territories, even if they are not known from currently available sources to have done so.[123] Indo-Muslim textile artisans are definitely known to have worked in early seventeenth-century Aleppo, where five were recorded as belonging to a local guild of cloth bleachers.[124] Apart from the significance of such men as indicators of the strength and geographic reach of India's world economy, they

---

[122] *Ibid.*, 60. Emile Tyan discusses the jurisdiction of the muhasib: *L'Organisation judiciare*, 645–48.
[123] It is important to remember that Turan became part of the Russian and then Soviet regime and documents have entered the archives there which would still be in the hands of mosque officials in Iran and India. It is precisely these types of documents, "sijill registers" and "tereke registers" that Inalcik emphasizes are critical sources for economic history in the Middle East: "Capital Formation in the Ottoman Empire," 108. The other critical sources are waqf deeds, such as those that E. A. Davidovitch has used to study prices and wages in sixteenth-century Turan in her work *Istoriia Denezhnogo Obrascheniia Srednevekovoi Srednei Azii.*
[124] Masters, *Western Economic Dominance*, 81. Masters refers to a residential street known as Zaqaq al-Hunud, "The street of the Indians."

also represented examples of the type of technology transfer that Russian authorities saw as a possible benefit of encouraging Indian merchants to settle in their newly conquered Caspian Sea port of Astrakhan. Russian policy towards Indian merchants and Russian goals in sending commercial missions to India were indistinguishable from their commercial and financial policies toward European merchants or states. In both cases Russian goals betrayed the status of the Muscovite state as an underdeveloped country that was as peripheral to the economies of Asia as it was to those of western Europe.

CHAPTER 4

Indo-Russian commerce in the early modern era

And these merchants and ambassadors are given leave to go to India . . . And when they arrive at the first Indian town they should tell its ruler that they are ambassadors of the great Tsar and great prince, Aleksei Mikhailovich, autocrat of all the Russias and ruler of many states, to their ruler, his majesty Shah Jahan.

Instructions to the first Russian embassy to India, June, 1646.[1]

Russian annexation of the Astrakhan khanate in 1556 gave the expanding Muscovite state a vital "window on the East," and for more than a century and a half the port of Astrakhan, located on the Volga's Caspian estuary, functioned as one of Russia's two most important links with the outside world. The other was the port of Archangel in the Russian arctic. Russian officials and merchants sought to use Astrakhan to gain direct access to Asian products to augment the state's customs revenue and to acquire silver for its currency. They tried to achieve these goals by inviting Indian and other Asian merchants to settle and trade in the city as well as through the dispatch of commercial-diplomatic missions to the Mughul court, along with others that were sent to Iran and the Uzbek khanates of Turan. In so far as their relations with Indians were concerned Russian governments were only moderately successful in attaining their economic goals. Russian merchants failed to derive any significant economic benefit from their contacts with Indians in Astrakhan or by initiating direct Russian commercial and diplomatic relations with Mughul India. Indians, on the other hand, took advantage of the Russian conquest and subsequent opening of Astrakhan to expand their mercantile activities into southern Russia, the last major advance of the Indian mercantile diaspora in the early modern era.

The Uzbeks of the Franks

In 1600, at a time when Indian merchants had probably already begun to visit Astrakhan, the Muscovite state encompassed a vast territory that was being

---

[1] Antonova, I, no. 24, 1646, 48.

rapidly augmented as Russian armies, fur traders and explorers pushed south into the steppe or eastwards through Siberia, reaching the Pacific coast by the middle of the seventeenth century. If the first Indian merchants who entered Russian territory in the late sixteenth or early seventeenth century had recorded their impressions of this sprawling empire their writings would probably have shown them to have been as astonished as western Europeans at the primitiveness of the country, the despotic barbarism of its rulers and the crudity of the populace. As members of communities with sophisticated cultural traditions and refined codes of personal conduct, including exceptionally high standards of personal hygiene, the Khattris and Marwaris and occasional South Asian Muslims who settled semi-permanently in Astrakhan are likely to have reacted to Russians in very much the same way as late seventeenth-century Iranians, who contemptuously referred to them as the "Yusbecs of the Francs."[2] Polished Isfahani courtiers used this derogatory phrase to indicate that Russians were the crudest Europeans they had encountered, as disorderly and generally uncivilized, that is, as their despised Turkic neighbors in Turan.

Outward cultural contrasts between Indians and Russians were matched by profound differences in their states and economies. In political terms Mughul India and Muscovite Russia differed from one another both at the beginning and end of the seventeenth century, although their roles were almost completely reversed over that 100-year period. In 1600 in the last years of Akbar's triumphantly successful reign Russia was passing through one of the most unstable phases in its history. At the time the country was in the midst of its euphemistically termed "Time of Troubles" (1584–1613), literally its "confused" or "disturbed" time, a chaotic three decades that followed and was substantially the consequence of the excesses of Ivan the Terrible (1547–84).[3] During those years five men briefly held power before Mikhail Romanov was elected to the throne in 1613, initiating his family's 300-year reign. While the effects of the Time of Troubles continued to be felt for decades Mikhail resumed the consolidation of the despotic Muscovite state that had reached its previous peak of power under Ivan the Terrible. He and his successors solidified the dynasty's absolutist control throughout the seventeenth century until Peter the Great ([1682] 1696–1725) largely completed the process that his predecessors had begun in the early fifteenth century. Princely independence had been destroyed; urban autonomy was never allowed to develop. The Muscovite tsars had succeeded where Mughul rulers by the early eighteenth century had conspicuously failed. They had successfully monopolized power, creating what has become known as the "service state," in which all members of Russian society from the largest

[2] Chardin, *Travels in Persia*, 89.
[3] Peter ruled jointly with his half-brother, Ivan V, from 1682 to 1696. Blum has a good survey of the growth of tsarist absolutism, *Lord and Peasant in Russia*, chapter 9.

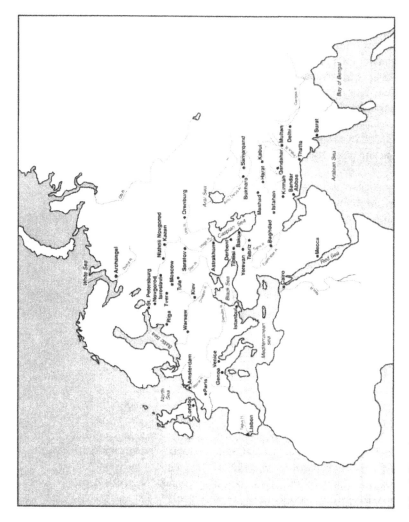

Map 4 Eurasia

gentry to the leading merchants had been rendered subordinate and subservient to the dynasty.[4]

In socio-economic terms Russia in 1600 was underpopulated and under-developed when compared with Mughul India – or with most other states on its periphery. If Jean Chardin had visited Russia in 1600 he undoubtedly would have found that its population was more scattered and much more isolated than that of Safavid Iran, although the villages and towns of Russia were separated by vast stretches of forest rather than by the desiccated stretches of soil that were found on the Iranian plateau. At the turn of the century Russia had a population that probably numbered no more than twelve million people.[5] Approximately 97 per-cent of them lived in rural areas, a striking contrast with the levels of urbanization in Mughul India, Safavid Iran and even Uzbek Turan. Most of the population made their living either directly or indirectly from agriculture or by exploiting Russia's natural resources, and throughout the seventeenth century the Russian economy's most valuable products were grain, timber, furs from its newly conquered Siberian territories, and leather and hides.[6] The agrarian sector of the economy had been devastated during Ivan the Terrible's reign and the subsequent Time of Troubles.[7] During those years agriculturalists abandoned immense tracts of previously cultivated land in the north-east and in the center of the country, with a consequent decline in production, commerce and state revenues. After Mikhail Romanov's accession those areas were gradually resettled, and agricultural production rose throughout most of the century, but the volume and diversity of agricultural produce was still modest when measured against Mughul India's enormous output of staple and cash crops.

Russia's rural and urban manufacturing sectors were also severely under-developed by Indian standards. Significant numbers of peasants may have become full-time artisans during the seventeenth century, and some men who were legally serfs may even have succeeded in becoming industrial entrepreneurs by the eighteenth century. Yet the scattered, unskilled population of rural Russia was

[4] See J. Michael Hittle, *The Service City, State and Townsmen in Russia 1600–1800* (Cambridge, Mass., 1979), 14–16, for a discussion of the service principle.

[5] As was the case in Mughul India, Safavid Iran and Uzbek Turan, no accurate censuses were taken in Russia at this period. W. H. Parker gives a figure of 12 million people for 1600. *An Historical Geography of Russia* (Chicago: Aldine, 1968), 94; but A. M. Sakharov says that the population in 1700 was still only 10.5 million with 200,000 people living in Moscow: "Rossiia i ee kul'tura v XVII stoletii," [Russia and its Culture in the 17th Century] in A. V. Artsikhovskii, ed., *Ocherki russkoi kul'tury XVII veka chast' pervaia* [Essays on Russian Culture in the 17th Century, part 1] (Moscow: Moscow University, 1979), 9; while Hittle, quoting V. M. Kabuzan for the first census revision of 1719, records 15.6 million people in that year: *The Service City*, 178. Blum offers a useful illustration of the variance of demographic estimates for this period. *Lord and Peasant in Russia*, 120 n. 9. For the Mongol census of Russia see Thomas T. Allsen, "Mongol Census taking in Rus' 1245–1275," *Harvard Ukrainian Studies* V/1 (March 1981), 32–53.

[6] For an introduction to the Russian economy in the sixteenth and seventeenth century see Blum, *Lord and Peasant in Russia*, chapters 8 and 10. A general economic history is Peter I. Lyaschenko's *History of the National Economy of Russia to the 1917 Revolution*, trans. L. M. Herman (New York: Macmillan, 1949).

[7] Blum, *Lord and Peasant in Russia*, chapter 10.

incapable of producing manufactures that were even remotely comparable in either quality or volume to India's remarkable village-level textile production.[8] In the decades following the Time of Troubles the state's military and bureaucratic requirements and the court's thirst for luxuries stimulated the building of iron foundries, paper mills, glass factories and cotton and silk enterprises.[9] However, it was symptomatic of the economy and of its society that the state stimulated most major new enterprises, while foreigners, in particular such Dutchmen as André Vinius, supplied much of their expertise and capital.

Mughul and Muscovite coinage offer visual and tactile metaphors of the contrasting levels of cultural sophistication and economic power of these two states. In 1600 at least, the differences in their coinage also appeared to reflect the relative strength of each regime. Their different levels of development are highlighted by comparisons between the Mughuls' heavy, beautifully designed and finely stamped gold mohurs and only slightly less-carefully produced silver rupees, and the poorly designed Muscovite silver kopeks of less than half a gram, crudely struck from silver wire.[10] In two general respects, though, Russian coinage did resemble that of the Mughuls – as well as the currencies of the Safavids and the Uzbeks. First, as was true of all three of those states, Muscovite currency was largely silver throughout the seventeenth century. Gold coins were produced solely for ceremonial purposes, and copper currency was issued only during the reign of Alexei Mikhailovich (1645–76), an experiment that ended with popular riots against the new issues.[11] Second, until silver mines began operating in Siberia at end of the century all metal for coinage had to be imported and paid for with Russian exports. Merchants had the right to both import silver and mint coins until the middle of the seventeenth century, when the purchase of precious metals and the manufacture of coins became a state monopoly.[12] Two principal coin types circulated. On the one hand there were the small "wire kopeks" that European merchants found so inconvenient to use as "they slipped through the pockets," whose value was too low for substantial business

[8] Hittle has a brief but stimulating discussion of the Russian economy in the eighteenth century with an analysis of the historiography of peasant trade and manufacturing. *The Service City*, 173–78. The existence of "peasant" or rural manufacturing as a precursor to industrial development in the iron and linen industries is briefly summarized by L. V. Koshman, "Manufaktura," in Artsikhovskii, ed., *Ocherki russkoi kultury XVII veka*, 105–8.

[9] Koshman, "Manufaktura," 105–21. See also the map in Lyaschenko, *National Economy of Russia*, 214–15, for the distribution of manufacturing in Russia at this period.

[10] A. S. Mel'nikova includes photographs of these wire kopeks in her book *Russkie monety ot Ivana Groznogo do Petra Pervogo* [Russian Money from Ivan the Terrible to Peter the First] (Moscow: Finance and Statistics, 1989). Compare those with the photographs of Mughul coinage in Stanley Lane-Poole, *The Coins of the Mughal Emperors of Hindustan in the British Museum*, repr. (New Delhi: Inter-India Publications, 1983), plates I–XX.

[11] I. G. Spasskii, *The Russian Monetary System*, trans. by Z. I. Garischina and L. S. Forrer (Amsterdam: Jacques Schulman N.V., rev. ed., 1967), 125–32 and Mel'Nikova, *Russkie monety ot Ivana Groznogo do Petra Pervogo*, 212–26. See Mel'nikova's general evaluation of the "archaic" state of the Russian monetary system in the seventeenth century, 154–7.

[12] Spasskii, *The Russian Monetary System*, 119–20.

dealings.[13] As a result many merchants refused to accept payment in kopeks and insisted upon receiving heavy silver coins known as "efimki" or thalers. These were Swedish, Dutch or German or other European heavy silver coins that were overstruck with Russian legends, although sometimes they were melted down and used for kopeks.[14]

Russia obviously enjoyed a trade surplus throughout most of the seventeenth century, since Muscovite rulers were able to import some silver for their coinage, but it is also evident that the amount of the surplus was never so great as to ensure a really satisfactory supply.[15] Merely the weight of the silver kopeks, usually around 0.48 grams, less than $\frac{1}{20}$ of the rupee, indicated that this surplus can never have been large. In some periods, such as Boris Godunov's short but effective reign (1598–1605),[16] supplies of silver are said to have been adequate for both state and private transactions. Later in the Time of Troubles in 1610 all treasury funds were dispersed to pay for Swedish mercenary troops, and currency reserves were virtually exhausted.[17] Throughout most of the early Romanov decades Russia suffered from an acute shortage of silver and Tsar Alexei Mikhailovich's introduction of copper coinage was partly a reflection of this problem. This perennial monetary crisis was publicly reflected in the Russian government's policy toward foreign merchants, which often hinged on whether or not they were willing to import silver or whether they, illegally, exported it. Officials preferred Dutch merchants to the English, because they were willing to pay for their purchases in silver, and they hoped to convince Indian merchants to do the same.[18]

Russia obtained her silver through a foreign trade that was consistent with her predominantly agrarian and raw material economy. She largely exported raw materials in exchange for manufactured goods. In the seventeenth and early eighteenth century most silver entered Russia through Archangel, the port on the White Sea that was founded in 1584, for Richard Chancellor's discovery of this route in 1553 and the subsequent formation of the English Muscovy Company two years later fundamentally reoriented Russia's northern commerce away from the Baltic to the Arctic sea-borne trade with England and the

[13] Mel'nikova, *Russkie monety ot Ivana Groznogo do Petra Pervogo*, 155. The coin's value was too low for foreign trade and too high for Russian local trade: *ibid.*, 156.

[14] Spasskii, *The Russian Monetary System*, 119–21, 128–9. See also Spasskii's useful summary of the monetary system in the seventeenth century: "Dengi i Denezhnoe Khoziaistvo," [Money and the Monetary Economy] in Artsikhovskii, ed., *Ocherki russkoi kultury XVII veka*, 145–60. In the mid-seventeenth century European "efimki" or thalers had slightly different values. In 1645 the Stockholm efimok was valued at 63–64 kopeks, while in 1661 in Holland the efimok was valued at 60 kopeks. Mel'nikova, *Russkie monety ot Ivana Groznogo do Petra Pervogo*, 197.

[15] Russia enjoyed a trade surplus throughout much of the eighteenth century. See Braudel, *Perspective of the World*, 463, and Ian Blanchard, *Russia's Age of Silver* (London: Routledge, 1989).

[16] Mel'nikova, *Russkie monety ot Ivana Groznogo do Petra Pervogo*, 77.

[17] Spasskii, *The Russian Monetary System*, 125.

[18] Israel describes the Dutch entry into the Russian market and the reasons why they were able to displace English merchants so quickly. *Dutch Primacy in World Trade*, 44–48.

Netherlands.[19] Russian natural resources were in great demand in western Europe, but it may have been Siberian furs which were most responsible for giving the Muscovite state a trade surplus as they were the single most valuable commodity shipped from Archangel. Otherwise, canvas, hemp and timber for British and Dutch ships, grain and leather, small quantities of wool cloth and specialized foodstuffs such as honey and caviar constituted the bulk of exports to European markets. Apart from silver Russia imported armaments, European cloth, paper, pins and other small metal products through its northern port. Then in the early seventeenth century the return of the first English and Dutch East India Company ships to northern Europe resulted in spices and Asian textiles being added to this list.[20]

Russia's conquest of Astrakhan altered her southern trading patterns virtually simultaneously with the shift in the north.[21] Before 1556 the Ottoman empire had been Russia's principal Asian trading partner, but after that date the focus shifted to Iran and Turan and, secondarily, to India. Russia is known to have exported combinations of its own natural resource products and re-exports of western European manufactured goods to Iran and Turan in the late sixteenth and early seventeenth century. Furs, leather, birchbark, walrus tusks, bridles and saddles, woolen cloth, "suits of armour" and paper were included among its exports to those areas.[22] By the mid-seventeenth century, though, it is quite likely that some of the small manufactured items being exported through Astrakhan were being produced by one of the thirty newly built industrial enterprises that had been developed after the Time of Troubles, largely in the Moscow–Tula region.[23] In terms of both cost and volume, Iranian, Central Asian and Indian cotton and silk textiles represented Russia's most important Asian imports through

---

[19] Paul Bushkovitch, *The Merchants of Moscow 1580–1640* (Cambridge: Cambridge University Press, 1980), chapter 2. Note that according to Antonova there are no extant sales records for the second half of the seventeenth century in Archangel. Antonova, I, 11.

[20] For the Archangel trade see Artur Attman, *The Russian and Polish Markets in International Trade* (Göteborg, Sweden: Meddelanden från Ekonomisk-historiska institutionen vid Göteborgs universitet, 1973); Simon Hart, "Amsterdam shipping and trade to Northern Russia in the Seventeenth Century," *Mededelingen van der Nederlands Vereniging voor Zeegeshiedenis* XXVI (March 1973), 5–30; Israel, *Dutch Primacy in World Trade*, 43–48; and Lyaschenko, *National Economy of Russia*, chapters 11 and 12; Arne Öhberg, "Russia and the World Market in the Seventeenth Century," *Scandinavian Economic History Review* III (1955), 123–52 and Willan, *Early History of the Russia Company*.

[21] Bushkovitch, *The Merchants of Moscow*, chapter 3.

[22] Anthony Jenkinson described Russian exports to Bukhara in 1558. *Early Voyages and Travels*, II, 88 n. 6 and 90. For other exports, which are very poorly documented for the sixteenth and early seventeenth century, see Parker, *An Historical Geography of Russia*, 94, and George Vernadsky, *A History of Russia*, V/2: *The Tsardom of Moscow 1547–1682* (New Haven, Conn.: Yale University Press, 1969), 653–56. For specific aspects of Perso-Iranian trade from the Iranian perspective see Robert Chenciner and Magomedkhan Magomedkhanov, "Persian Exports to Russia from the Sixteenth to the Nineteenth Century," *Iran* XXX (1992), 123–30, and Rudolph Matthee's unpublished essay, "Anti-Ottoman Politics and Transit Rights: The Seventeenth-Century Trade in Silk between Safavid Iran and Muscovy." There is a summary of Russo-Indian commerce in 1800 in Antonova, II, no. 216, 1800, 415.

[23] Koshman, "Manufaktura," 105.

Astrakhan,[24] although Iranian and Turanian horses sometimes also entered the country by this route.

At both Archangel and Astrakhan non-Russian merchants dominated Russia's import and export trade, a fact unequivocally recognized by the Russian historian, Iokotevskii, who stated that "Factually, the trade of Russia abroad in the eighteenth century was largely found in the hands of foreign merchants and the role of Russian merchants consisted in buying up of goods in border ports from foreign merchants and in the sale to them of goods of Russian production."[25] Indeed, with few exceptions, most notably the state-organized caravans to China that began in the late eighteenth century, few Russian merchants ever ventured abroad.[26] One exception was the fifteenth-century Tver merchant, Afanasy Nikitin, who was probably one of the first Europeans to visit India in this period. He traveled overland through Iran to the Persian Gulf and sailed from there to India's Gujarat coast.[27] Yet Nikitin's voyage was a wholly atypical Russian mercantile adventure. He had not originally planned to visit India, but did so only as a desperate attempt to recoup his fortune after his goods had been seized in the Caucasus. While he was the first Russian who is known to have traveled to India prior to the dispatch of official trade missions to the Mughul court in the seventeenth century, he actually discouraged others from following in his path!

There is a vast historical literature on the characteristics and inadequacies of the Russian mercantile bourgeoisie, and various explanations have been advanced to explain Russian merchants' largely passive role in foreign commerce, but there seems little doubt that four factors were especially important.[28] Compared both to their European and Asian counterparts Russian merchants were few in number, poorly educated in accounting techniques, not to speak of the intricacies of international trade, lacking in substantial capital resources and usually subordinate to and dependent on state power. This latter trait, the lack of mercantile autonomy, may cause the Russian merchant class to seem to resemble its South Asian counterparts, who lacked the independent urban institutions of European merchants, but the extent of Russian government control was qualitatively different. This was reflected in the existence of the state-chartered merchant guilds.

In the seventeenth century Russia's most influential merchants totaled only about 300 individuals,[29] and they were concentrated in Moscow, the focal point of

---

[24] See below, chapter 4, for a discussion of this trade in the seventeenth century.

[25] Quoted by Hittle, *The Service City*, 107.

[26] Clifford M. Foust describes the China caravans in *Muscovite and Mandarin: Russia's Trade with China and its Setting, 1727–1805* (Chapel Hill, N.C.: University of North Carolina Press, 1969).

[27] Afanasy Nikitin, *Khozhenie Za Tri Moria Afanasiia Nikitina* (Leningrad: Nauka, 1986). His trip extended from 1466 to 1472.

[28] See especially the discussion of Bushkovitch, *The Merchants of Moscow*, preface and chapter 1.

[29] For a brief introduction to the administrative/juridical status of Russian cities see Hittle, *The Service City*, 26–37. See also Bushkovitch, *The Merchants of Moscow*, and Samuel H. Baron, "Ivan the Terrible, Giles Fletcher and the Muscovite Merchantry: A Reconsideration," *The Slavonic and East European Review* LVI/4 (Oct. 1978), 563–85 and Baron, "Who Were the Gosti?" *California Slavic Studies* VII (1973), 1–40.

the country's commerce.[30] These men were members of three "officially created and sustained"[31] state-affiliated mercantile guilds or corporations known as the *gosti*, the *gostinaia sotnia* and the *sukhonaia sotnia*. Many of the elite, Moscow-based gosti possessed substantial capital, but there were usually only twenty to thirty gosti at any given time, and most members of the other corporations possessed only modest financial resources.[32] Men of these corporations functioned as the Muscovite state's commercial and financial service class, the urban equivalent of the service-obligated landed gentry. Apart from their own trade they worked as tax collectors, financial advisors and bureaucrats. It was a measure of the interpenetration of these top merchants with the state that eight gosti were among fifty men who were appointed as chancellery secretaries during the century.[33]

The service obligations of this small group of privileged merchants have often been viewed in a negative light, as another indication, that is, of the Russian mercantile bourgeoisie's lack of financial strength and absence of legal autonomy. While that is true in one sense, their government links also enabled this relatively underdeveloped class to exert pressure on the government to enact measures that would restrict the activities of foreign merchants. Russian merchants openly conceded that they were incapable of successfully competing with their foreign rivals on equal terms, so throughout the seventeenth century there was an ongoing struggle in Moscow over commercial policy.[34] Thus while the state welcomed foreigners in order to achieve specific fiscal and monetary goals, merchants attempted to prevent them from competing too freely within the country's internal markets.

The Indian "guest-house" in Astrakhan

Muscovite officials may not have developed a formal policy to encourage foreign merchants to settle in Astrakhan until the early seventeenth century, although the city's governors must have made ad hoc arrangements with visiting merchants from the first days of Russian rule. The Romanov dynasty undoubtedly decided to welcome foreigners to the city because of their need to rebuild the country after the Time of Troubles. Yet their underlying reason for doing so must have been the weakness of the Russian merchant class, especially their well-known inability or unwillingness to trade abroad in sufficient numbers. The Russian conquest of Astrakhan did not stimulate Russian merchants from Moscow or the Volga cities

[30] Lyaschenko, *National Economy of Russia*, 221.
[31] Baron, "Who Were the Gosti?" 7. This article is the best introduction to the recruitment, privileges and responsibilities of the gosti.
[32] The resources of some of these men in relation to Indian merchants is discussed below, chapter 5.
[33] Richard Hellie, *Enserfment and Military Change in Muscovy* (Chicago: University of Chicago Press, 1971), 70. Most other secretaries came from bureaucratic families.
[34] Bushkovitch's argument that Russian merchants held their own internally seems slightly over-stated in the economic sense as they consistently invoked state aid to prevent sustained competition from foreigners. *The Merchants of Moscow*, 170.

to visit Iran, Turan or India in numbers that were significant enough to be noticed – apart from the one recorded visit of the merchant Kotov – any more than English and Dutch visits to Archangel resulted in substantial Russian commercial settlements being established in England or the Netherlands. Russian merchants in Astrakhan, whose numbers were undoubtedly quite modest in the late sixteenth century, waited for Armenian, Iranian, Central Asian and Indian traders to visit the city, market the goods and make local purchases. Therefore, Ivan the Terrible's reported interest in obtaining reasonably priced Indian spices and augmenting his treasury by opening up trade with India could not have been accomplished by relying on his indigenous merchant class.[35]

Indian knowledge of Russian markets undoubtedly antedated the Russian conquest of Astrakhan, since Turkic traders from the khanate had well-established contacts with two areas frequented by large numbers of South Asian merchants in the sixteenth century – northern Iran and Turan. Anthony Jenkinson and other members of the English Muscovy Company met Indian merchants in Kashan and Qazvin in the 1560s and 1570s who must have been quick to learn about the Russian conquest.[36] These merchants must also have realized quite soon that this gave them access to markets in the vast Volga basin. However, no evidence exists to show that Indian merchants actually began to reside semi-permanently in the city before the first quarter of the seventeenth century. According to an early nineteenth-century Russian source they first arrived in Astrakhan from Iran and the Caucasus in 1615/1616 A.D.[37] The Indian diaspora probably expanded from these nearby areas initially because it would have been easy for Indian merchants to have sent their assistants or relatives to visit Astrakhan to explore its new commercial possibilities; some Indian merchants in the city still operated as agents of Iranian-based firms in the mid-eighteenth century. It is also important to remember that under Shah 'Abbas the Safavids exercised hegemony over the Araks–Kura duab in the eastern Caucasus, only a short distance by ship or land from Astrakhan. This date is also likely to be at least approximately accurate, as is suggested by the testimony of the Indian merchant Sutur, for in a 1648 petition he said that he had been living and paying customs duties in the city for the past twenty-five years.[38]

Whatever the exact year of the initial settlement the Indian Astrakhan community probably began growing rapidly during the 1620s. During this decade Moscow officials repeatedly instructed their subordinates to create more favorable trading conditions for all "eastern Merchants who arrive in Astrakhan with all sorts of eastern goods . . . and allow them to go upstream along the Volga to Kazan

[35] Antonova, I, Introduction, 6.
[36] Jenkinson, *Early Voyages and Travels*, I, 149 and 428–29.
[37] Antonova, I, Introduction, and Baikova, *Rol' Srednei Azii v Russko-Indiiskikh Torgovykh Sviaziakh*, chapter 2, for discussions of early Indian contacts. Some Indian merchants were known to trade along the Terek river in the northern Caucasus, the setting of Leo Tolstoy's *Caucasian Sketches*.
[38] Antonova, I, no. 36, 1648, 88–89.

and other cities."[39] This was the period, after all, immediately following the Time of Troubles when the Russian government was desperately short of cash, a situation exacerbated by the closure of the Baltic ports to Russian trade.[40] Russian officials may reasonably have expected to offset these difficulties to some degree by encouraging Asian traders. These policies were probably directly responsible for the fact that when Sutur wrote in 1648 a sizeable Indian mercantile community was present in Astrakhan. He himself had publicized its existence in the previous year when he asked Russian authorities to grant Indians permission to construct their own *gostiny dvor*, literally their "guest-house," a kind of residential bazar.[41] Shortly after the building was completed in 1649 the earliest known census of Indian merchants revealed that the new building housed twenty-six long-time residents of the city.[42]

Sutur provided considerable additional information about the Indian Astrakhan community in the numerous petitions that he addressed to the tsar between 1647 and 1658 concerning his commercial disputes and bureaucratic problems. The information is of two kinds, references to his own business activities and a general explanation for the growth of Indian commerce in Russia. In the course of pleading his case with Russian authorities Sutur reported that he traded in "all kinds of goods," and it is clear from his description of his affairs that in the mid-seventeenth century he regarded himself primarily as an Astrakhan merchant. Nonetheless, he operated over a distance that extended from Isfahan to Moscow, and at one point he lived in the Russian capital for three years. Sutur may well have been the archetype of the successful Indian businessman who migrated from Iran to Russia in the prosperous and stable 1620s, using capital generated from cloth sales and financial operations. This was the time, after all, at the height of Shah 'Abbas' power, when the Russian merchant Kotov visited Isfahan and described settlements of Multani merchants there. It is obvious from a trip that Sutur made to Iran in 1651, during which he sold, among other goods, Russian sables in Iran in exchange for Iranian silk, that he had extensive business connections in Isfahan, undoubtedly some of the thousands of "banias" who worked in the Safavid capital. Two of Sutur's brothers also traded in Qazvin in northwestern Iran. One of these men may have been the brother whom he had originally persuaded to join him from India.[43]

In one petition that Sutur wrote because he wanted to see a troublesome Astrakhan official dismissed he offered an analysis of the origins of Indian trade in Russia. It was probably symptomatic of the self-serving, inevitably calculated

[39] Goikova, *Essays*, 161.
[40] *Ibid.*, 161.
[41] Antonova, I, no. 33, 1647, 84. Hittle discusses the use of the term dvor. *The Service City*, 25. Nikitin, *Astrakhan' i ee Okrestnosti*, 57, includes a small but clear photograph of the eighteenth-century Indian dvor in Astrakhan. It is a substantial and impressive stone building. The book also includes photographs of the Iranian dvor and other major buildings in the city.
[42] *Ibid.*, no. 38, 1649, 90–91.
[43] *Ibid.*, nos. 34, 1647, 85–86; no. 48, 1651, 97–99 and no. 57, 1654, 126–30.

rhetoric of the genre that his explanation for Indian migration to Astrakhan stressed business conditions rather than new market opportunities. Still, even with its predictable slant Sutur's account represents a unique perspective on the foundation of the Indian mercantile settlement. In his statement he excoriated Iranian authorities for their treatment of the 10,000 Indian merchants he estimated to be living in Safavid dominions at the time, writing that

the Shah takes much in customs from them . . . and each person in the Shah's provinces steals from the Indians . . . and the khans and all the court people call them to dine . . . and they do not care that many Indians in the Shah's cities live in desperate situations.[44]

While these conditions do not appear to have differed radically from those of merchants in many European and Asian countries, Sutur evidently spoke from personal experience when he reported that Iranians in the provinces regularly extorted money from Indians. At least in 1651 he claimed that several Iranians in Tabriz had in effect stolen some of his sables, and his testimony was corroborated in general terms by the experience of Russian merchant-diplomats of the second Russo-Indian mission who lost many goods to local officials in northwestern Iran.[45] Sutur said that in Russia Indians were much better off. Russian officials, he said, were both just and solicitous of Indian merchants' welfare. He cited as evidence of Russian treatment his own experience of being allowed to travel from Astrakhan to Kazan and then on to Moscow, trading in complete freedom throughout the country, an experience that may after all have reflected official directives of the 1620s regarding the treatment of "Eastern merchants." He went on to report that customs dues were charged to him solely and "directly" at customs houses, implying that no extraordinary exactions had been extorted from him at intermediate points along the road. With the single exception of an Astrakhan Turk, whom Russian authorities employed as a "translator," and whose actions had originally triggered some of his petitions, Sutur reported that he had never been injured by any local officials.[46] Urging that the translator be dismissed he pointedly remarked that if Russian officials continued to treat Indian merchants well all his compatriots who were then doing business in Iran would move to Astrakhan, proportionately raising Russian customs receipts.

Indian merchants never shifted their operations to Iran en masse; their familiarity with Iran and Persian, the relatively impoverished Russian population and the resistance of Russian merchants which had just begun to coalesce into organized opposition to foreign traders, probably ensured that a large-scale migration never occurred. Sutur may well have been correct, though, when he asserted that the Muscovite state was more concerned and capable of protecting foreign merchants than were Iranian officials whose control over provincial areas,

[44] *Ibid.*, no. 33, 1647, 84–85.
[45] *Ibid.*, no. 54, 1662, 116–18.
[46] *Ibid.*, no. 33, 1647, 84–85. The "translator," whose name is given as Devlet 'Ali, seems to have been functionally equivalent to the "dragomans" of the Ottoman empire. For a brief description of this office see Masters, *Western Economic Dominance*, 96.

especially those where Qizilbash amirs still governed, was relatively weak.[47] Russian authorities were certainly exceptionally responsive to Sutur's own particular complaint, for in 1647, shortly after he had denounced the translator, the man was transferred.[48] The incident demonstrated what Sutur undoubtedly knew and implied in his petition, that Russian enthusiasm for Russian trade was dependent to a large degree on the level of customs receipts that it produced. The tsar explicitly made this connection in a letter that he sent to his Astrakhan governor in the same year, for he ordered him to protect Indian merchants "above others" just because their trade generated substantial customs revenue.[49]

In retrospect, though, 1647 marked the end of the initial phase of Russia's Indian commercial policy, for already in the previous year this largely passive policy with its unambiguous welcome of Indian merchants had begun to change. Two major developments occurred in 1646. First of all Russian merchants and foreign officials took the initiative to make direct contact with Mughul Indian rulers and merchants by dispatching the first combined diplomatic–commercial mission to India. At the same time Russian merchants began to campaign aggressively to limit the freedom and ability of foreign merchants to compete in Russian markets.

Borzois and gyrfalcons

The internal dynamics of the Muscovite bureaucracy that led to the dispatch of the four missions to India in the seventeenth century can only be guessed at, but the gosti and members of the other trading corporations probably lobbied for them in the first instance. Merchants from Kazan and Astrakhan who were presumably knowledgeable about the Indian trade headed the first delegation in 1646,[50] and the enthusiasm of merchants for these trips was expressed in their petition that prefaced the second mission in 1651, in which

the merchants and trading people humbly asked the reigning Tsar and Prince of all the Russias Alexei Mikhailovich [for permission] to depart India for trading purposes and to send the Qizilbash Shah their State Letter about that so that he would allow the gosti and trading people to go to India.[51]

Merchants also led the third mission in 1676, and headed the last delegation in 1695, the only one of the four that successfully reached the Mughul court.

Merchants may have been the prime movers of the Indian missions, but leaders

[47] As was suggested above, the issue is not only one of centralized control but of state policy. The Russians may simply have valued Indian and other Asian merchants at this time more than the Iranians did.

[48] Antonova, I, no. 35, 1647, 86.

[49] *Ibid.*, no. 35, 1647, 87. Antonova mentions that the Muscovite government's Secret Department had begun collecting information on India by 1632. Antonova, I, 14.

[50] *Ibid.*, no. 25, 1646, 62.

[51] *Ibid.*, no. 49, 1651, 99. A similar petition may have prefaced papers of the first mission, but part of the text of those instructions has been lost.

of each delegation also functioned as tsarist emissaries. They carried elaborate diplomatic instructions, which like many such documents of the period were prefaced by blatant state propaganda. In these letters the tsars dwelled at length on their titles and the extent of their sovereignty – specifically alluding at one point to the inclusion of fur-rich Siberian territories in their possessions. In the instructions envoys were commanded to follow strict standards of conduct – they were, characteristically, urged in one letter not to drink excessively,[52] and to observe detailed protocols for contacting Mughul officials. Each mission was given multiple diplomatic, commercial and intelligence-gathering objectives, which show that tsarist officials had developed more ambitious goals for their commercial relations with India than that of simply relying upon Indian merchants to increase their customs revenues. It is also important to note that their state objectives were not always consonant with those of the merchant class, whose representatives carried their instructions.

The leaders of the first mission were instructed, first of all, to withdraw from the state account 3–4,000 roubles' worth of goods that would be suitable for sale in India.[53] Their sense of what Russian goods might be appropriate for the Indian market was not indicated in these documents but the second delegation of 1651 is known to have carried with it at least two commodities, "Tver copper" and sable pelts.[54] Prior to the third embassy in 1675 Russian officials sensibly sought out expert commercial advance and were told by Indian merchants in Moscow that

In the Indian state the highest demand for Russian goods is for high-priced sables – 10, 20, 30 roubles a pair, good red broad cloth and green broad cloth, red leather, walrus teeth, coral, large middle sized and small mirrors, gold and silver velvet and Turkish velvet. And if honouring gifts are sent to the Indian ruler then the above mentioned goods [should be sent]; other Russian goods are not much used in India. And it will be best of all and most gratifying to the Indian rulers [if the tsar] allows to be sent gyrfalcons and hawks. And the Indian rulers love Borzoi dogs.[55]

This Indian's list is a useful reminder that in India as well as in Europe Siberian furs were likely to produce the greatest response – or the largest profit – but that unlike Britain and Holland, where Russian forest products were in great demand for shipping, nearly all of the Russian goods that could be easily sold in India were luxury products that would have only a limited market among the Mughul elite.

Once the two emissaries reached India they were ordered to acquire information

---

[52] *Ibid.*, no. 50, 1651, 100. This particular admonition refers to a possible meeting with the Iranian shah on the emissaries' proposed route through Iran. It may have reflected a knowledge of the Iranians' own proclivity for alcohol as well as concern for Russians' intimate knowledge of their countrymen's drinking habits.

[53] *Ibid.*, no. 24, 1646, 48.

[54] *Ibid.*, no. 54, 1662, 116.

[55] *Ibid.*, no. 108, 1675, 189–90. The Russians eventually sent sables, broadcloth, coral, leather and mirrors valued at 800 roubles, although a single sable pelt represented 600 roubles of that amount, and also 300 roubles' worth of unspecified goods.

on an encyclopedic variety of subjects that included: Shah Jahan's religion and
that of his subjects, whether religious buildings were constructed from wood or
of stone, the extent of the Mughul kingdom and the number and identity of its
subordinate monarchs, the size of the Mughul empire's military forces, including
specifics on cavalry and infantry, the manner in which towns were constructed,
the population, whether or not western India was under Mughul control and how
many ships came to trade via "the German Sea."[56] The last question reflected the
commercial goals of the mission which were delineated in particularly great
detail. The two men were to collect commercial intelligence, covertly if necessary,
on the following subjects: the availability and prices of local products, the
trading activities of "Germans" and other Europeans in India, what German,
Russian and European goods the Indians preferred, customs duties charged and
what were the best land and sea routes to India. They were also to find out if a wide
variety of cotton and silk textiles, precious stones, "vegetables" and spices could
be purchased in the country.[57] The specificity of these latter requests probably
indicated that Russian merchants in the lower Volga cities already possessed
considerable information about Indian products that had been imported into
Russia via Astrakhan. Even Russians in the north might have been familiar with
certain Indian products as more and more English and Dutch ships arrived in
Archangel carrying East Indian goods.

Apart from intelligence gathering, the mission's two leaders were instructed
to encourage Shah Jahan to reciprocate by sending a diplomatic or combined
diplomatic and commercial embassy to Moscow.[58] If the Mughul ruler permitted
merchants to accompany the mission they would be allowed to trade duty-free
throughout the country,[59] a promise which, if fulfilled, would have deeply
angered Russian merchants, who were just then organizing to demand that
restrictions be placed on foreign competition by limiting their access to internal
Russian markets. The Muscovite government's rationale for threatening the
interests of its own merchant class was not made completely clear in the letters of
instruction that were given to the 1646 or to the 1651 delegations, but in 1675 the
tsar made two specific requests of the reigning emperor, Aurungzeb, and his
ministers to send 2–3,000 *puds* (72,000–108,000 lbs) of silver annually with
ambassadors or merchants. In exchange for the precious metal Indians would be
offered sable and ermine pelts, skins, broadcloth and other goods "abundantly
available in Russia."[60] This almost endearingly naive request reflected the
continuing currency shortage in Russia and a poor sense of the demand for
Russian goods in India. The tsar's second request was indicative of the relative

---

[56] *Ibid.*, no. 29, 1646, 69–70. Note that in this letter the Russians mentioned by way of an apology for
any protocol mistakes they might make with Shah Jahan's titles that they had never before had any
communication from the Mughul court: *Ibid.*, no. 50, 1651, 106.

[57] *Ibid.*, no. 24, 1646, 57–58.

[58] *Ibid.*, no. 24, 1646, 54.

[59] *Ibid.*, no. 24, 1646, 54.

[60] *Ibid.*, no. 113, 1675, 200.

level of skills among some Russian artisans, for he asked that experienced Indian stone masons be sent to Russia.

The request for stone masons partly reflected the fame of these Indian craftsmen whose predecessors in the fourteenth century had been abducted by Timur and sent to Turan to aid in the construction of his capital, Samarqand.[61] The tsar's request was typical of his predecessors' well-established policy of recruiting outside technical expertise. They had begun doing so almost immediately after Chancellor had discovered the White Sea passage to Russia, and the policy later reached its climax with Peter the Great's massive recruitment of European artisans to develop the Russian economy. The obvious difference in the two cases is that Russia was seeking new technology from Europe, but traditional craft skills from India. The Russian government had made a similar request for Indian help ten years earlier when Kazan and Muscovite officials had written to the Astrakhan governor instructing him to find Indian artisans who practiced the crafts for which they were most famous, the preparation and decoration of cotton and linen cloth. If located they were to be invited to Moscow to establish their industry there. However, the Iranian or "tazik" merchants to whom the governor entrusted this task reported that no Indian craftsmen lived in the city, an indication, perhaps, of the relatively more modest and recent Indian business presence there when compared with Darya Khan's complex business operations in Samarqand. In fact, Russian officials seemed to be looking for exactly the kind of artisans who had been supplying Darya Khan in the late sixteenth century. No further attempt seems to have been made to locate Indian textile craftsmen, probably because Iranians and a Bukharan "master dyer" who possessed the necessary skills were located in the city.[62]

The elaborate diplomatic preparation and ambitious goals of the first three missions were ultimately irrelevant because none of them succeeded in reaching the Mughul court; they are mainly interesting because of what they revealed about Russian economic policy. The first two missions had been sent via Iran, probably because of Russia's well-established ties with that country. Both had failed virtually before they began. Persian officials had refused the first mission permission to proceed because, they claimed, frontier disturbances threatened its safety, a possible allusion to Safavid–Mughul quarrels and warfare over Qandahar. The second never advanced beyond northwestern Iran, because most of the goods that the emissaries were carrying for trade in India were extorted, plundered or allowed to be extorted by Safavid provincial officials in Ardebil, the site of the dynasty's original *khangah*, or devotional center, but also an important commercial city near the Caspian Sea. Russian officials complained that other government officials in Isfahan itself had also extorted goods from their

[61] Beveridge, *The Babur-nama in English*, 76.
[62] Antonova, I, nos. 78–80, 1665, 156–57. See also A. I. Iukht, "Indiiskaia koloniia v Astrakhani" [The Indian Colony in Astrakhan], *Voprosy Istorii* no. 3 (March 1957), 137, where Iukht says that there were no Indian craftsmen in Astrakhan, but this sweeping statement seems to be based only on data from 1746.

emissaries.[63] Russians then turned to an experienced Bukharan merchant and resident of the Bukharan gostiny dvor to head the third mission which traveled to Kabul via Balkh, but the merchant, Muhammad Yusuf Qasim(ov), was not allowed to proceed further than the Afghan capital because of a major Afghan–Mughul war which disrupted travel and trade in the region for several years.[64] The only apparent result of these first three missions was that they enabled Russian officials gradually to acquire a more sophisticated geographical and political appreciation of both Iran and Turan. At least by the end of the seventeenth century they knew that no water route existed by which they could travel from Turan to India![65] Their commercial interest in a Central Asian route also seems to have given some Russians one additional justification for supporting Muscovite expansion in that region.[66]

Even the final, successful fourth Russian mission to India in 1695, the only one that Peter the Great sanctioned, did not have perceptible long-term consequences. Indian trade may have held only minor interest for Peter at a time when Russia was beginning to mine its own silver and the importation of Asian products was made infinitely easier by the opening of St. Petersburg. At least this last mission appears to have been a purely commercial one. Not only was it led, as usual, by merchants, in this case by two members of the gostinaia sotnia merchant corporation, but its letters of instruction were perfunctory when compared with the elaborate documents of the first missions. Peter's government approved the trip, but otherwise did not order the Russians who led it to perform diplomatic duties or to seek commercial intelligence – the tsar primarily asked Aurungzeb to assist the Russian merchants with their trade.[67] These men traveled to India through Iran by a similar route to that which Nikitin had taken in the fifteenth century, and then they went onwards by ship from Bandar Abbas to Surat.[68] They met Aurungzeb, who was then camped with his army at "Barunpur," probably Burhanpur, a city due east of Surat where the emperor was then on campaign, and were granted the right of free trade during their prolonged stay in Mughul territories. Later at Delhi and the other north Indian cities they purchased indigo and varieties of cotton textiles, classic Indian export commodities, an indication, perhaps, of their desire

[63] The documents for the first mission are Antonova, I, nos. 24–30, 1646–47, 48–73, and for the second mission, *ibid.*, nos. 49–55, 1651–67, 99–103. The reference to disturbed conditions is *ibid.*, no. 30, 1647, 73. The complaints about the missions' treatment in Ardebil is *ibid.*, no. 55, 1667, 73. The losses were principally in Ardebil and Isfahan to a value of just over 837 roubles.

[64] Antonova, I, no. 126, 1676, 220–21.

[65] *Ibid.*, no. 110, 1675, 191–2.

[66] In the seventeenth century Russian enquiries about trade with India through Central Asia were also combined with requests for information on the military and political situation in the Central Asian khanates. See, for example, Antonova, I, no. 110, 1675, 191–92. By the middle of the eighteenth century the Russians were established at Orenburg and expressed interest in the khanates as intermediary points between Orenburg and India. *Ibid.*, no. 139, 1751, 283–84, and no. 214, 1800, 406–8.

[67] Antonova, I, no. 251–60, 1695–1716, 356–77. This collection, which includes reproduction of original letters, is an interesting example of diplomatic correspondence of the period.

[68] *Ibid.*, no. 258, 1716, 371.

to circumvent Indian merchants in Iran and Astrakhan, or even Europeans in Archangel. They also learned at Agra that Indian merchants were prepared to buy Russian hides and leather, two staple Russian commodities that Jenkinson had seen in Bukhara a century and a half earlier, and an indication of the severely limited demand for Russian goods among the general populace.[69] The entire trip took five years, though, and one of the principal merchants died on the return journey just before he reached Astrakhan.

The New Trade Regulations

Simultaneously with the approval of the first Russian missions to India in 1646 Russian merchants and traders of all classes, from the elite gosti to peasant traders, began a concerted effort to limit the commercial privileges of foreigners.[70] The growing Russian resentment against the unconditional welcome shown to foreign merchants by Russian authorities in the chaotic conditions of the late sixteenth and early seventeenth century was viscerally expressed by a Croatian Catholic missionary who arrived in the Ukraine in 1659, Iurii Krizanic. Krizanic, who resented foreigners' treatment of Slavs in general, said of their role in Russia that

Under the guise of commerce, the foreigners reduce us to extreme impoverishment. Here in Russia (except for the tsar's treasury), one cannot see or hear of riches anywhere; instead there is wretched, empty-handed poverty everywhere. All the wealth of this realm . . . are carried away by foreign tradesmen or thieves . . . Foreign tradesmen, Germans, Greeks and Bokharans, rake in all the wealth and products of this land for themselves . . . They travel freely throughout the land and buy our goods at lowest prices; while they bring to us many useless but expensive foreign wares . . . And finally, being sly, they cheat our tradesmen out of large sums of money.[71]

Initially the merchants directed their complaints mainly at Europeans, who were numerous, highly visible and active in Archangel, Moscow and northern Russia. In 1646 gosti merchants and members of the other two privileged corporations in the capital presented a petition to the tsar in which they complained forcefully about the English, who had enjoyed free trade and other privileges since the formation of the Muscovy Company in the mid-sixteenth century.[72] In response the tsar, who was far more secure than his predecessors, approved the abolition of free trade for all Europeans, and three years later cancelled all the special privileges for the English. He also expelled English merchants from the interior, ordering them to confine their activities to border

---

[69] *Ibid.*, no. 258, 1716, 371–72. The following currency equivalents were given in this letter. One rupee was said to be the same weight as a Russian poltinka and equal in value of 13 altins and 2 dengas.

[70] See the petition reprinted in George Vernadsky, ed., *A Source Book for Russian History from Early Times to 1917*, I: *Early Times to the Late 17th Century* (New Haven, Conn.: Yale University Press, 1972), 246, which was sent by members of the three trading corporations.

[71] "Krizanic on Russia in the 1660s," in Vernadsky, ed., *Source Book*, I, 252.

[72] *Ibid.*, 246.

cities such as Archangel.[73] Merchants who resided in Astrakhan were later included in a 1665 regulation that forbade all foreigners from residing and conducting business in Moscow. In 1667 these piecemeal restrictions were climaxed by the enactment of the comprehensive New Trade Regulations. This latter act recapitulated earlier commercial restrictions on foreigners, essentially confining them to border cities and restricting them to wholesale trade with their Russian counterparts.[74] Exceptions were permitted, but if foreign merchants were allowed to proceed beyond Archangel, Astrakhan or other border cities with government passes they were required to pay double the usual customs duties.[75] Foreigners were also forbidden to purchase gold or silver for export, another reminder of Russian chronic currency shortage and, many would argue, an indication of Russia's increasing commitment to a·mercantilist foreign trade policy.[76]

The 1667 legislation had the intended effect of further concentrating Asian mercantile activity in Astrakhan, but it did not inhibit the continued growth of the Indian mercantile community in that city. If anything the opposite was true. By the 1670s and 1680s more than one hundred Indian men permanently resided there, four times the 1647 census figure.[77] Nor did the regulations pose an insurmountable obstacle to Indian or other merchants doing business in the Volga basin or even in Moscow itself. This was partly due to the difficulty of enforcing regulations that included, among other restrictions, a prohibition on foreigners trading among themselves. Sometimes Indian merchants simply ignored the restrictions; more than a century after they were passed Indians were still purchasing Russian currency and smuggling it out of the country.[78] More often

---

[73] *Ibid.*, 246, and Hittle, *The Service City*, 70.

[74] Hittle has one of the most lucid, concise summaries of these regulations. *The Service City*, 71–72 and n. 37. Details of gosti complaints that were directed specifically at Iranians, Indians and Armenians are contained in their 1672 petition: Antonova, I, no. 95, 172–73. Details of the implementation of customs collection and restrictions on the movements of Indians and other "eastern" merchants are contained in an order of the Astrakhan governor: Antonova, I, no. 98, 1672, 174–79. See also no. 104, 1673, 182 where Indians were ordered to confine all their trading to the gostiny dvor. Letters detailing the restrictions were sent to authorities in every major city.

[75] Hittle estimates that this meant that foreigners were paying 16% duties on goods taken into the interior. *The Service City*, 70. However, Baikova argues that Indians who took goods to Moscow paid 25% of their value by the time they were sold: 10% at entry into Astrakhan, 10% for departure to Moscow and 5% for sale in Moscow: Baikova, *Rol' Srednei Azii v Russko-Indiiskikh Torgovykh Sviaziakh*, 105.

[76] Golikova, *Essays*, 164. Golikova and most Russian and western historians classify Russia's commercial policy at this period as mercantilist. Hittle, citing the Russian historian Bazilevich, suggests that specific western European mercantilist thinkers helped to shape the New Trade Regulations, and that the government actually initiated these regulations even if they reflected long-standing goals of merchant groups. *The Service City*, 71. Fernand Braudel pointedly remarks that the term mercantilism, which was invented after the fact, has been given a variety of meanings, "But if one of those meanings was to be paramount, it would be that which implied a defence against others. For mercantilism was, above all, a means to self-defence." *The Perspective of the World*, 53.

[77] Golikova, *Essays*, 163.

[78] Antonova, II, no. 192, 1777, 364–68.

than not, though, Indians, Armenians and others were simply able to obtain special exemptions. The Armenian company from the Isfahan suburb of Julfa was granted an exemption in 1667, the very year that they were promulgated. Russian officials allowed them to trade freely in Moscow and beyond the western borderlands to Europe, while paying standard customs fees for imported goods.[79] Armenians found it particularly easy to obtain concessions because they controlled a significant portion of Iranian silk exports, but other Asians, including Indians, also regularly received passes that permitted them to trade on the same basis as Armenians. These were granted because, in the words of the head of Russian customs who in 1678 pressed the government to exempt Indians from the regulations, "their payments enriched the treasury."[80]

Enriching the treasury, the original reason for welcoming Indian merchants to Astrakhan and the upper Volga cities, always seems to have been the most compelling justification for issuing passes to Indians that exempted them from the New Trade Regulations. Such exemptions were common, illustrating that while members of the three merchant corporations might influence legislation they could not compel officials to enforce provisions which conflicted with the interests of the state. The gosti and others made repeated anguished protests about the continued involvement of Indians in Russian internal trade. More than 160 of them signed a 1684 petition protesting such exemptions. Alluding to the 1667 code, gosti, representatives of the gostinaia sotnia, urban shopkeepers, trading peasants and even members of the *strel'tsi*, the musketeer-tradesmen, complained about damaging competition from all foreign merchants and singled out Indians for special mention.

To the ruling Tsar and Great Prince, Ioann Alekseevich, Autocrat of Great and Small and White Russia . . . all of your Moscow state gosti and gostinaia sotni . . . [protest] the injury to all trade from foreigners of various states but especially from Indians because they live in Moscow and Astrakhan many years without leaving and falsely call themselves Astrakhan inhabitants although they have wives and children overseas in India. They trade in all types of goods. They sell at retail and lend money at high rates of interest. They carry on their various sales in all arcades of Moscow shopkeepers and in the Gostiny Dvor of all cities where merchants arrive . . . From Armenians and Persians . . . these Indians in Astrakhan and Moscow take goods when they arrive impoverished and with us, your slaves and orphans, they trade and exchange for our goods poor rejected goods which themselves cannot get rid of for a long while. They take their own high quality goods with themselves to Moscow and to cities in Great Russia and to towns in Great Russia and to Makarevskii market and they sell at retail and buy, living in Moscow . . . They sit in Moscow in the old Gostiny Dvor in the very best shops roofed with tiles. And these Indians sell their own goods and buy overseas goods from many Russian merchants and sell at retail and lend money at great rates of interest and Moscow inhabitants purchase from them, the Indians, our goods at a dearer price than from us. And these Indians who live in Astrakhan without paying tribute, enrich themselves because they never serve our state,

---

[79] Golikova, *Essays*, 164.
[80] *Ibid.*, 165.

they do not pay taxes . . . And enriching themselves in the Muscovite state they go overseas to their wives and families in their state.[81]

Indians responded to this petition against their relentlessly effective marketing as they had in the past. Using their most persuasive retort they reminded authorities that Russia derived "great profits" from their trade, particularly as they paid twice the usual customs duties. A year earlier, in fact, they had claimed that they paid 24,000 roubles customs duties on goods worth 80,000 roubles that they had brought to Moscow.[82] If these figures were accurate they would explain why Russian customs officials were so enthusiastic about encouraging Indian trade, although Russian merchants challenged the accuracy of these figures in their 1684 petition.

In what must have been for Russian merchants and tradesmen a maddeningly familiar sequence of events, Russian authorities responded to the 1684 petition by reiterating the restrictions on foreign merchants that were included in the New Trade Regulations – and then largely refusing to enforce them. A year later "foreigners" again were told that they were prohibited from trading in the "upper [Volga] cities of Kazan, Simbirsk, Saratov and Tsaritsin,"[83] but five years later when Peter the Great assumed direct control of the Muscovite state he acted to increase foreign trade by encouraging foreign merchants to trade inside Russia. In 1697 Astrakhan foreigners were explicitly welcomed to travel to Moscow once again,[84] and throughout Peter's reign foreign merchants were treated with great consideration, even to the extent that Russian envoys in Iran intervened on behalf of permanent foreign residents of Astrakhan when they visited Iranian territories to trade. By the 1720s some Indians had even gone so far as to petition the government for permission to extend their trips to the important Baltic port of Riga, and to Peter the Great's new capital of St. Petersburg, and to be allowed to pass through Russia on their way to western Europe and to China via Russia's Siberian territories.[85] At this time Indian merchants seemed poised to follow the Armenian example, and expand their diaspora into the rich markets of western Europe.

Merchants and the state

The success that Indian merchants had in penetrating Russian markets in the seventeenth and early eighteenth century should not obscure the fact that the Muscovite state initiated and closely regulated Russian–Indian commercial

[81] Antonova, I, no. 225, 1684, 306–7.
[82] *Ibid.*, 312–19, where two Indian merchants explain in detail the customs that they paid when bringing goods from Astrakhan to Moscow. These figures approximate Baikova's estimates for the customs and sales percentages that the government charged Indian and other foreign merchants. See above, n. 74.
[83] *Ibid.*, no. 226, 1685, 339.
[84] Golikova, *Essays*, 176.
[85] Antonova, II, nos. 32 and 37, 1720 and 1723, 54–55, and 57–59.

relations. Sutur may have been genuinely pleased that the Muscovite state was able to regulate its subordinates effectively enough to prevent them from extracting arbitrary payments of the kind that Iranian officials took from him, other Indians and even members of Russian diplomatic missions. Yet the obverse of this relative commercial security was the high degree of centralized control that Russian monarchs exerted over foreign trade and the movement of non-Russian merchants within their territories. Indians and other foreigners may have been able to evade the spirit of some regulations, but after the New Trade Regulations were promulgated the necessity of having to apply for passes for each trip into the Russian interior severely limited their ability to expand their own businesses beyond Astrakhan. Not only did they have to apply for permission to city authorities each time they wanted to make a trip to Moscow, Saratov or any other Volga city, they also had to do so each time that they wished to carry on commerce in the nearby steppe.[86]

Given the degree of control that Muscovite authorities exercised over their own merchant class and over the activities of all residents of *posads* or urban communes, it is scarcely surprising that they insisted upon closely monitoring and regulating foreign businessmen. Yet their desire and ability to supervise closely foreign merchants contrasted sharply with the relatively laissez faire attitude that Safavid officials had toward foreign merchants who traded in Iran. The difference did not stem from fundamental differences in economic outlook. As far as he was able Shah 'Abbas implemented an unmistakably mercantilist foreign economic policy that was designed to solve many of the same problems that plagued Russia in the seventeenth century. He even co-opted Armenian merchants into the state apparatus to serve in a limited way as his gosti. Yet it is questionable if his form of absolutism had sufficient ideological or political strength to have achieved the kind of unitary state despotism that the tsars had attained. In any event neither he nor any of his successors ever seem to have attempted to regulate the movement or settlement of Indian merchants – the story that banians bribed one of his successors is the only known hint that such a policy might ever have been tried. Otherwise some Safavid shahs sought only to prevent the export of currently issued coinage, although it is impossible to say if this policy was systematically enforced over an extended period of time.

There is little reason to doubt that if Indian merchants had been able to operate as freely within Russia as they had long been able to do in Iran they would have used their resources and marketing talents to extend their influence from their well-established Iranian base deeply into the markets of the upper Volga urban centers and possibly to enter western Europe. Yet even while operating within the constraints of increasingly effective Muscovite absolutism, Indians were able to exert significant economic influence in the Astrakhan region. Expanded documentation of the Petrine era offers exceptional insight into both the mechanics and magnitude of their achievement. These sources demonstrate that

[86] Antonova, II, no. 25, 1721, 56–57.

outbursts from Russian merchants who objected to Indian competition were far more than manifestations of Russian xenophobia; they were instead protests that reflected the fundamentally unequal relationship of the skills and capital assets of the two merchant classes.

CHAPTER 5

The Indian diaspora in the Volga basin

Astrakhan stands at the mouth of the river Volga, on an island formed by two of its branches
. . . in the middle of the town is the principal square, about two hundred yards wide N. and
S., and one hundred E. and W. On the east are the houses of the Governor and the Vice-
Governor. Opposite is the house occupied by the [Scottish] missionaries. On the south is
the Gostenoi Dvor, a range of shops, which, being uniform, have a pleasing and grand
appearance . . . The natives of every country enjoy religious toleration here. The town is
full of temples of Hindoos and Kalmucks, of the mosques of the Mahometans, and of the
churches of different Christian sects. Astrakhan is considered as the see of the Armenian
Archbishop in Russia.

> George Keppel: *Personal Narrative of a Journey from India*
> *to England . . . in the Year 1824*

The Indian mercantile settlement of Astrakhan represented a bridgehead of the
Indian world economy into the most underdeveloped or "peripheral" European
state in the early modern era. Primarily an extension of the substantial Indian
commercial presence in Iran, the Indian community came to exercise significant
economic influence in the Volga basin by the late seventeenth and early
eighteenth century. Using the family firm as the nucleus of their businesses,
Indians successfully combined commercial and financial activities to accumulate
substantial amounts of capital. At the height of their influence during the reign of
Peter the Great their financial resources not only exceeded those of other
merchant communities in Astrakhan, but they were also greater than those held by
Russian merchants in all but a few Russian commercial and manufacturing
centers. The Indians' success in Russia was continued evidence of the dynamism
of Indian mercantile capital in the latter years of the Mughul empire.

The Indian community in Astrakhan

Astrakhan was not the sole Russian city where groups of Indian merchants were
allowed to reside for long periods of time. As the number of Indians entering
Russia rose during the latter half of the seventeenth century increasing numbers of
them traveled up the Volga river to Moscow, the center of Russian commercial

life. By 1684 twenty-one Indians resided in Moscow, where most of them had lived since 1679 in the stone gostiny dvor near the coaching inn that was situated in the Kitaegorod suburb. This dvor had also been allotted to Armenian, Bukharan and Iranian merchants.[1] Some Indians came to Moscow on their own initiative – and without a knowledge of Russian – while others arrived as agents of their relatives or other partners in Astrakhan. This was true, for example, of three Indians known in Russian sources as Ardash China, Banda Mingal(ova) and Lahori Ban'ia, all of whom conducted business in Moscow in 1675 for their brothers in Astrakhan.[2] Several Indians in Moscow subsequently petitioned to extend their trade to St. Petersburg after Peter the Great had constructed his new capital.[3] However, this potentially important community of Indian merchants in Moscow was not allowed to grow significantly larger, because pressure from Russian merchants increasingly prompted officials to limit the Indians' travel beyond Astrakhan. This effectively prevented the diaspora from spreading much further north or west. By the middle of the eighteenth century no Indian merchants who were not converts are known to have been living in Moscow; at that time all commercial agents of Indian merchants in Astrakhan appear to have been either Armenians or Russians.

The best records for reconstructing a picture of the Astrakhan Indian mercantile community date to the early and middle of the eighteenth century and, therefore, this analysis of the socio-economic characteristics of the community will focus on this period, although not to the exclusion of earlier data. Throughout the seventeenth century the semi-permanent Indian population of Astrakhan had grown steadily until it reached 209 people in 1725.[4] Fifty to one hundred of these individuals seem to have been merchants, moneylenders and bankers, or, more accurately, to have engaged in all these activities, with relatives, assistants, servants and "priests" making up the remainder of the total. Not all Indians lived in the main Indian gostiny dvor. Some lived scattered about the city in other dvors. Other merchants or individuals of mixed Indian-Turkic parentage lived in the "Agrizhan" suburb of the city and would not normally have been included in census counts, although they usually maintained close economic ties with members of the principal Indian house.[5] Some "Indians," possibly Afghans, apparently resided in the Bukharan dvor, for in 1746, when a census showed that 469 people inhabited that dvor, at least six of those counted were Multanis who had, by this evidence, reached Astrakhan via Turan.[6]

Indian merchants and their relatives and servants enjoyed the same legal status

---

[1] Antonova, I, no. 225, 2684, 329 and no. 182, 1679, 287.
[2] *Ibid.*, no. 140, 1675, 240.
[3] Antonova, II, no. 32, 1720, 54; no. 35, 1721, 56; and no. 37, 1723, 57–58.
[4] Golikova, *Essays*, 169–70. Golikova points out that her figures significantly exceed Antonova's much smaller estimates because Antonova failed to take into account that Indians had more than one dvor and that some lived in the Agrizhan or Indo-Turkic suburb.
[5] *Ibid.*, 170. 109 people lived in the Agrizhan suburb in 1744–46, p. 169.
[6] *Ibid.*, 170. In 1725 the Armenian colony numbered more than 500 people, p. 169.

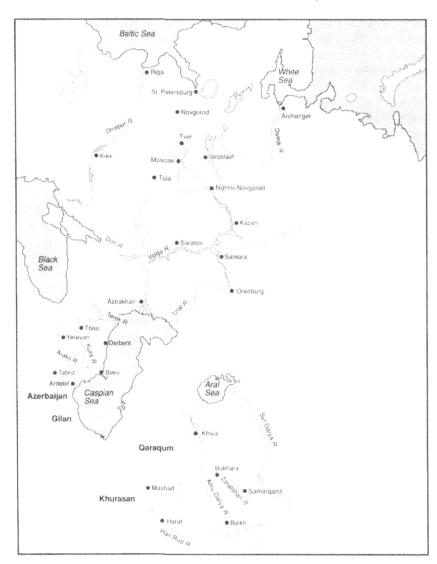

Map 5 Russia

as members of other officially recognized foreign mercantile communities in Astrakhan. This status was similar in general terms to that which Indian rulers granted to Mediterranean or European merchants from Roman times to the modern era or to the well-known "capitulations" that Ottoman rulers accorded to foreign mercantile communities within their territories.[7] Russian authorities classified all foreign merchants as members of particular, semi-autonomous commercial communities.[8] Each one was free to observe its own customs, including the right to practice the various faiths. Bukharan Turks and Iranians each built their own mosques. Hindus not only constructed a temple within their dvor, they also received permission to cremate their dead, much to the disgust of Russian residents who vociferously objected to the practice and to the ceremonial scattering of the corpses' ashes in the river and to the wind.[9]

Russian merchants often expressed their revulsion as Christians to Hindu ceremonies, but they seem to have done so primarily because they wanted to reduce Indian merchants' freedom to compete with them in Russia. They also repeatedly complained about the fact that Indian and other foreign merchants were not subject to the taxes that were levied on all Russian citizens, although in addition to customs dues all non-Russian merchants had to pay a rent of 12 roubles for their shops and a fee for the privilege of living within the city. All resident foreigners were also expected to affirm their commitment to observe local laws and customs in their relations with Russian citizens and local administrators. Disputes among Indians, Armenians, Bukharans or Iranians were, on the other hand, usually adjudicated within each community, but Russian courts exercised jurisdiction over personal or commercial disputes between foreigners and Russian subjects. Indian merchants sometimes had recourse to Russian judicial authorities to settle disputes among themselves, although Russian officials usually expressed a reluctance to become involved in these matters. An illustration of why Russians preferred not to interfere was a complex claim that Narayan Chanchamal(ova) filed with Russian authorities against the property of a deceased Indian merchant, Vishnat Narmaldas(ov), who had died while on a trip to Kizil Yar on the Terek river. They referred this dispute and many others like it back to the Indian community for adjudication, where, they said, it should be decided on the basis of customary law.[10]

---

[7] Masters discusses aspects of seventeenth-century Ottoman capitulatory agreements in *Western Economic Dominance*, 67, 76–78 and 88. The privileges that Indian rulers granted to Mediterranean and Arab traders in South Asia are discussed by Stephen F. Dale in *Islamic Society on the South Asian Frontier: The Mappilas of Malabar, 1498–1922* (Oxford: Clarendon Press, 1980), 29.

[8] See Golikova, *Essays*, 172–80, for the status of these communities.

[9] Antonova, I, no. 225, 1684, 308 and no. 223, 1683, 305 in which Russian authorities granted permission for cremation.

[10] Antonova, I, no. 48, 1727, 80–81. The deceased, "Vishnat," had asked another Indian "Ardial," to take his property back to India to his father and relatives, but a third Indian merchant, Narayan, had claims against the deceased's property and petitioned Russian authorities to prevent Ardial from leaving the city.

In social terms the Indian mercantile community shared certain characteristics of early European trading enclaves in Asia. Most Indian expatriates who lived in Astrakhan on a semi-permanent basis, and those for whom biographical information is available left home at a young age. They resided in the city for years or even decades at a time before returning to India, if indeed they ever did return. By a Russian order promulgated in 1681, Indians, along with Georgians and Armenians, were allowed to live in Astrakhan permanently if they carried on trade.[11] In the most complete census of Indian residents of the city, although one unfortunately taken in 1747, well after the community had gone into decline, fifty-two Indian residents of the gostiny dvor were recorded whose ages ranged from eighteen to sixty-five. While a few of these men had arrived only that year one individual had come from Multan thirty years earlier and five had lived in the city for twenty years or more. The average period of residence for men whose ages and dates of arrival are given was eight years.[12]

Thus, far from representing a transitory group of itinerant traders whose composition changed completely with the arrival of each new ship from northern Iran or each caravan from Turan, the Indian community of Astrakhan represented a relatively stable social group. They constituted a modest, incremental expansion of the Indian diaspora whose membership may have altered by as few as a half-dozen new residents in any given year. That should not obscure the fact, though, that many more Indian merchants arrived each year for short visits. The prominent Marwari merchant and financier, Marwar Bara(ev), estimated that approximately 200 Indian merchants annually came to the city via Iran and Bukhara in the early eighteenth century.[13] This figure seems very high and is not confirmed by other evidence. Still, even if the actual number was much smaller, the regular arrival of merchants from India and Turan indicated that Astrakhan merchants could easily maintain their social and economic ties with Multan, Lahore or Marwar, and remit their profits in goods or specie to their homes. As will be seen, many Indians in the city also regularly traded back and forth each year between Russia and Iran, where so many Indians had lived for decades and where so much of their commerce was concentrated.

Most of those who stayed on, even for decades, seem to have lived and worked largely within the gostiny dvor, and to have maintained their caste identities and ritual life with little change. In the earliest first-hand account of the community by an outsider, the Scottish doctor, John Bell, said of the Astrakhan Indians in 1716 that, "In Astrakhan there are a few Indians or banians who paint their foreheads with saffron . . . they are good-natured, innocent kind of people, and live almost entirely on fruit."[14] Bell himself seems to have been somewhat naive in his

---

[11] Golikova, *Essays*, 165.
[12] Antonova, II, no. 132, 1747, 265–69.
[13] *Ibid.*, no. 69, 1735, 129. Bara(ev) may have been referring to Indians coming *from* Iran or Bukhara, but the text clearly states that they came "cherez," through or via Safavid or Uzbek territories.
[14] John Bell, *Travels from St. Petersburg in Russia to Diverse Parts of Asia* (Glasgow: Robert and Andrew Foulis, 1753), I, 39.

presumption of Indian innocence, but his sympathetic if superficial description offered a rare, humanizing characterization of a group of merchants whom Russian officials and Russian merchants often spoke of in derogatory tones. Interestingly enough Bell's opinions were echoed seventy years later by the Russian author, I. G. Georgi, who not only agreed with his brief description, but wrote a much longer, sensitive and informed ethnographic and commercial sketch of the Indian community. His account showed that these Khattris and Marwaris observed common pollution restrictions and practiced everyday religious observances characteristic of an upper-caste Indian community. He reported on their fastidious preference for simple but exceptionally clean clothes, said that they ate porridge with raisins, as well as melons and other fruits, and kept their individual plates for meals. They worshipped, Georgi said, in a small "temple" within the dvor, and observed daily prayers in the morning and evening at the river, where they were able to perform traditional ablutions. Georgi's comments about their mercantile life are especially revealing, for they represent one of the few unemotional or unprejudiced accounts of Indian commercial life in Russia, most of which are suffused with a visceral dislike that resembles Russian anti-semitism. After describing the outlines of their textile trade he wrote with evident admiration of their financial practices, saying that, "They have all the character-istics of good moneylenders; good stocks of money and caution, they do not charge more than the usual percentage, they do not harass their debtors."[15]

The most detailed description of the worship of the community was given less than twenty years later in 1794 by P. S. Pallas, a German official of the Russian court. Pallas, who was making a second trip to the lower Volga region, wrote that, "during my stay at Astrakhan, I attended with pleasure at the idolatrous worship of the Indian merchants who reside together in the Indian court called the Indeiskoi Dvor." According to Pallas, worship was then supervised not by a Brahman, but by a "Dervish," applying the Arabic term for a mendicant or even a sufi to a Hindu officiant.[16] It is impossible to know if Pallas was completely accurate, or if a non-Brahman had always presided in the temple of the Astrakhan dvor, for just a few years later, when George Forster visited Hindu merchants in the Iranian town of Tirshiz, northwest of Harat, he found that a Brahman who was referred to locally as a *pirzadah*, the son of a *pir* or sufi, presided over their worship.[17] Pallas showed the merchants to have been principally Vaishnavites, as

[15] I. G. Georgi, *Opisanie vsekh obitaiushchikh v Rossiiskom gosudarstve narodov i ikh zhiteiskikh obriadov, obyknovenii, odezhd, zhilishch, veroispovedanii i prochikh dostopamiatnostei, ch. iv-o narodakh mongol'skikh, ob armianakh, gruzinakh, indeitsakh, nemtsakh, poliakakh i o vladychestvuiushchikh rossianakh s opisaniem vsekh imenovanii kazakov, tazhke istoriia o Maloi Rossii i kupno o Kurliandii i Litve* [A Description of all the people living in Russia and their every-day ceremonies, habits, dress, and other memorable things . . .] (St. Petersburg, 2nd ed., 1777), 58–62. Quoted in Antonova, II, 518–21.

[16] P. S. Pallas, *Travels Through the Southern Provinces of the Russian Empire*, trans. by Francis W. Bludgon (London: Longman and O. Reed, 1802–3), 254–59. I am indebted to Thomas Allsen of Trenton State University for this reference.

[17] Forster, *A Journey from Bengal to England*, II, 166.

they stood before a "shrine" that not only contained images of Vishnu and Brahma but a pantheon of mainly Vaishnavite deities, including Rama, Lakshmi, and Hanuman as well as "three black stones," evidently *shaligrams*, "brought from the Ganges and regarded by the [Vaishnavite] Indians as sacred."[18]

These residents of the main dvor seem to have represented the prosperous core of the community and to have eventually retired to India with their profits. Others, though, took mistresses or occasionally even married locally. In Astrakhan a number of Indians formed liaisons with or married local Turkic women, who represented the predominant population in the surrounding countryside. By the eighteenth century the number of children born of these alliances had been sufficient to generate a distinct Indo-Tatar community which occupied the Agrizhan suburb. At least some Indian men who married Turkic women moved into this part of the city and remained there permanently, as did one Rampur Bulanat(ov) who, when his name appeared in a 1744 document, was sixty-four and had lived in the city for twenty years.[19] He was then married to a Turkic woman and lived in this Agrizhan quarter. His children and those of other Indian men were Muslims, as is clearly indicated by the occasional instances in which their names are given.[20] These children appear to have become thoroughly Turkicized as well as becoming Muslims, and their original Indian identity may have disappeared within two or three generations.

References to Indian–Turkic marriages are quite numerous in eighteenth-century records. It is not easy to categorize Indians who married or formed alliances with Turkic women, as their lives were usually not documented. Most were clearly poor. They seem to have worked on the economic margins of Astrakhan commercial life as they were notably less prosperous than residents of the main dvor. Several instances are recorded where Agrizhan Indians took loans from their compatriots or, more usually, accepted charity from them, as did Rampur Balanat(ov) himself. One Indian, "Bujak Lachiram," a 67-year-old man in 1744, had become completely assimilated and lived with his family in a yurt on the steppe.[21] The much rarer instances of Indians who converted to Russian orthodox Christianity might also be classified with these Agrizhan residents as men who had been unsuccessful, and possibly saw conversion as a way of improving their chances to compete more effectively. This may have been the reason for the conversion of a man whose name is given as "Dzhukki" in 1675. He had come to Moscow in the train of the Shemakh khan's ambassador and was engaged in an acrimonious dispute with the three Indians who acted as commission agents for their brothers in Astrakhan. However, this man lived with an Indian orthodox Christian in the Kitaegorod suburb who could have been his original contact and may have influenced his own subsequent decision to

[18] Pallas, *Travels Through the Southern Provinces of the Russian Empire*, I, plates 8 and 9 and 257–58.
[19] Antonova, II, no. 112, 1744, 208.
[20] *Ibid.*, no. 41, 1725, 52.
[21] *Ibid.*, no. 112, 1744, 208.

convert.[22] Financial and legal troubles seem to have been the immediate reason for the later conversion of Marwar Bara(ev). His obvious exasperation at his inability to collect debts that he said were owed to him appears to have driven him to take this step.[23]

Patterns of Indian commerce

As the Indian merchant Sutur implied in 1647 and 1648, the first Indian merchants who traded in Russia probably came initially from commercial centers in northern Iran or from the nearby Caucasus where they and other Indians had long conducted business. This established the dominant pattern of Indian commerce in Russia for the next two centuries, for it is virtually certain, if not statistically demonstrable, that Indian merchants in Russia acquired most of the goods that they marketed there from "correspondents" in the Caspian ports of Baku and Derbent or in important Iranian commercial centers such as Tabriz, Kashan, Qazvin and Isfahan.[24] Indians arriving directly from India and Bukhara must have brought significant amounts of merchandise. However, in the mid-eighteenth century most Indian merchants are known to have been supplied by relatives, assistants or superiors in Iran, who would have had stocks of Indian goods on hand or been able to purchase Iranian merchandise at competitive prices. Eighteen Indians who arrived in Astrakhan from Iran for brief stays in 1746 may well have been acting in this capacity.[25] The same Indian correspondents in Iran are likely to have acted as sales agents for Russian and European goods that Astrakhan Indians exported to Safavid territories, but details about the mechanics of this aspect of the trade are virtually non-existent.

Depending on the period, Indian merchants in Astrakhan primarily marketed variable mixtures of Indian and Iranian textiles, although in the seventeenth century they sometimes also sold spices. Armenians from India also conducted a specialized trade in gems and jewelry that they designed specifically for the tsarist court.[26] Typical of the imports that Indians brought for sale in the seventeenth century were goods recorded by officers of the governor of Kazan in 1638. In reporting to Moscow that an Iranian trade delegation had arrived in the city on its

---

[22] Antonova, I, no. 142, 1675, 248. The Shemakh khan ruled in the area of the confluence of the Araks and Kura rivers.

[23] Golikova, *Essays*, 177–78.

[24] For a discussion of the Iranian cities see Barthold, *Historical Geography*. The significant reference to the Indians' "correspondents" in Iran is contained in a 1750 petition. Antonova, II, no. 134, 1750, 272.

[25] Antonova, II, no. 131, 1746, 264. All of the men on this list, including some who were not merchants, had arrived in the city within the previous year.

[26] Antonova, I, no. 66, 1663, 141–42. Three Armenians brought among other jewels a crown covered with diamonds, star rubies and sapphires topped by a double eagle and a gold cross itself encrusted with diamonds, rubies and star sapphires. It was valued by Armenians at 7,348 roubles and by jewelers at between 5,000 and 5,600 roubles. If the Armenian museum is still intact in the Isfahan suburb of Julfa the visitor can quickly see what close ties existed between Indian and Iranian Armenians by the evidence of bibles printed in India, etc.

way to Moscow, the governor mentioned that the group included a large number of Iranian merchants and two Indians. These Indians may have been genuine peddlers, although it is equally likely that they were agents for other Indians in Iran. They carried two bundles that contained twenty-eight different varieties or sizes of cotton and silk textiles, according to the list prepared by the customs officer. Included among these were 4,600 "kindiak" cotton piece goods of unspecified origin, cloth that was often used for men's outer garments, 900 "aranei" cotton piece goods of "eastern manufacture," 120 pieces of Ardebil silk from northwestern Iran and 150 pieces of Indian silk. Much of the eastern manufactured cloth or that specifically identified as calico or muslin was probably woven in India, but most silk and some cotton in these Indians' possession that was not specifically identified probably had been produced in Iran – in Ardebil, Gilan province or Kashan.[27] A Khattri merchant, Mutra Kapur Chand, who resided in Astrakhan nearly fifty years later, carried a similarly diverse collection of textiles to Moscow in 1680,[28] and comparable lists are found in customs records of Indian imports to Russia at the end of the century.

Indians continued to import textiles into Russia in the eighteenth century, but the mixture of types of fabrics was noticeably different from the earlier period. Other manufactured items and raw materials also completely disappeared from customs lists. Indian silk was no longer mentioned and records of identifiable Indian cotton pieces became increasingly rare, although some Indian cotton cloth continued to be sold by Astrakhan Indians as late as 1800.[29] By the mid-eighteenth century most Indian merchants in Astrakhan had become Eurasian "country traders": that is, just as European merchants in Asia rarely sold many European goods before the industrial revolution reversed the balance of trade between Europe and Asia, by the mid-eighteenth century Indian merchants in Russia came to conduct business almost entirely in non-Indian goods and primarily in Iranian textiles.

The most likely reason for this shift is that Europeans began selling Indian textiles to Russians in Archangel and later in St. Petersburg, and were able to compete successfully against imports of Indian textiles via Astrakhan because of the cost advantage they enjoyed with sea transportation. English merchants, presumably agents of the Muscovy Company, began selling Indian cotton and silk textiles in Archangel at least as early as 1616. By that time small but

---

[27] Antonova, I, no. 12, 1638, 38–39. Ardebil was in Azerbaijan province. Gilan province was located immediately to Ardebil's southeast. For a description of Ardebil see Aziz Allah Bayat, *Kulliyat-i Jugrafiyayi tabi'i va Tarikh-i Iran* [A Survey of the Natural and Historical Geography of Iran] (Tehran: Amir Kabir, 1367), 235–40.

[28] Antonova, I, no. 184, 1680, 288.

[29] Antonova, II, no. 211–17, 1800, see especially 402–4. Together these seven documents represent a comprehensive analysis of Indo-Russian commerce and trade routes in 1800. Note that Indians were sending Indian textiles from Astrakhan to Bukhara in 1722. Antonova, II, no. 36, 1722, 57, and as late as 1777 I. G. Georgi referred to their importation of Indian cotton, linen and silk goods. Antonova, II, 518. However, the overwhelming weight of customs reports and census data quoted below is that Indians were marketing few Indian goods in Russia by the early eighteenth century.

well-connected and well-capitalized Dutch "firms" had superseded the Muscovy Company as the dominant European commercial presence in northern Russia. They supplied most of Russia's demand for pepper and much of its cloth requirements. Indian textiles were included in Dutch sales as they had been earlier in English shipments. An explicit reference to Dutch sales of Indian cloth to Russia is included in a 1722 report of the Dutch ambassador to the Hague.[30]

The apparent decision that most Indian merchants made to cease marketing Indian textiles in Russia may also have been influenced by two other factors. First, as Indonesian and Indian pepper glutted European markets by the mid-seventeenth century, European merchants increasingly depended on sales of Indian cloth for their profits, sales that increased with shifts in European tastes and a gradual rise in general prosperity.[31] Then, following Peter the Great's construction of his new capital of St. Petersburg on the Baltic, Russian markets instantly became more accessible than they had been when ships had to make the dangerous voyage to Archangel. Prices of all commodities must have fallen, increasing the Europeans' competitive advantage. Indians, Armenians and Iranians continued profitably to market Iranian goods in Russia in the late eighteenth century, but these merchants' costs of carrying Indian cloth to Russia via Iran and Turan may have exceeded those of their European competitors who shipped textiles from Bengal, Gujarat or the Sind to the Baltic.[32]

As far as Indian exports from Russia are concerned, Indian merchants usually purchased combinations of western European and Russian goods in Astrakhan, Moscow, Kazan and other cities. In 1676, for example, eleven different Indian merchants sent goods from Astrakhan to Derbent, the Caspian port located northwest of Baku. Included in these shipments were western cloth, Russian leather, fox and sable pelts, iron and needles.[33] Fifty-five years later an Indian merchant in Astrakhan named Ram Chand provided Russian customs authorities with a similarly diverse list of goods that Indians were shipping to Bukhara and Khiva. These included Dutch and English broadcloth, hides, otter and beaver pelts, tanned leather, vegetable dyes, bronze rings, locks and scissors.[34] Most notable in later lists of Indian exports from Russia is the increasing prevalence of Russian or western European manufactures, especially varieties of cloth and metal products such as locks and scissors, a foreshadowing of the torrent of European industrial goods that were to appear in Asian markets by the end of the century.

One misleading feature of these lists of goods of Indian exports from Russia is that they never included what was probably Indian merchants' most valuable commodity, silver currency. Yet it was well known that Indian merchants – and

---

[30] Israel, *Dutch Primacy in World Trade*, 44–48 and Antonova, II, no. 50, 1722, 84–85.

[31] Chaudhuri has an admirably lucid discussion of the relation between the Indian and English textile trade in *Trading World*, see especially chapters 11 and 12.

[32] For a general introduction to the relative costs of land and sea trade see n. 3, chapter 3 above.

[33] Antonova, I, nos. 149–63, 1676, 258–66.

[34] *Ibid.*, II, no. 59, 1731, 116.

others – regularly smuggled currency out of the country to Iran, probably the most profitable way of repatriating their profits. In 1667, for example, some Indian merchants exchanged 7,860 roubles' worth of Russian silver kopeks for Iranian currency in Shemakh.[35] Russian officials forbade currency exports that contributed to the country's chronic currency shortage, but seemed helpless to prevent the common practice that was described at length in 1777 by the angry governor of Astrakhan, I. Yakobi.

It is not a secret that they, the Indians, having trade with Russian subjects, attempt, in exchange for Russian money and for goods, to receive Russian silver money, and especially heavy silver of the best kind with the portrait of Peter the Great. And for this they keep in Moscow a correspondent who . . . acquiring various silver money sends it to them secretly in sea-going vessels . . . hiding the money in various goods and foodstores . . . And in Persia they sell silver money at a markup of 20–30 kopeks per rouble or more . . . silver is in short supply in Russia and is aggravated by these non-citizens, the Indians.[36]

Thus, as was true of Indian merchants in Iran, those in Russia also contributed to the silver stream entering the Mughul empire. As was the case of Indians in Iran, those in Russia obtained this currency both from trade and their financial operations.

As these periodic but discontinuous customs reports indicate, Astrakhan Indian merchants largely conducted their commerce on a north–south axis. In the early eighteenth century Indians primarily sold Iranian goods in Russia and Russian commodities in Iran, but only occasionally did they trade with Bukhara or other cities in Turan. Most Indian merchants who operated within Russia either had business in Moscow, the final destination of most of these journeys from Astrakhan, or at the Makarevskii market near Nizhnii Novgorod, the modern Gorki, the site of a major commercial fair each July.[37] Indians who exported Russian or western European products generally did so by ship to the western Caspian ports of Derbent or Baku or smaller ports on the southern Caspian littoral. Southward journeys are more difficult to trace than those to Moscow, since Russian records cite only the ships' initial destinations, such as Baku, not alluding to markets further south in Iran or even in India.[38]

By the end of Peter the Great's reign Indians seem to have dominated this commerce, even at that time overshadowing the Armenians, their principal

---

[35] Antonova, I, no. 84, 1667, 161. I am assuming that silver kopeks were being exchanged as they were the standard silver commercial currency. The report refers to 7,860 roubles' worth of silver. This perfunctory report does not indicate how many Indian merchants were involved nor does it offer any hint as to how common the practice was at this period. This must have been a chance report. It is very unlikely that Russian officials had reliable knowledge of financial transactions in the Shemakh khanate at any period!

[36] *Ibid.*, no. 192, 1777, 366–67.

[37] B. B. Kaufengauz describes this extremely important fair in detail in his book *Ocherki Bnutrennego Rynka Rossii Pervoi Poloviny XVIII v.* [Essays on the Internal Markets of Russia in the first half of the 18th century] (Moscow: Akademiia Nauk, 1958), "Makarev'skaia Iarmarka," 114–90.

[38] Golikova, *Essays*, 182.

competitors in the Astrakhan foreign mercantile community. Indians made the most trading trips to Moscow of any community between 1718 and 1726, 71 of a total of 129, although the capital invested in these journeys is not, unfortunately, known in most cases.[39] In terms of trade with Iran, not only did more Indians import goods than did members of any other merchant community in 1725, the last year of Peter's reign, but the forty-seven Indians who did so brought in 35,059 roubles' worth of goods to the 11,672 that forty-three Armenians imported in the same year.[40] Indian merchants had achieved their dominance even though Armenians enjoyed privileged status both in Iran and Russia.

The Indian "firm" in Astrakhan

It is impossible to attribute the relative commercial success of Astrakhan-based Indian merchants to their unique or innovative forms of business organization, for in that respect the Khattris and Marwaris who resided semi-permanently in the city were absolutely typical of their Russian and non-Russian counterparts. Like those merchants, Indians used kinship ties to form the nucleus of their businesses. As the example of Sutur and his brother has suggested, these ties were probably responsible for bringing most Indians to Russia in the first instance. The resulting family firms that were formed can be seen operating in the examples of the brothers who traded between Astrakhan and Moscow in the 1670s.[41] The prevalence of this standard pre-modern, Eurasian model of commercial organization among Astrakhan Indians was especially marked in the results of the 1747 census of the community.

The 1747 census was the first detailed survey that Russian authorities are known to have taken of the inhabitants of the principal Astrakhan Indian dvor. It was a census, and not an exhaustive commercial survey, but the Indians' answers still revealed a great deal about the operation of Indian firms in the city. They were asked to state their business and to give their name, the names of their children and to identify "from what Persian domicile they came."[42] Their answers revealed three patterns in the personal and commercial life of the inhabitants: the prevalence of Multanis, the importance of kinship ties in their commerce and existence of close kinship and business ties between Astrakhan Indians and members of the Indian diaspora in Iran.

All of the fifty-one Indians listed in 1747 appear to have been Hindus or Jains. Forty-three were merchants, four others were casual laborers and the remaining four were charity cases, supported by other Indians. Nearly half of the merchants came from Multan city, and many others appear to have been natives of the southern Panjabi entrepôt, although the variable spelling of Indian names makes

[39] *Ibid.*, 182.
[40] *Ibid.*, 184–85.
[41] Antonova, I, no. 140, 1675, 240–41.
[42] Antonova, II, no. 132, 1747, 265. Whether Russian officials classified Multan as a Persian town at this time is not clear, but in earlier documents they occasionally did so.

Indian gostiny dvor in 1747

Names	Age	Origin, occupation and years of residence
1 Kasiram Pera(yev), son of Ryndana	52	Came from Multan in 1721; has business in various Persian goods which he buys from Iranians who arrive in Astrakhan. He sends goods for sale to Iran with his assistant.
1a Razharam Pera(yev), a relative [brother] of Kasiram, son of Ryndana	47	See no. 1 above.
2 Tolaram Nebagu(yev),	60	Came from Kotobpur village ten years ago; has business in various Persian goods which are sent by friends from Iran.
3 Khemchand Tavar(ov),	42	Came from Gagar village five years ago; has business in various Persian and Russian goods and for the sale and import of goods into Astrakhan he sends an assistant within Persia.
4 Zhodaram Kevlram(ov),	25	Came from Multan three years ago; has business in various Persian goods which are sent by his assistant in Persia.
4a Zhodaram's assistant, Kasiram Madodas(ov), son of Chek(ov)	35	See no. 4 above.
5 Kulavra Lalchand, son of Mutmezha(ev)	51	Came from Multan fourteen years earlier; has business in various Persian goods brought from arriving Persians and his assistant in Iran sends goods to Astrakhan.
6 Kulamar[-ram?] Chadna(ev), son of Dany(ev)	32	Came from Multan two years earlier; has business in various Persian goods and sends assistant to Iran to bring goods to Astrakhan.
6a Lachiram Chanda(ev), Kulamar's natural brother	50	See no. 6 above.
6b Chantulala(ev), son of Lund(ov and Kulamar's assistant		See no. 6 above.
6c Lezhan Nisora(ev), son of Rindany(ev)	35	Evidently worked with no. 6 above.
7 Tekchan Lal(ev), son of Asyzha(ev)	38	Came from the small town of Dunikpur eleven years ago; has business in various Iranian goods sent to him from Gilan by his uncle.
8 Sukhanat Dyrymdas(ov), son of Vagi(ev)	55	Came from Multan thirty years ago; has business in various Persian goods sent to him from Persia by order of Indian friends.

Names	Age	Origin, occupation and years of residence
9 Gordan Balaki(ev), son of Sety(ev)	40	Came from the village of Ziravad three years ago; has no business, lives by casual work.
10 Jesu Naum(ov), son of Ryndana (see above 1, 1a and 6c)	35	Came from Multan six years ago; has business in various Persian goods and to import goods he sends an assistant to Iran.
10a Charan Naum(ov), natural brother of Jesu Naum(ov) and son of Ryndana	40	See no. 10 above.
11 Bansiram Azhandak(ov), son of Vadva(ev)	30	Came from the village of Gugar [see no. 3 above]; has business in various Persian goods sent to him by his uncle.
12 Tavar Balaki(ev), son of Tutezha(ev) (see above no. 2)	47	Came from the small town of Adavai fourteen years earlier; has business in various Persian goods for which he sends an assistant within Russia and Persia.
13 Brazinat Bavanidas(ov), son of Kazhirani(ev)	31	Came from the village of Gosar this month; has business in various Persian goods for which he sends an assistant into Persia.
14 Basiram Balu(ev), son of Khirbat(ov)	40	Came from the small village of Adavain [see no. 12 above]; has no business; subsistence is given him by other Indians.
15 Chantu Lachiram(ov), son of Batura(ev)	40	Came from the small town of Kirob eleven years ago; has business in various Persian and Russian goods, for purchasing which he sends an assistant. His natural brother sends him goods from Gilan.
16 Peru Zhivanda(ev), son of Kalra(ev)	21	Came from the small town of Jilapur five years earlier; has business in various Persian goods. His natural brother sends him goods from Gilan.
17 Bagari Alamchand(ov), son of Sagadi(ev)	41	Came from the village of Alipur seven years earlier; has business in various Persian goods that are sent him from Gilan by his natural brother.
18 Zhigatra Fatichant(ov), son of Regezha(ev)	49	Came from the village of Badarat twenty years earlier; has business in Persian goods. His natural brother sends him goods from Gilan.
18a Kasira Chatu(ev), son of Regezha(ev	18	See no. 18 above.

Names	Age	Origin, occupation and years of residence
19 Ramdas Dzhasu(ev), son of Michirani(ev)	40	Came from Multan twenty-three years earlier; has business in various Persian goods that are sent to him from Gilan by his uncle.
20 Zhokupal Arzhandas(ov), son of Dagum(ov)	33	Came from the village of Kushap twelve years earlier. Has no business but is given subsistence by his brother Indians.
21 Divani Nebagu(ev), son of Kukur(ov)	60	Came from the village of Advanid eighteen years earlier; has business in various Persian goods. He sends an assistant to Iran for buying and importing goods.
21a With him is his son, Lahori	34	See no. 21 above.
21b and his relative, Tavar	29	See no. 21 above.
22 Talaram Alimchand(ov), son of Chavlak(ov)	45	Came from the village of Jalalpur five years earlier; has business in various Persian goods acquired by his assistant.
23 Lary Dadyla(ev), son of Chaba(ev)	41	Came from the village of Davar four years earlier; has business in various Persian goods for which he sends an assistant into Iran.
24 Amardas Multani(ev), son of Regechdap(ov)	25	Came from the village of Badagaty [see no. 18 above, possibly the same village] four years earlier; has business in various Persian merchandise and his natural brother sends goods from Gilan.
25 Tolokchan Kola(ov), son of Buchany(ev)	22	Came from Multan two years earlier. Has business in various Persian goods and for business sends his assistant into Russia and has goods sent to him from Gilan by his master.
26 Pop Balibu Mingirali(ev), son of Dangaar(ov)	45	Came from Multan ten years earlier; has no business but subsists as a pauper from his fellow Indians.
27 Asanat Ruphand(ov), son of Dangaar(ov)	45	Came from Multan five years earlier; has business in various Persian goods sent to him from Gilan by his master.
28 Lazharom Bindraban(ov), son of Naryn(ov)	50	Came from the village of Duniapur eleven years earlier; has no business but subsists as a pauper from his fellow Indians.
29 Lala Bandur(ov), son of Manizhak(ov)	50	Came from Multan ten years earlier; has business in various Persian goods sent to him from Gilan by order of his brother Indians.

Names	Age	Origin, occupation and years of residence
30 Lachiram Gulara(ev), son of Chegira(ev)	41	Came from the village of Davar [see no. 23 above, the same village] ten years earlier; has business in various Persian goods sent to him from Iran by his natural brother.
31 Isardan Chanda(ev), son of Saluzha(ev)	25	Came from the village of Adavar this year; does not have business but exists at his own expense.
32 Kosordas Kirpuram(ov), son of Chu(ev)	23	Came from Multan two years earlier; has business in various Persian goods that are sent to him from Gilan by his natural brother.
33 Baliram Talaram(ov), son of Vadva(ev)	39	Came from Multan two years ago; has business in various Persian goods that are sent to him by his natural brother.
34 Vaporta Alychand(ov), son of Nadana(ev)	40	Came from the small town of Duki Apora [Dunikpur? see no. 7 above]; has business in various Persian goods that are sent to him from Iran by his fellow Indians.
35 Lacharam Multand(ov), son of Saichal(ov)	35	Came from the village of Dera three years earlier; has business in various Persian goods that are sent to him by his brother Indians.
36 Rutandu Parsram(ov), son of Miany(ev)	22	Came from Multan six years earlier; has business in various Persian goods that are sent to him from Gilan by his uncle.
37 Iserdas Chada(ev), son of Dydezha(ev)	42	Came from Multan eleven years ago; has various Persian goods sent to him from Iran by his brother Indians.
38 Kulavra Iserdas(ov), son of Salnysi(ev)	65	Came from the village of Chenoi seven years earlier; has no business; subsists on casual labor.
39 Kirparam Kavalram(ov), son of Mikizhas(ov)	40	Came from the village of Adavan [Adavai? see nos. 12 and 14 above] fourteen years earlier; has business in various Persian and Russian goods and goes within Russia and Iran to purchase them.
40 Tarachan Zhesav(ov), son of Panulzha(ev)	45	Came from the village of Sabychkovov twenty years earlier; does not have business but subsists on itinerant work.
41 Asanat Devidas(ov)	45	Came from Multan nine years earlier; has no business but subsists at his own expense.
42 Lakmidas Pallia(ev), son of Banian(ov)	38	Came from the village of Dega two years ago; has no business but subsists on itinerant work.

it difficult to locate these villages precisely.[43] One man carried the Lahori nisba, but since his father did not it is difficult to understand the significance of the designation without further information.

One of the most important aspects of the census is that it demonstrates that kinship ties linked many Indian merchants both within the city and between the city and other Indian merchants in the Caspian ports and northern Iran. It is particularly significant that many Indians themselves identified these ties as the basis of their firms. At least five sets of brothers jointly conducted trade within Astrakhan and twelve Astrakhan Indians received goods from their uncles or brothers in Gilan province, the littoral at the southwestern edge of the Caspian Sea. These obvious, stated, immediate family relationships almost certainly do not reveal every aspect of kinship ties among Indian merchants in Astrakhan. Less direct blood ties that are sometimes alluded to in other documents were not identified here, although some may be surmised from the common village backgrounds of many individuals. Apart from origin and kinship relations, what stands out in this survey is that all of these Indian merchants in Russia dealt almost entirely in Iranian goods.

The 1747 census was the most detailed survey of the Indian dvor that Russian authorities compiled up to that time. However, not only was it done two decades after the Indian community had reached the apex of its prosperity and influence, but like all such surveys it was limited in the type of information that it provided. Based upon the census it would be reasonable to assume that Indians invariably did business with their own relations or assistants, who were also Indians, and that they confined themselves to mercantile pursuits within Astrakhan. Other documents show that no such limitations existed either as to their business associates or the range of their commercial activities. They show first, that however restrictive Astrakhan Indians may have been in their commensal and social relations they concluded agreements that spanned the entire ethnic and religious spectrum of Astrakhan society. The same is true of their financial activities. Nearly every Indian who traded in Russia also regularly lent funds as an integral part of his overall business activities to Armenian, Russian and Turkic merchants and occasionally to other Indians as well.

In the seventeenth century Indians regularly sent their kinsmen as assistants or agents to Moscow or the upper Volga cities,[44] just as Indians in the 1747 census reported that they regularly sent relatives to Iran. In the first half of the eighteenth century, though, the dispatch of relations within Russia is rarely mentioned. It may

[43] In the 1746 census fifty-two Indians are listed and one is specifically identified as an Indian Muslim. This suggests that Russian authorities would have used this classification at other times if Indian Muslims had arrived in Astrakhan via Iran. Apart from Multanis in the Bukharan dvor one of the few references to an Indian-Muslim merchant in Russia occurs in 1676. Antonova, I, no. 166, 1676, 267. Note that in cases where villages on this list can be identified they are, like Kotobpur, located in Multan District. I am indebted to Professor Kenneth Jones of Kansas State University who has helped me to locate some of the villages in this census.

[44] Antonova, I, no. 185, 1680, 288–90.

have always been the exception. The fact that the pre-Petrine period was so much less well-documented than the first quarter of the eighteenth century makes it impossible to be certain – Peter the Great modernized his country in terms of the systematic collection of information as well as in other aspects of Russian life. At the same time it is very likely that Indians began to rely more on non-Indian merchants after the New Trade Regulations began to be enforced systematically against them. The most obvious reason for doing so would have been financial; Russians, Turks and Armenians with their special privileges were exempt from paying the substantial extra duties that were levied on Indians or other non-citizens. Thus by using merchants from these communities as agents, Indians could reduce their cost of doing business, they could, that is, lower their trans-action costs by temporarily expanding their firms beyond the circle of their relatives or assistants.[45] In any event during the first quarter of the eighteenth century Indians rarely traded within Russia without the help of Armenians or citizens, whether ethnic Russians or Turks. Often Indians dispatched men from one of these communities as their agents, but they seem to have marketed most of the goods that they sold in Russia by concluding formal, legally enforceable contracts with them. In general these were the same type of commercial agree-ments used by Armenian merchants in this period.[46]

Innumerable examples of such enterprises are recorded in eighteenth-century documents, and the varieties of these arrangements or organizations are as great as those that merchants used in early modern Europe.[47] Most agreements seem to have been concluded for relatively short periods – sometimes merely for the duration of a single Caspian voyage or a trip to Moscow, although some other joint ventures endured for as long as ten years.[48] Details of contracts varied enormously but seem to have fallen into two general categories: partnerships and commenda. Partnership is used here as a term that describes ventures known as *shirka* or *khulta* in the eleventh-century Arab world, that is, joint ventures in which both partners or larger groups of investors pooled their capital, although not necessarily or even usually in exactly equal amounts.[49] In Astrakhan what distinguished these contracts from others was the relatively equal status of the investors, which was reflected in the language of the agreements, as it was in the document that one Balaki(ev) concluded in 1725 with an Armenian for the sale of Russian goods in Iran.[50] Balaki(ev) committed 2,600 roubles while the

[45] For an introduction to the ramifications of transaction costs see Sherwin Rosen, "Transaction Costs and Internal Labor Markets," in Williamson and Winter, *The Nature of the Firm*, 75–89. Edmund Herzig points out that Armenians signed temporary agreements with non-relatives for particularly capital intensive operations. "Armenian Merchants," 181.
[46] Herzig, "Armenian Merchants," chapter 4, "Partnership and Agency," 213–37.
[47] Pierre Jeannin, *Merchants of the Sixteenth Century*, trans. by Paul Fittinghoff (New York: Harper and Row, 1972), 43–49.
[48] Golikova, *Essay*, 189.
[49] Goitein, *A Mediterranean Society*, I, 169–71.
[50] Antonova, II, no. 42, 1725, 65. Such contracts were recorded by the city magistrate. See Hittle, *The Service City*, 82–83 and 133–34.

Armenian gave 1,400 roubles, and they jointly stipulated that the Armenian, Egorov, would actually sell the goods in Iran. After each recovered his original capital the profits were to be divided equally, and if the two men suffered losses they were to bear them equally. A similar type of agreement was concluded in the same year between an Indian and two "trading peasants," who committed 800 and 400 roubles respectively to purchase goods for the purpose of trading in the upper Volga region. The peasants were to conduct the trade, and, as was true of the first agreement, the profits were to be shared equally among the three men after the original capital was recovered.[51] In another case, two Armenians from Tiflis pooled their 4,300 roubles with 8,600 roubles that three Indians provided. The Armenians were to buy and market goods, and the profits were then to be divided into nine parts, with four going to the Armenians and five to the Indians.[52]

One of the advantages of most of these partnership agreements that Indians signed during this period is that they avoided the physical risks of long, overland journeys as well as avoiding additional customs duties. The danger inherent in trips to Turan was always great. Even the semi-annual armed caravans that traveled up and down the Volga guarded by *strel'tsi* could be risky in the seventeenth century, considerably more dangerous than journeys in India or Iran in the seventeenth century. In 1667, for example, the famous Stenka Razin plundered a caravan in which Indian merchants were traveling, and this was apparently the first of many attacks that the Don Cossack leader made on commerce that eventually triggered widespread revolts throughout the lower Volga region.[53] Normally in shirka or khulta agreements any partner could have been charged with marketing the goods. Indians might not always have been able to do so because of restrictions on their movements, although they could certainly travel with passes in the Petrine period. However, they may have been able to avoid this responsibility because in virtually all of these contracts they supplied much greater amounts of capital than any of their partners, and it seems to have been understood that this exempted them from the actual trading process. What seemed to be implicit in these partnership agreements was, however, the dominant and explicit feature of the second and most common form of joint venture that Indian merchants subscribed to, the commenda.

Known in Arabic as *qirad* or *mudaraba*, mutual participation in an enterprise,[54] the commenda had long been a standard legal and financial device for organizing long-distance trade in the Mediterranean world. The basic principle of commenda contracts was simple; one or more merchants would provide all the capital while

[51] Antonova, II, no. 42, 1725, 66.

[52] *Ibid.*, 66.

[53] Antonova, I, no. 83, 1667, 160–61. Stenka Razin (Stephan Timofeevich Razin, 1630?–1671). Along with other river traffic there were fall and spring caravans that were guarded by strel'tsi between Nizhnii Novgorod and Astrakhan. For references see Samuel H. Baron, *The Travels of Olearius in Seventeenth Century Russia* (Stanford, Calif.: Stanford University Press, 1967), 310, n. 30.

[54] Goitein, *A Mediterranean Society*, I, 171.

trader(s) with no significant funds would take the risk of delivering or marketing the goods. If a particular venture was successful, the profits were divided with two-thirds going to the investor and one-third to the trader. If on the other hand a caravan was attacked or destroyed the investor could lose his entire capital while the trader might well lose his life. Commenda contracts were standardized throughout the early modern Islamic world, as examples from seventeenth-century Aleppo demonstrate.[55] Their basic financial inequality gave these agreements the appearance of investors acting as employers for impecunious traders, and this quality particularly is what distinguished them from shirka or partnership.[56]

Indians typically concluded commenda agreements with Russians traveling to Moscow, with Turks of the Bukharan dvor who were experts in making perilous journeys to Turan, or with local Turks who dealt with their compatriots in the surrounding steppes, "Tatars of the yurt," as they were described in Russian documents. That is, Indians may sometimes have used the commenda principally as a means of economizing on the transaction costs of higher customs dues, as in the case of trading trips within Russia. However, when they wished to ship goods to Turan through Bukharan Turks they apparently employed this type of agreement primarily as a contractual device to pay mediatory traders to move goods across especially dangerous territory. Khattri, Marwari or Afghan merchants in Multan, Kabul or Bukhara are likely to have signed commendas and for precisely this same reason when they wished to have Luharni or other powindah tribes move their goods across either the Sulaiman range or the Hindu Kush.

Several agreements that Indians concluded with Astrakhan merchants in 1725 offer examples of commenda contracts. In one an Indian, listed as Nebagu Chadzhu(ev) signed an agreement with two residents of the Bukharan dvor in which Chadzhu(ev) gave the two Muslim merchants 1,288 roubles to conduct trade in the nearby Kalmuck *ulus*, the steppe encampment of the Kalmuck Turks.[57] The two men agreed that when they returned they would truthfully "square their accounts" with Chadzhu(ev), making an honest statement of their profits, which were to be divided into three parts, two for the Indian and one for the Bukharan residents. The original investment was then to be returned to the Indian in full. A second document recorded an arrangement between two Indians and a Bukharan Turk in which the latter took 2,000 roubles from the Indian to trade at the Makarevskii market. The terms of the agreement were precisely the same as the other commenda contract.[58] In a third example three Indian merchants concluded exactly the same type of agreement with an Armenian, Moses Meskun, who received 8,000 roubles to buy goods that he planned to sell in Moscow.[59] In all these cases the contracts were affirmed by several witnesses.

[55] Masters, *Western Economic Dominance*, 50–51.
[56] Goitein, *A Mediterranean Society*, I, 170, 174–75.
[57] Antonova, II, no. 41, 1725, 63. One man was a Turk, the ethnic identity of the other is not clear.
[58] *Ibid.*, 63.
[59] *Ibid.*, no. 42, 1725, 66–77.

"Companies" and capital

When groups of Indian merchants joined together to finance trading ventures they were probably members of one of three groups within the Indian dvor that Russian authorities identified as "companies." In 1727 these companies were reported to have had 39, 49 and 10 members respectively.[60] The organization and significance of these groups is not entirely clear from the sources that allude to them only when internal disputes among Indians spilled out of the dvor into the Astrakhan administrative and judicial system. It is obvious that they were not commercial organizations, although they may have represented informal spheres for business cooperation. The companies appear to have constituted factions within the dvor that were based on kinship and capital assets; they were not corporate entities and evidently had no special status in Russian law. Membership in each company was at least partly derived from kinship connections and may have been originally generated through the kind of family ties that were conspicuous in the 1747 census. However, the companies also represented an economic hierarchy of the dvor. Two relatives, Anbu Ram Mulin and Nebagu Chadzhu(ev) were successive leaders of the first, most well-capitalized company in the first quarter of the eighteenth century,[61] and while the exact nature of their relationship is not made clear it is a good example of how difficult it is to trace all the ramifications of kinship influence from fragments of occasional documentary evidence. They were sufficiently powerful to be able to dictate to their fellow Indians on certain occasions, and they were officially recognized by Russian authorities as "principal company men," those Indians who represented the dvor in discussions or negotiations with local officials.[62]

Anbu Ram Mulin and Nebagu Chadzhu(ev) evidently represented a class of Indian merchants who controlled the largest amounts of capital among all the non-Russian merchants – and probably among Russian merchants as well – in Astrakhan in the first quarter of the eighteenth century. A rare insight into the resources that such men possessed was provided by the drawn-out legal wrangling over the estate of a deceased colleague of these "principal company men," known in the sources either as Sukhanant Dermu(ev) or Sukhanant Dyrymdas. Sukhanant had come to Astrakhan from Multan in 1717; he died in 1759 at the age of sixty in Moscow.[63] At the time of his death the value of his estate was estimated at 300,000 roubles, a remarkable figure for any merchant at that time, including gosti and members of the other privileged corporations. Even though Russian officials indignantly referred to him as one who "had gathered considerable capital by the illegal means [of charging] a high percent [of interest],"[64] it is obvious from their records that Sukhanant was much more than a mere moneylender. His estate

---

[60] *Ibid.*, no. 48, 1727, 82.
[61] *Ibid.*, 82. They belonged, that is, to the "company" of 39 individuals.
[62] *Ibid.*, no. 42, 1725, 66.
[63] *Ibid.*, no. 132, 1747, 266, and no. 163, 1760, 320.
[64] *Ibid.*, no. 163, 1760, 322.

consisted of cash, goods, letters of credit and promissory notes. That is, he lent small sums to individuals, larger sums to other merchants and himself participated in commenda trading ventures with other merchants – such as the agreement he concluded in 1725 with several trading peasants to market goods in the upper Volga cities.[65]

It is impossible to analyze the total capital worth of Anbu Ram Mulin and other prosperous Indian merchants whose affairs were not recorded as comprehensively as those of Sukhanand. Knowing the full scope of Anbu Ram's resources would be especially valuable as he was one of several Indians who petitioned Peter the Great in 1723 to be permitted to trade in St. Petersburg and Archangel and to transit Russia to trade in both Germany and China.[66] Still it is obvious that this upper strata of Indian merchants had more funds available than other foreign Astrakhan merchants at this time. In 1724–25, for example, twenty-three Indians traded in Russia with more than 1,000 roubles' worth of goods each.[67] While this figure does not seem exceptional in view of the fact that Sutur invested more than 5,000 roubles in one trading trip in the mid-seventeenth century,[68] in the previous year only six Armenians had this much working capital to commit to a single venture.[69] This was the time, after all, when Indians imported into Astrakhan from northern Iran and the Caspian port three times the value of Armenian imports, and Indians were also the most active of all foreign merchants in conducting trade between Astrakhan and Moscow as well as between Astrakhan and Derbent, Baku and Iran.[70]

Many of the same individuals who directly invested in trade, either by themselves or through partnership or commenda agreements, also lent substantial sums of money as another dimension of what was for virtually all of them a multifaceted complex of economic activities. While it is obvious from both Iranian and Russian evidence that the bania stereotype of expatriate Indian merchants has inaccurately portrayed them exclusively as moneylenders, Astrakhan statistics show that certain Indian merchants in the city did *concentrate* on moneylending or banking rather than on trade. It is also clear that Indians as a group lent funds more often than other ethnically defined merchant communities. That is, while Armenians and Russians also lent money at interest Indians did so with greater frequency, although this should scarcely be surprising considering their greater capital resources.[71] In 1724–25, 127 Indians granted loans, although 70 percent of these came from only nineteen individuals, men who also possessed the largest amount

[65] *Ibid.*, no. 43, 1725, 66.
[66] *Ibid.*, no. 37, 1723, 57–59.
[67] Golikova, *Essays*, 186.
[68] Antonova, I, no. 48, 1651, 97–99.
[69] Golikova, *Essays*, 186–87.
[70] *Ibid.*, 184–86.
[71] *Ibid.*, 200. In her article, "Rostovshchestvo v Rossii nachala xviii v i ego nekotorye osobennosti," [Usury in Russia at the beginning of the eighteenth century and some of its peculiarities] in S. D. Shazkin, ed., *Problemy genezisa kapitalizma* (Moscow: Nauka, 1970), 242–90, Golikova discusses the subject of Indian usury in Russia at greater length.

of capital for the purpose.[72] In 1724 ten Indians lent more than 1,000 roubles each, although most loans were quite small. Marwar Bara(ev), for example, lent a total of 4,372 roubles that year, but did so in fifty-four separate transactions.[73] These figures indicate only his working capital, not his total assets, for he always seems to have had a large number of unpaid loans outstanding, such as the debt of 3,047 roubles that one individual had accumulated over two decades between 1706 and 1725.[74] He appears to have been the most prominent example of an Indian who concentrated almost exclusively on moneylending. He also exemplified the dangers of such specialization, for later it was his inability to collect several large loans that almost certainly led him to become a member of the Russian orthodox church.

Bara(ev)'s loans are a good example of the variety of an Indian's financial operations, for his clients ranged from a clerk who had borrowed 12 roubles to a Turkic shopkeeper who had taken 57, to a market gardener who owed him 215 roubles, to an Armenian textile merchant who was indebted to him for 1,550 roubles.[75] A small number of his loans and those of other Indians may have been used for personal expenses, such as the 12-rouble loans to the clerk, but the important, often unstated purpose of most agreements appears to have been commerce. To a certain extent this purpose was reflected in the short durations of most loans, ranging from a few months to a year, for the repayment period was usually geared to the estimated length of a trading journey. Indians concluded such commercial loan agreements with men at every level of Russian society, but the majority of them appear to have been arranged with Tatars of the yurt.[76] One example of a simple agreement that involved only one Indian lender was that in which "Chantu Lala(ev)" agreed in 1725 to give 340 roubles to a group of Turks on the understanding that the debt would be repaid in full on their return to Astrakhan from Moscow.[77] In a more complex deal the previous year multiple Indian creditors joined together to loan five Turks 983 roubles to buy goods for sale in Moscow. The Turks agreed to repay the loan with interest when they returned to Astrakhan.[78]

Interest rates on the loans are not indicated in most documents which were witnessed and filed with Russian authorities. They may have been omitted because lending money at interest was technically illegal until 1754.[79] It has been estimated, though, that rates varied from 30 to 120 percent a year in the seventeenth century, while in the late eighteenth century the governor of Astrakhan

---

[72] *Ibid.*, 201. In 1724 Indians granted loans that totaled 95,054 roubles.

[73] *Ibid.*, 202.

[74] Antonova, II, no. 44, 1726, 69.

[75] *Ibid.*, no. 35, 1721, 56; no. 42, 1724, 61; no. 42, 1726, 67.

[76] This is, however, an impression rather than a statistical fact.

[77] Antonova, II, no. 41, 1725, 63.

[78] *Ibid.*, no. 40, 1724, 62.

[79] Hittle, *The Service City*, 109. In a 1727 loan contract, for example, the debtor was to repay the loan "s naddacheiu," that is, with interest, but the actual rate is not stipulated: Antonova, II, no. 48, 1727, 75."

reported that Indians, Armenians and Russians in the city lent money at between 20 and 50 percent interest per annum. Large loans commonly cost 3 to 4 percent a month while smaller ones were offered at 4 to 5 percent for the same period.[80] In every case creditors had legal recourse to Russian judicial authorities in case of default; merchandise, immovable property and even land served as collateral. Marwar Bara(ev)'s debtors mortgaged cloth, vegetable gardens and shops among other things, and on several occasions he had such property seized for bad debts. In one case he demanded that a Turk who had not paid his 57-rouble debt should relinquish all the shops that he owned, including two that were located in the "Tatar bazar" that he had previously concealed.[81] Such actions undoubtedly explain why in the eighteenth century Indians in Astrakhan worked as market gardeners and shopkeepers as well as merchants and moneylenders/financiers.

At a period when banking institutions did not exist in Russia, private capital represented the only source of credit. While Indians may have been perceived by the "national masses" as "rapacious, cruel, alien men of wealth dwelling in the dark, cramped shops of the Indian dvor,"[82] the Russian scholar I. G. Georgi obviously did not react to the Indians that way in 1777. In any event the use of that type of colored, anti-semitic quality rhetoric to characterize Indian merchants overlooks the fact that Indians were supplying scarce capital to Russian merchants just as they had apparently long done for Iranians in a similarly capital-poor if not quite so extremely underdeveloped society. Russian merchants lent capital in precisely the same way and almost certainly at exactly the same high interest rates. What distinguished Indian merchants from Russians is that Indians were exceptionally effective in accumulating capital. Apart from a relatively small group of wealthy merchants in St. Petersburg, Moscow and the nearby industrial complexes at Tula, Indian merchants in Astrakhan appear to have become far better capitalized than their Russian counterparts in most other Russian cities in the early eighteenth century.

A study of Russian merchants in the upper Volga cities in the seventeenth and eighteenth centuries has shown that in Afanasy Nikitin's city of Tver in 1723 there were 266 merchant families. Of these thirty-two were "principal Tver merchants," but only five of them had more than 1,000 roubles capital. Two hundred and thirty-two families possessed less than 100 roubles capital,[83] and Tver had the largest, best capitalized merchant class of any of the five adjacent cities that were included in this study. Even as late as 1759 the average capital of the most well-to-do Russian merchants in the nearby important commercial and manufacturing city of Iaroslavl' was only 32 roubles and 21 kopeks![84] Yet in 1724 thirty-seven

---

[80] Golikova, *Essays*, 204.

[81] Antonova, II, no. 48, 1727, 77–78.

[82] Golikova, *Essays*, 206.

[83] A. V. Demkin, *Russkoe kupechestvo XVII–XVIII vv* [The Russian merchant class in the 17th and 18th centuries] (Moscow: Nauka, 1990), 45.

[84] Hittle, *The Service City*, 108. L. V. Danilova offers some idea of the relative importance of privileged merchants in Iaroslavl' in 1691 in her article, "Torgovye Riady Iaroslavlia v kontse

Indians in Astrakhan possessed more than 100 roubles of working capital and twenty-eight of them invested more than 1,000 roubles in commerce and loans that year.[85]

The disparity in these figures may seem remarkable when it is remembered that at its height the Astrakhan Indian community numbered only slightly more than 200 individuals, and no more than half that number were actually businessmen. Yet apart from the Indians' commercial acumen, which the underdeveloped Russian merchant class understandably feared, it is impossible to understand the significance of the Indians' success without remembering that the Indian merchants in Astrakhan represented an extension of the Indian world economy in Iran. Originally the settlement probably represented a transfer of capital resources from the massive Indian commercial presence in Safavid territories. The first Indian merchants who arrived in the city quite likely possessed greater capital than most of their Russian counterparts. Even in 1747 many Indians acted as agents for Iranian-based firms and may have been using profits from the sales of Indian goods in Iran to help finance the purchase of Russian and European commodities in Russia.

Legal disputes offered occasional glimpses into this elaborate, well-established network and documented a few of the ways that Indian merchants in Iran and Russia might be linked and how funds could be transferred. A particularly interesting case occurred in 1727, when a Marwari in Tabriz planned to transfer funds to a colleague in Astrakhan by the device of lending funds to an Armenian who was planning to travel to Astrakhan, probably on a trading venture, as was so often the purpose of taking such loans. When the Armenian reached the city he was to repay the loan, with interest, to the Indian there.[86] It is impossible to be certain how these funds would have been used had not the Armenian died before he could complete the transaction, but the case hints at the importance of these links, which in this instance would have generated additional capital for the merchants in Astrakhan by transferring funds as a loan. Money was probably repatriated back to India through Iran using the same network. It was not necessary to transfer specie, although many Indians obviously chose to do so, probably because they could exploit the exchange rates to make considerable profits in the process. They could also have arranged for shipments of sables to Isfahan through one of their correspondents in the Safavid capital, probably also a relative, and have those profits repatriated through the Indian financial network in Isfahan, Bandar 'Abbas or Qandahar. Given the resources at their command it

XVII v.," [Trading Arcades of Iaroslavl' at the end of the 17th century] in N. V. Ustiugov, ed., *Voprosy Sotsial' no-Ekonomisheskoi Istorii i Istochnikovedeniia Perioda Feodalizma v Rossii* (Moscow: Nauka, 1961), 86, in which she shows that gosti and gostinaia sotnia merchants possessed 8.5% of the shops in the city. Evidently these merchants sold goods produced outside of the city, linking it with the wider Russian and international markets.

[85] Golikova, *Essays*, 207. This figure represents a combination of Golikova's tables, 16 and 23.

[86] Antonova, II, no. 48, 1727, 75.

is perhaps only surprising that the disparity in resources between Indian and Russian merchants was not greater.

Peddlers, merchants and moneylenders

The Astrakhan documents are limited in scope and content and they cannot illuminate all aspects of mercantile life in the Indian diaspora. In particular they offer virtually no information on the credit network that was known to link remnants of the diaspora in the early nineteenth century and undoubtedly did in the previous century as well. Yet it is likely that the Indian credit system was at least as sophisticated as the financial ties that linked Armenians and facilitated their trade.[87] It would be particularly interesting to know if this network was sufficient for Indians in Russia to remit substantial profits to India via bills of exchange or *hundis*. These sources are more than sufficient, though, to dispose of two archaic typologies of Indian merchants whose use has distorted the nature and significance of this diaspora: the peddler thesis and the erroneous dichotomy that artificially divides Indian businessmen into distinct categories of merchants and moneylenders.

It will be readily apparent, first of all, that the peddler model is irrelevant as a guide to understanding the management of commerce in this diaspora. The idea that Eurasian trade was carried out through an early modern form of perfect competition by poorly informed, economically vulnerable undercapitalized individuals who were constantly in motion over the seas and land masses of Asia bears little resemblance to the activities of highly capitalized merchants of Astrakhan. These men used partnerships and commenda both to reduce costs by avoiding additional customs duties and also to extend the range and expand the volume of their commerce by employing intermediaries on dangerous caravan routes. Astrakhan itself was only a modest representative of a diaspora in which there were far more substantial settlements of Indian merchants. Bukhara with its estimated 300 Indian merchants was one such city; Qandahar was almost certainly another. Above all there was Isfahan. These cities constituted a constellation of interconnected urban centers where Indian merchants conducted most of their business, and this type of network represents the most satisfactory model for understanding how Indians traded in the diaspora. Nearby cities such as Astrakhan and Tabriz were closely linked by frequent trips of merchants or their assistants, who were often their brothers, sons or nephews. More distant centers such as Lahore or Multan were connected to Isfahan or Astrakhan by yearly caravans. Many Indians in these cities were extremely well-capitalized. As their Russian competitors could attest, they possessed an intimate knowledge of local market

---

[87] For detailed information on the credit network of the Armenian diaspora in Iran and India see Edmund M. Herzig, "Commercial Credit and Long-distance Trade: The Julfa Armenians in the Seventeenth Century," Paper presented at the "Workshop on the Political Economies of the Ottoman, Safavid and Mughal States during the 17th and 18th Centuries," Istanbul, Turkey, 16–20 June 1992.

conditions and market exchange rates, and they cooperated with members of other mercantile communities as a matter of course. Peddlers may have been their servants, but they themselves were tujjar or mercantile capitalists.

The other common assumption about Indian trade in the diaspora that cannot now withstand scrutiny is the over-intellectualized classification of Indian businessmen into discrete categories of merchants and moneylenders. This is a false dichotomy that still vitiates attempts to interpret the significance of large Indian settlements in Safavid Iran. This habit of conceiving that Indian business-men were divided into at least two distinct occupational groups betrays a failure to appreciate well-documented patterns of commercial life across early modern Eurasia. Whatever doubt may have existed about actual Indian mercantile patterns in this period, the Astrakhan documents make it unmistakably clear that trade and moneylending were absolutely indivisible aspects of merchants' business affairs. Indians in Astrakhan either traded directly through their assistants or relatives, they formed partnerships or participated in commenda with other merchants, and they also lent capital to other merchants for their own trade and therefore collected these commercial profits as interest. This was ordinary, typical merchant behavior – for Indian merchants in Astrakhan, Russian merchants in the upper Volga cities or Italian merchants in the Renaissance city-states.[88]

---

[88] Demkin has breakdowns of the commercial and financial investments of Russian merchants in Tver and other upper Volga cities, *Russkoe kupechestvo*, 22–25. Italian parallels are discussed in the conclusion below.

CHAPTER 6

Imperial collapse, mercantilism and the Mughul diaspora

Previously there were favorable conditions for trade from India to Russia and merchants comfortably went [abroad]. Each year about two hundred exported . . . goods, and then when disturbances occurred in Persia and passage became difficult because of robbers the number of merchants declined year by year. Now exceedingly few came, less than eighty.

Marwar Bara(ev), 15 February 1735

When Anbu Ram Mulin petitioned Peter the Great in January 1723, asking permission to expand his trade to St. Petersburg, Archangel and beyond Russia to the German state and eastwards to China, he unknowingly represented the apogee of the Indian mercantile diaspora.[1] Not only did Anbu Ram himself fail to advance the diaspora a stage further and make direct contact with European and Asian markets, but the Indian business community rapidly declined after 1723 both in terms of its numbers and its economic influence. Already in 1747 the census showed that the Indian merchant population in the city had fallen to less than half of its former size, and when P. S. Pallas visited forty Indians who still lived in the city in 1793–94 he reported, based upon his knowledge of an earlier visit, that "Everything here . . . appeared in a more miserable state than formerly, since a part of this people have abjured the religion of their ancestors, and have been incorporated among the citizens of Astrakhan."[2] The community was swiftly atrophying and within a half century it ceased to exist. Indian merchants in the city had been acutely conscious of their deteriorating condition for decades. In 1750 they had addressed a petition to Russian authorities in which they attributed their decline to two factors: the interruption of Russian trade with India and Persia and renewed Russian prohibitions against their participation in internal trade.[3] These men were correct. Political events rather than competition from other merchants had eviscerated the Indian diaspora in Iran and southern Russia.

[1] Antonova, II, no. 37, 1723, 57–59.
[2] Pallas, *Travels Through the Southern Provinces of the Russian Empire*, 254.
[3] Antonova, II, no. 134, 1750, 272..

Multanis and Multan

Less than a year before Anbu Ram wrote his petition the remnants of the impressive Safavid army that Shah 'Abbas had developed failed to defend his capital, Isfahan, against a poorly equipped contingent of Ghilzai Afghans. Following the battle the Ghilzais sacked the city, destroying most Safavid administrative records in the process, and terminated Safavid rule, creating a power vacuum on the Iranian plateau that endured for three-quarters of a century. During that period the security which had been a distinguishing feature of Iranian life in the second century of Safavid rule disappeared, while pastoral nomadic contingents, many of them remnants of Qizilbash tribal formations, contended for power. The Ghilzai sack of Isfahan badly damaged the prosperous base of what was probably the largest community of Indian businessmen outside of the South Asian subcontinent at that time, while the ensuing country-wide disorder allowed various combatants to plunder merchants throughout the country.[4] Then in 1745/46 Nadir Shah Afshar's relentless campaigns and fiscal exactions dealt the decisive blow to the prosperity of the mercantile communities in Isfahan and the economy of the country as a whole.[5]

These events fatally compromised the stable hinterland of Astrakhan Indian merchants, immediately threatening the vitality of their community in two substantial ways. Fewer Indians arrived in Astrakhan from Iran and India, and a precipitous decline in Iranian textile production drastically reduced supplies of cloth that had become the staple commodity of Indian commerce in Russia. By 1735 the number of Indians who traveled to Astrakhan each year had dropped to less than half the number that had arrived annually before 1722, and by 1758 the value of silk and cotton exports from Iran and the Caucasus to Astrakhan had declined to 40,000 roubles per year, down from the 230,000 roubles' worth of cloth that had been shipped to the city in 1744.[6] These trends translated into a dramatic deterioration of the commercial influence of Astrakhan Indian merchants. Whereas as late as the 1730s and 1740s Indians still carried on about one-third of the value of Russia's average trade with Iran and the Caucasus, by 1785 their share of this trade had fallen to between 7.3 and 5.6 percent.[7]

This dramatic deterioration in Indian mercantile fortunes in Astrakhan was not solely a factor of Iranian political disorder; the vitality of the Indian community was also weakened by the Mughul empire's simultaneous decline and eventual dissolution. This was a more prolonged process than the astonishingly swift disappearance of Safavid rule, and the causes were more complex, although the final collapse was directly related to events in Iran. It was partly rooted in the

---

[4] Moreen, *Iranian Jewry*, 35 and 45.
[5] Herzig, "Armenian Merchants," 107–9.
[6] Antonova, II, no. 69, 1735, 129 and Iukht, "Indiiskaia koloniia v Astrakhani," 141.
[7] Iukht, *ibid.*, 142.

evanescent quality of Mughul legitimacy in South Asia and the residual vitality of Afghan and Hindu lineages. However, the unraveling of the empire also stemmed more immediately from military overextension and related financial strains, deterioration of dynastic leadership and the aggressiveness of such newly evolving social and sectarian groups as the Marathas and Sikhs. The incremental decline of Mughul centralized control was evident in the early eighteenth century, but its unmistakable climax occurred in 1739 when Nadir Shah of the Afshar Qizilbash tribe defeated a provincial Mughul army in the Panjab, occupied and sacked Delhi and appropriated the Mughul treasury. The collapse of Mughul authority that this invasion both revealed and accelerated dislocated commerce in many areas of northern and northwestern India as Mughul notables and indigenous groups vied for control of India's wealthy agricultural heartland.[8] The fate of the Multani entrepôt exemplified the way that this disarray exacerbated the difficulties already faced by Indian merchants who were involved in regional commerce with Iran, Turan or Russia.

As has been seen, Multan was the principal dispersal point for the Indian mercantile diaspora in the seventeenth and early eighteenth century, an apparent continuation of the role that it had played in regional trade at least since the fourteenth century. In certain significant respects the city resembled a regional version of the contemporaneous Dutch world entrepôt. That is, in addition to acting as a production center for cotton and silk textiles and a distribution center for textiles as well as for sugar, indigo and tobacco, it also possessed, as was exemplified by Darya Khan Multani and his cadre of Multani master textile artisans, "a powerful merchant elite with the expertise and resources to undertake 'grande enterprises commerciales.' "[9] The manufacture of silk cloth from Central Asian raw silk was indicative of its status in the region. At least Multan possessed these advantages relative to the economies and merchant classes of Iran, Turan and Russia, even if it was a traditional entrepôt and did not display Amsterdam's "originality . . . in new forms of productive efficiency and technological innovations in manufacturing" which helped that Dutch city attain its unprecedented position as the first truly world-wide entrepôt.[10]

If the Safavid collapse irreparably damaged the Multani merchants' base in Iran, the disintegration of the Mughul empire eventually led to the devastation of Multan itself. The decline of the city can be seen as part of a general pattern of deterioration of Mughul entrepôts that Ashin Das Gupta has analyzed in the case of Surat, whose decay he attributed to the collapse of both the Mughul and Safavid states.[11] Following Nadir Shah's invasion Multan continued to be ruled by

---

[8] For a discussion of the historiography of Mughul decline and a specific analysis of that decline in the Panjab see Muzaffar Alam, *Crises of Empire*, Introduction and chapter 1. Bayly has a good discussion of the magnitude and duration of this disruption, *Rulers, Townsmen and Bazaars*, 63–73.

[9] Israel, *Dutch Primacy in World Trade*, 409.

[10] *Ibid.*, 415.

[11] Das Gupta, *Indian Merchants and the Decline of Surat c. 1700–1750* (Wiesbaden: Fritz Steiner, 1979), 8–10.

Mughul governors, but in 1749 the invasion of the Afghan monarch, Ahmad Shah Durrani, led to the city's annexation to the Afghan state three years later. During the next three-quarters of a century Multan and the southwestern Panjab were ravaged by a succession of invasions and sieges, beginning with a destructive Maratha occupation in 1759 and concluding with a nearly half-century of ruinous warfare between its Afghan rulers and the new Sikh kingdom in the Panjab. Sikh forces first occupied Multan for eight years between 1772 and 1780. Then, following twenty-eight more years of intermittent warfare during which Sikhs mounted four direct assaults on the city, they finally staged a successful attack in June, 1818. Afterwards they sacked Multan, seriously damaging much of its lingering prosperity.[12] A corollary effect of these Afghan–Sikh struggles was that commerce no longer flowed freely from the Panjab through the Khyber Pass to Kabul. The earlier conquest of Sind in 1786 by the Baluchi Talpur amirs had already interrupted the free movement of traffic down the Indus to Thatta and Lahori Bandar.[13] Both textile production and trade revived in Multan after the final Sikh conquest, partly stimulated by the Sikhs themselves, but the city never regained its central role. Its loss of economic importance was indicated by the fact that many of the largest Multani merchant capitalists shifted their base of operations to Shikarpur, a desiccated bazar located near the eastern entrance to the Bolan Pass. In the late nineteenth century Hindu and Jain merchants in Central Asia were no longer known as Multanis, but as Shikarpuris.[14]

These tumultuous, disruptive events in Iran and northern India radically altered the significance of the Astrakhan Indian community. Previously the extension of a dynamic mercantile diaspora, by the mid-century it was rapidly being reduced to the status of a socio-economic artifact of the Indian world economy. The Indian authors of the 1750 petition evocatively conveyed their sense of isolation, of being cut off from their mercantile "correspondents" who supplied them with goods and presumably also assisted them with repatriation of funds. These men also argued, though, that their "destitute, indebted and wretched" state was partly due to the Russian government's departure from Peter the Great's liberal policies toward foreign merchants and the imposition of newly rigid prohibitions against their trading within internal Russian markets.[15] As is true of all such documents the emotive rhetoric must be read skeptically, if not entirely with a grain of salt. As late as 1777 Indians were still able to partly evade these restrictions on internal trade often enough to provoke Astrakhan's governor, A. Yakobi, to say within a long, belligerent letter about Indian merchants:

---

[12] Ahmad Nabi Khan summarizes the history of Multan from Mughul times to the Sikh conquest, *Multan, History and Architecture* (Islamabad: Islamic University, 1983), 85–140. See also Alam, *Crises of Empire*, 292–98.

[13] Burnes, *Travels into Bokhara*, I, 26–27.

[14] Burnes, *Cabool*, 54–55.

[15] Antonova, II, no. 134, 1750, 272.

They have entered into the internal trade not permitted to them . . . They give money to Astrakhan Tatars and Armenians and [the latter] trade in their property, going abroad into Asia and internally into Russian towns, or in Astrakhan, for a price fixed by the Indians or for one-third of the profit.[16]

In spite of the governor's complaints there is little doubt that Indian merchants did suffer from the reimposition of earlier seventeenth-century regulations that confined Indian and other foreign merchants to frontier cities such as Astrakhan and Archangel. They were able to circumvent these regulations to some degree by hiring Armenian or Russian agents, but that device was still a poor substitute for directly employing their own marketing and financial skills in Kazan, Saratov, Moscow – or in Germany and China. European merchants would have been similarly hampered in India if they had been confined to Surat or Thatta rather than being allowed to conduct their business personally in Ahmedabad or Lahore. By denying Indians unrestricted access to its internal markets the Russian government prevented these merchants from exploiting the weakness of its own mercantile bourgeoisie and also prevented them from reaching European markets. The diaspora's forward progress was blocked just as its markets and manufacturing bases in Iran and India were being disrupted or destroyed.

Russia's unitary state absolutism allowed it to exert an exceptional degree of control over both its own mercantile class as well as foreign traders, but its policies also must be viewed as an aspect of a general European trend in the first half of the eighteenth century. Jonathan Israel has argued that the basic reason for the decisive decline of the Dutch world-trading system in the 1720s and 1730s

was the wave of the new-style industrial mercantalism which swept practically the entire continent from around 1720. This was an immensely important change which has often been stressed in relation to particular countries such as Prussia, Russia, and Sweden-Finland but has never been taken into account of sufficiently as a European phenomenon with vast international reverberations.[17]

One unappreciated international consequence of this trend was the effective exclusion of the Indian mercantile diaspora from Russian markets. Partly as a result the number of Indians in Astrakhan continued to decline throughout the eighteenth century. Those who remained increasingly made their living by trading in Russian goods to Turan,[18] where the Indian diaspora was still intact in Bukhara and Samarqand. By the first quarter of the nineteenth century few Indians continued to trade in Astrakhan and by 1840 the colony had disappeared.

---

[16] Antonova, II, no. 192, 1977, 364–68.
[17] Israel, *Dutch Primacy in World Trade*, 383.
[18] Iukht, "Indiiskiai koloniia v Astrakhani," 142.

Indian entrepreneurs and Eurasian trade

The characteristics of the Indian mercantile diaspora, its economic significance and the reasons for its demise provide vital new data for the complex debate on Eurasian commercial/economic relations in the early modern era. The commercial ethos and financial skills of Hindu and Jain merchants in particular show them to have been the equal of any mercantile community or organization of the period. Their presence in the thousands in Iran and Turan should, first of all, be sufficient to give the coup de grace to any lingering, antiquated notions about the willingness of members of Hindu and Jain mercantile castes to trade beyond the boundaries of Hindustan, which were not solely defined by the "black waters" of the Indian Ocean but were also marked by Attock – Atak-Banaras on the Indus river. Caste restrictions no more confined Khattris and Marwaris to the subcontinent in the seventeenth century than it discouraged mercantile castes and Brahmans from eastern India from contributing to and perhaps initiating the Indianization of Southeast Asia in the early Christian era. Indeed, the example of Indian merchants traveling with their "priests" to Astrakhan and Moscow suggests a complex and dynamic model for imagining how Indianization might have been initiated in Southeast Asia, one that seems more satisfactory than the rigidly formalistic explanations that are commonly advanced to explain this process.[19]

These Indians' risk-taking enterprises in Russia, even in competition with formidable and privileged representatives of the Armenian mercantile diaspora,[20] may also help to refute outdated assumptions about the commercial conservatism of Indian mercantile castes – or even those same assumptions about Afghan tribesmen! Thin-blooded Indians traveling to do business in the primitive Muscovite state seem no less adventurous or risk-taking than Anthony Jenkinson traveling to Bukhara for the English Muscovy Company. The example of their initiative and success makes modern socio-psychological critiques of Indian entrepreneurial potential seem ill-informed and largely irrelevant to twentieth-century discussions of economic development.[21] Their expansion into Russia and the attempts of some of them to reach European markets also refute casual Eurocentric assumptions about the inherent limitations of their family firms.

Evaluating the significance of the Indian diaspora would be easier if it were

---

[19] André Wink summarizes some of these theories in *Al-Hind: The Making of the Indo-Islamic World* (Leiden: E. J. Brill, 1990), 337–40.

[20] Apart from the dissertation of Edmund Herzig, see especially the article by Michel Aghassian and Keram Kevonian, "Le commerce arménien dans l'Océan Indien aux 17e et 18e siècles," in Denys Lombard and Jean Aubin, eds., *Marchands et hommes d'affaires asiatiques* (Paris: Editions de l'Ecole des Hautes Etudes en Sciences Sociales, 1988), 155–81.

[21] David C. McClelland, *The Achieving Society* (Princeton: D. Van Nostrand, 1988), 155–81, offers a good example of western social science theorizing that seems quite plausible if one has no more than a superficial knowledge of Asian societies. As an undergraduate who studied economic development with little knowledge of Asia I was enormously impressed with McClelland's book. As a student of Islamic and South Asian culture it now strikes me as a classic piece of western social science orientalism.

generally understood that the standard commercial organization and contractual arrangements of Indian merchants represented general Eurasian types rather than archaic Asian precolonial artifacts. Analyses of world economic relations in the early modern era ought to focus on the study of commonalities in the Eurasian firm rather than perpetuating outdated oriental and occidental stereotypes. In this instance it is worth echoing Frank Perlin's insistence "that the proper comparative focus for precolonial India is not the colonial imperium of the late nineteenth century, but contemporary pre-industrial Europe."[22] That is, the economies of mercantile societies ought to be compared rather than inappropriately contrasting the mercantile east with the industrial west. Perlin's comments should, in turn, act as a reminder that comparative historical studies generally, and those of Eurasian commerce and economic development in particular, are still often conducted in an extremely casual fashion, with little thought for systematic method. Even Marc Bloch's more than half-century-old essay, "Pour une histoire comparée des sociétés européenes," seems to be largely unknown – at least most of Bloch's most elementary suggestions have gone largely unheeded.[23]

Successful Multani merchants of Isfahan and Astrakhan appear to have possessed the same entrepreneurial spirit and to have engaged in a similarly wide range of economic activities as Gino Luzatto's "great merchant" of the Italian Renaissance cities; Luzatto writes of the Italian prototype:

The great Italian merchant of the Renaissance was no narrow specialist, dealing in certain kinds of goods and engaging in certain activities only. He was a businessman in the complete sense. Equipped with some personal capital but also with daring, initiative, and the gift for organization, he engaged in all kinds of ventures; trading at home and abroad, wholesale and retail; dealing in cloth, wool, spices and other goods, financing industries; changing moneys; lending to private individuals and governments; and collecting customs dues under contract.[24]

If Luzatto's portrayal is generally applicable to the Italian merchant class then there was no fundamental difference between them and their Indian counterparts. Not all the details may have been shared by each group of merchants. Khattris in Iran did not function as government officials, but those in Mughal India, Afghanistan and Balkh certainly did.[25]

The nature of Astrakhan Indian firms and the types of contracts that they generally employed also suggest that the business organization and techniques

---

[22] Frank Perlin, "Proto-Industrialization and Pre-Colonial South Asia," *Past and Present* XCVIII, 91–92.

[23] Marc Bloch, "Towards a Comparative History of European Societies," trans. by J. C. Riemersma, in Lane, ed., *Enterprise and Secular Change*, 494–521. For other discussions of comparative history see Raymond Grew, "The Case for Comparing Histories," *American Historical Review* LXXXV/4 (October, 1980), 763–78 and the mathematical model that K. N. Chaudhuri proposes in his new work, *Asia Before Europe* (Cambridge: Cambridge University Press, 1990).

[24] Luzatto, "Italian Cities of the Renaissance," in Lane, ed., *Enterprise and Secular Change*, 52.

[25] Apart from the example of Todar Mal see Ibbetson's comments in Rose, *Glossary of Tribes*, 506 and Boileau, *Personal Narrative*, for descriptions of Marwari businessmen acting as officials for Rajput courts.

of Indian merchants were virtually indistinguishable from those of Italian Renaissance merchants of Florence and Siena, Genoa and Venice. Even some of their *havelis*, the palazzo-like houses which they constructed for their extended families in Indian cities, appear almost as architectural reminders of that similarity. The resemblance seems to have been especially marked in the case of Genoese and Venetian firms.[26] In Astrakhan as in these two latter Italian cities the family firm continued to be the basic unit of business organization. The three Indian brothers who traded between Astrakhan and Moscow were good examples of kin-based firms operating over long distances, as were the many instances of Indians who received their goods from relatives in Iran. In Astrakhan as in Genoa and Venice the occasional temporary arrangement of commenda was the norm for large investments in long-distance trade. The Indians also resembled the Italians – and probably the majority of early modern European merchants – in that they concentrated on two primary activities: the cloth trade and finance. If the same statistics were available for Isfahan that are extant for the Italian cities a similarity would also undoubtedly be found in the substantial social differentiation that was common among merchants in large Italian cities. Information on the Astrakhan "companies" has shown that some stratification was indeed the norm in the Indian dvor, and the relative poverty of the men of the Agrizhan community demonstrates that it existed throughout the city as well. Yet Astrakhan was a modest and, in retrospect, a tentative extension of the Indian mercantile diaspora. The really large branches of Multani firms would have been found in Isfahan, or even in Qandahar and Bukhara.

The Indian and Italian Renaissance business firms were fundamentally similar in organization and method, an identity that validates Irfan Habib's tentative, pensive thoughts about banias and other "merchant communities in pre-colonial India."[27] After reviewing the peddler thesis and other interpretations of commercial practices of Indian mercantile castes Habib writes, "one begins to wonder how Indian or Asian trade could have been different from commerce within western or central Europe."[28] In fact, "innovations that lowered transaction costs," which scholars of western European history too readily assume to have been unique developments of early modern western Europe, were usually not at all peculiar to that region, but may often have developed later there than in parts of the Middle East and Asia.

The one major institutional innovation that western Europeans brought to Asian trade was the joint-stock company, but the time has long since passed when it could be argued that this innovation by itself resulted in the European seizure of Asian markets or the large-scale displacement of Asian merchants. The example of English and Dutch competition in Russia is an important illustration of the fact

[26] Luzatto, "Italian Cities of the Renaissance," in Lane, ed., *Enterprise and Secular Change*, 48–49.
[27] Irfan Habib, "Merchant Communities in Precolonial India," in James D. Tracy, ed., *The Rise of Merchant Empires* (Cambridge: Cambridge University Press, 1990), 371–99.
[28] *Ibid.*, 398.

Plate 4　Haveli, Indian merchant's house in Jaisalmir

that joint-stock organization by itself did not confer a critical competitive edge. Small Dutch firms displaced the English in Russia partly because their ships had greater capacity but mainly as a result of the fact that they were much better capitalized than their English counterparts, which also made it easy for them to satisfy the Russian thirst for silver specie.

The Indian diaspora did not decline because the family firm, or that firm contractually expanded by partnership and commenda agreements, was incapable of competing with the representatives of the Dutch and English East India companies. Only the low cost of sea transportation seems to have undercut the sales of Indian cloth in southern Russia, but the Indian diaspora continued to grow in Russia well after that effect had begun to be felt. The Astrakhan Indians' links with compatriots in Iran, their relatively high levels of capitalization and their sophisticated mercantile skills helped to ensure their continued success. Nor was the diaspora significantly affected by western military action, as Irfan Habib suggests was true of Asian merchants generally when he asks rhetorically:

Could it be that the European triumph over Indian (and Asian) merchants was not, then, one of size and techniques, of companies over peddlers, of joint-stock over atomized capital, of seamen over landsmen. Might it not have been more a matter of men-of-war and gun and shot, to which arithmetic and brokerage could provide no answer.[29]

The critical difference between Europe and Asia that led to the decline of the Indian mercantile diaspora was not European superiority in either economic organization and method or in military technology, however important that technology had been or was to be in other contexts. The critical difference was one of political organization, and to understand the diaspora's decline it is essential to bring the state back into the equation, as several European historians have recently insisted upon doing in order to appreciate the divergence in historical development in different areas of early modern Europe.[30]

In the case of the diaspora the defining contrast was that between the political fragility of the early modern Islamic empires, especially Mughul India and Safavid Iran, and the steadily increasing strength of European nation-states, in this instance the economically backward but triumphantly absolutist Russian state. In the seventeenth century both the Mughul and Safavid states possessed many of the characteristics that Thomas J. Brady Jr. has used to distinguish upwardly mobile "new" European states from old European monarchies,[31] but these two Islamic states also differed from their European counterparts in several important ways.

---

[29] Habib, "Merchant Communities in Precolonial India," 399.
[30] Thomas . Brady Jr., "The Rise of Merchant Empires, 1400–1700: A European Counterpoint," in James D. Tracy ed., *The Political Economy of Merchant Empires* (Cambridge: Cambridge University Press, 1991), 117–60, and Theda Skocpol, "Bringing the State Back In: Strategies of Analysis in Current Research," in Peter B. Evans, Dietrich Roeschemeyer and Theda Skocpol, eds., *Bringing the State Back In* (Cambridge: Cambridge University Press, 1985). As is so often the case this essay focuses on modern western states and the issues associated with them, but it still raises a number of useful comparative issues for early modern polities.
[31] Brady, "The Rise of Merchant Empires," 139.

The political ideology of both states was exceptionally weak, whether this ideology is conceived of as legitimacy or the articulation of a broadly accepted ideal of sovereignty. This deficiency was most obvious in the Mughul case, but the "inescapable illegitimacy of the state" in a predominantly Shi'i country was also a fundamental contradiction of the Safavid regime.[32] The structural obverse of these ideological problems was the obvious failure of the Mughul and Safavid regimes to eliminate compelling political and social groups and monopolize the use of armed force within their territories. Even the British, of course, found it impossible to control the Afghans, but Mughul and Safavid failures were of a far greater order of magnitude. As Muscovite Russia evolved in the late sixteenth and early seventeenth century into imperial Russia with its successful elimination of all intermediary groups within the state, such groups picked over the political remains of Mughul India and Safavid Iran.

Even so the Indian diaspora in Iran and Turan never entirely disappeared. In fact, it revived again under British colonial rule. However, during the nineteenth century the Khattri and Marwari diaspora in those areas, as was true of the Chettiar caste in southeast Asia, gradually fell under the dominance of European capital.[33] In the late nineteenth and early twentieth centuries these diasporas eventually became extensions or personifications not of Indian economic influence, but of a newly triumphant European world economy.

[32] Hamid Algar, *Religion and the State in Iran, 1785–1906* (Berkeley: University of California Press, 1969), 5. See also John Foran, "The Long Fall of the Safavid Dynasty: Moving Beyond the Standard Views," *International Journal of Middle Eastern Studies* XXIV/2 (May 1992), 281–304.
[33] Hans-Dieter Evers, "Chettiar Moneylenders in Southeast Asia," in Lombard and Aubin, eds., *Marchands et hommes*, 199–219.

Appendix

Dynasties (regnal dates)

Mughuls

Babur: 1526–1530
Humayun: 1530–40, 1555–1556
Akbar: 1556–1605
Jahangir: 1605–1627
Shah Jahan: 1627–1658
Aurungzeb: 1658–1707

Safavid

Ismail I: 1501–1524
Tahmasp I: 1524–1576
Muhammad Khudabanda: 1578–1588
'Abbas I: 1587–1629
Safi I: 1629–1642
'Abbas II: 1642–1666
Sulayman I: 1666–1694
Tahmasp II: 1694–1722

Russia

Ivan IV, the Terrible: 1547–1584
Theodore I: 1584–1598
Boris Godunov: 1598–1605
False Dimitri: 1605
Basil Shuisky: 1606–1610
Michael Romanov: 1613–1645
Alexis: 1645–1676
Theodore III: 1676–1682
Ivan IV and Peter I: 1682–1696
Peter I, the Great: 1696–1725

Uzbeks

No attempt has been made to list Uzbek rulers because of the complications of the separate appanages. Uzbek dynastic history of the early modern era is generally divided into two periods: the Shibanid (1500–1600) and the Janid (1600–1750). For discussion and details of the appanages see Martin Dickson, "Shah Tahmasp and the Uzbeks," unpublished Ph.D. dissertation, Princeton, 1958, chapter 2, and McChesney, "Central Asia, VI. In the 10th–12th/16th–18th Centuries," *Encyclopaedia Iranica* V, fasc. 2, 176–93.

Coinage

Mughul India (1594–1605)

gold mohur (10.9 g)
silver rupee (11.6 g)
copper dam (20.9 g)

1595: one muhr = 9 rupees
    one rupee = 100 dams
1695: one muhr = 13.25 rupees
    one rupee = 205.02 or 222 dams

Source: Deyell, "Akbar's Currency System and Monetary Integration," 36, and Habib, "A System of Trimetallism in the Age of the Silver Influx on the Mughul Monetary System," 148–49, both in Richards, ed., *The Imperial Monetary System of Mughal India.* See also *The Coins of the Mughal Emperors of Hindustan in the British Museum.*

Iran

gold 'Abbasi (1588–1629) (9.33 g)
silver 'Abbasi (1588–1629) (9.33–7.77 g)
copper – a local currency which varied with location

Source: Borgomale, *Coins, Medals and Seals,* Table II.

Uzbeks

silver tanka-i shahrukhi of Shibanids (6 g)
silver tanka-i shahrukhi of Janids (4.25 g)

Source: Lowick, "Shaybanid Silver Coins," 258; and Davidovich, "Klad serebrianykh monet Sheibanidov" (for full citations see n. 77, chapter 2).

Russia

silver kopek (1613–45) (48 g)
silver kopek (1645–96) (40–46 g)

Source: Mel'nikova, *Russkie monety ot Ivana Groznogo do Petra Pervogo,* 308–16

Equivalencies

'Abbasi – one 'Abbasi = 1s 4d (English) (1677)
        one 'Abbasi = one Reichsthaler (1673–38)
Tuman – one tuman = 24 rupees (1694)
Tuman – one tuman = 50 'Abbasis (1664–67)

Source: Borgomale, *Coins, Medals and Seals*, 4–5 and 38.

Rupee – one rupee = 13 altins and 2 dengis or forty kopeks (1695–99)

Source: Antonova, I, 1717, 371–72.

Astrakhan Indian trade in 1680

List of goods taken by Mutra Kapur Chand to Moscow in 1680

40 pieces of "eastern" cotton cloth
64 pieces of muslin cloth of "eastern" manufacture, probably Caucasian
14 pieces of silk cloth of Indian manufacture
8 half-silk [and?] leather veils
14 pieces of silk cloth of Indian manufacture
36 pieces of wide Kashan silk cloth
12 pieces of gold or silver brocade cloth
60 pieces of Shemakh silk cloth
27 pieces of coarse cloth used for window coverings
13 pieces of narrow cotton cloth
5 pieces of silver and gold lace
7 pieces of narrow, multicolored cotton cloth
180 cotton sashes
7 pieces of half-silk, cotton cloth
3 multicolored half-silk pieces
18 narrow girdles
3 medium width Kashan girdles
40 pieces of Kashan silk
30 pieces of white muslin

"These pieces in two bundles for customs stamping."

Source: Antonova, I, no. 184, 1680, 288.

Bibliography

Abu-Lughod, Janet L., *Before European Hegemony: The World-System A.D. 1250–1350* (New York: Oxford University Press, 1989).

Aghassian, Michel and Kevonian, Keram, "Le commerce arménien dans l'Océan Indien aux 17e et 18e siècles," in Lombard and Aubin, eds., *Marchands et hommes d'affaires asiatiques*, 155–81.

Ahmad, Khwaja Nizam dl-Din, *The Tabaqat-i-Akbari*, trans. by Brajendranath De and ed. by Baini Prashad (Calcutta: Asiatic Society of Bengal, 1937).

Ahmed, Akbar, "Nomadism as Ideological Expression: The Gomal Nomads," in *Islam, Ethnicity and Leadership in South Asia*, repr. (Karachi: Oxford University Press, 1981), 211–27.

Akhmedov, B. D., *Istoriia Balkha* (Tashkent: Fan, 1982).

Istoriko-geograficheskaia literatura Srednei Azii XVI–XVII vv. (Tashkent: Fan, 1985).

Alam, Muzaffar, *The Crises of Empire in Mughal North India, Awadh and the Punjab, 1707–1748* (New Delhi: Oxford University Press, 1986).

Algar, Hamid, *Religion and the State in Iran, 1785–1906* (Berkeley: University of California Press, 1969).

'Ali, M. Athar et al., "Mughals," *Encyclopaedia of Islam*, new ed., VII fasc. 119–20 (Leiden: E. J. Brill, 1991), 313–36.

'Allami, Abu'l Fadl, *The A'in-i Akbari*, trans. and ed. by H. Blochmann and D. C. Phillott, repr. (New Delhi: Crown Publications, 1988), 3 vols.

The Akbar Nama of Abu-l Fazl, trans. by H. Beveridge, repr. (New Delhi: Ess Ess Publications, 1987), 3 vols.

Allsen, Thomas T., "Mongol Census Taking in Rus', 1245–1275," *Harvard Ukrainian Studies* V/1 (March 1981), 32–53.

"Mongolian Princes and their Merchant Partners," *Asia Minor*, 3rd ser., II/2 (1989), 83–125.

Anderson, Perry, *Lineages of the Absolute State*, repr. (London: Verso Editions, 1980).

Antonova, K. A., Gol'dberg, N. M. and Lavrentsov, T. D., eds., *Russko-Indiiskie Otnosheniia v XVII v.* (Moscow: Nauka, 1958).

Antonova, K. A. and Gol'dberg, N. M., eds., *Russko-Indiiskie Otnosheniia v XVII v.* (Moscow: Nauka, 1965).

Artsikhovskii, A. V., ed., *Ocherki russkoi kul'tury XVII veka chast' pervaia* (Moscow: Moscow University, 1979).

Attman, Artur, *The Russian and Polish Markets in International Trade* (Göteborg; Meddelanden från Ekonomisk-historiska institutionen vid Göteborgs universitet, 1973).

Bacqué-Grammont, Jean-Louis, "Études Turco-Safavides, I: Notes sur le blocus du commerce iranien par Selîm Ier," *Turcica*, VI (1975), 68–88.

Le Livre de Babur (Paris: Imprimerie Nationale, 1985).

al-Bada'uni ['Abd al-Qadir ibn Muluk Shah], *Muntakhabu-T-Tawarikh*, trans. by G. Ranking and ed. by B. P. Ambashthya, repr. (Patna: Academica Asiatica, 1973), 3 vols.

Baikova, B. N., *Rol' Srednei Azii v Russko-Indiiskikh Torgovykh Sviaziakh* (Tashkent: Nauka, 1964).

Bakhari, Sayyid Muhammd Ma'sumi, *Tarikh-i-Sind*, best known as *Tarikh-i-Ma'sumi*, ed. by A. M. Daupotra (Poona: Bhandarkar Oriental Research Institute, 1938).

Ball, J. N., *Merchants and Merchandise, the Expansion of Trade in Europe 1500–1630* (London: Croom Helm, 1977).

Balland, Daniel, "Census II. In Afghanistan," in E. Yarshater, ed., *Encyclopaedia Iranica* V, fasc. 2 (Costa Mesa, Calif.: Mazda, 1990), 152–59.

Baron, Samuel H., "Ivan the Terrible, Giles Fletcher and the Muscovite Merchantry: A Reconsideration," *The Slavonic and East European Review* LVI/4 (Oct. 1978), 563–85.

The Travels of Olearius in Seventeenth Century Russia (Stanford, Calif.: Stanford University Press, 1967).

"Who Were the Gosti?" *California Slavic Studies* VII/4 (1973), 1–40.

Barthold, V. V., *Four Studies on the History of Central Asia*, trans. by V. and T. Minorsky (Leiden: E. J. Brill, 1962).

An Historical Geography of Iran, trans. by Svat Soucek and ed. by C. E. Bosworth (Princeton: Princeton University Press, 1984).

Bayly, C. A., *Rulers, Townsmen and Bazaars* (Cambridge: Cambridge University Press, 1983).

Beale, T. W., *An Oriental Biographical Dictionary*, repr. (New Delhi: Manohar Reprints, 1971).

Beckwith, Christopher I., "The Impact of the Horse and Silk Trade on the Economies of T'ang China and the Uighur Empire," *Journal of the Economic and Social History of the Orient* XXXIV/2 (June 1991), 183–98.

Begley, Wayne E., "Four Mughal Caravansarais Built during the Reigns of Jahangir and Shah Jahan," in Oleg Grabar, ed., *Muqarnas* (New Haven, Conn.: Yale University Press, 1983), I, 167–79.

Begley, W. E. and Desai, Z. A., *The Shah Jahan Nama of 'Inayat Khan* (Delhi: Oxford University Press, 1990).

Taj Mahal: The Illumined Tomb (Seattle: University of Washington Press, 1980).

Bell, John, *Travels from St. Petersburg in Russia to Diverse Parts of Asia* (Glasgow: Robert & Andrew Foulis, 1753), 2 vols.

Bentley-Duncan, T., "Niels Steensgaard and the Europe–Asia Trade of the Early Seventeenth Century," *Journal of Modern History* XLVII (1975), 512–18.

Beveridge, Annette Susannah, trans. and ed., *The Babur-nama in English*, repr. (London: Luzac, 1969).

Beveridge, Henry, ed. and Rogers, Alexander, trans., *The Tuzuk-i-Jahangiri*, repr. (New Delhi: Manoharlal, 1978), 2 vols.

Biddulph, Michael A. (Major-General), "Pishin and the Routes between India and Candahar," *Proceedings of the Royal Geographical Society*, n.s. II (1880), 212–46.

Blackwell, William L., *The Industrialization of Russia* (New York: Thomas Y. Crowell, 1970).

Blake, Stephen P., "The Hierarchy of Central Places in North India during the Mughal Period of Indian History," *South Asia* VI/1 (1983), 1–32.

"The Urban Economy in Premodern Muslim India, Shahjahanabad, 1639–1739," *Modern Asian Studies* XXI/3 (1987), 447–71.

Blanchard, Ian, *Russia's Age of Silver* (London: Routledge, 1989).

Bloch, Marc, "Towards a Comparative History of European Societies," trans. J. C. Riemersma in Lane, ed., *Enterprise and Secular Change*.

Blum, Jerome, *Lord and Peasant in Russia* (Princeton: Princeton University Press, 1961).

Boileau, A. H. E., *Personal Narrative of a Tour Through the Western States of Rajwara in 1835 . . .* (Calcutta: Baptist Mission Press, 1837).

Borgomale, H. L. Rabino di, *Coins, Medals and Seals of the Shahs of Iran, 1500–1941* (Oxford: Oxford University Press, 1951).

Bornford, Henry, "Henry Bornford's Account of his Journey from Agra to Tatta [? March 1639]," in William Foster, ed., *The English Factories in India, 1637–41* (Oxford: Clarendon Press, 1912), 134–36.

Boyle, J. A., ed., *The Cambridge History of Iran*, V: *The Saljuq and Mongol Periods* (Cambridge: Cambridge University Press, 1968).

Braudel, Fernand, *Civilization and Capitalism 15th–18th Century*, trans. by Siân Reynolds, III: *The Perspective of the World* (London: Collins, 1984).

Brucker, Gene, *Renaissance Florence* (Berkeley: University of California Press, 2nd ed., 1983).

Burnes, (Sir) Alexander, *Cabool, Being a Personal Narrative of a Journey to, and Residence in that City in the Years 1836, 7 and 8* (London: John Murray, 1842).

Burnes, (Sir) Alexander et al., *Reports and Papers, Political, Geographical and Commercial . . .* (Calcutta, Military Orphan Press, 1839).

Burnes, (Sir) Alexander, *Travels into Bokhara* (London: John Murray, 2nd ed., 1835), 3 vols.

Bushkovitch, Paul, *The Merchants of Moscow 1580–1640* (Cambridge: Cambridge University Press, 1980).

Calmard, Jean, "Les marchands iraniens: formation et montée d'un groupe de pression, 16e–19e siècles," in Lombard and Aubin, eds., *Marchands et hommes d'affaires asiatiques*, 91–107.

Carswell, J., "The Armenian and the East–West Trade through Persia in the XVII century," *Sociétés et compagnies de commerce en Orient et dans l'océan Indien* (Paris: 1970), 481–86.

Chakravarti, Ranabir, "Horse Trade and Piracy at Tana (Thana, Maharashtra, India): Gleanings from Marco Polo," *Journal of the Economic and Social History of the Orient* XXIV/2 (June 1991), 159–82.

Chandra, Satish, "Commercial Activities of the Mughal Emperors during the Seventeenth Century," in Satish Chandra, ed., *Essays in Medieval Indian Economic History* (New Delhi: Manoharlal, 1987), 163–69.

Chandra, Satish, ed., *Essays in Medieval Indian Economic History* (New Delhi: Munshiram Manoharlal, 1987).

Chardin, (Sir) John (Jean), *Travels in Persia 1673–1677*, repr. (Mineola, N.Y.: Dover Books, 1988).

Chardin, Jean, *Voyages du Chevalier Chardin, en Perse* . . . , ed. by L. Langles (Paris: Le Normant, 1811), 4 vols.

Chaudhuri, K. N., *Asia Before Europe* (Cambridge: Cambridge University Press, 1990).

"Markets and Traders in India during the Seventeenth and Eighteenth Centuries," in K. N. Chaudhuri and Clive J. Dewey, eds., *Economy and Society: Essays in Indian Economic and Social History* (New Delhi: Oxford University Press, 1979), 143–62.

The Trading World of Asia and the English East India Company, 1660–1760 (Cambridge: Cambridge University Press, 1978).

Chekovitch, O. D., "Gorodskoe samoupravlenie v Tashkente XVIII v.," in B. G. Gafurov and B. A. Litvinskii, eds., *Istoriia i Kul'tura Narodov Srednei Azii* (Moscow: Nauka, 1976), 149–60.

Chenciner, Robert and Magomedkhanov, Magomedkhan, "Persian Exports to Russia from the Sixteenth to the Nineteenth Century," *Iran*, XXX (1992), 123–30.

Cirtautas, Ilse Laude, "On the Development of Literary Uzbek in the last Fifty Years," *Central Asian Review* XXI (1977), 36–51.

Coulson, N. J., *A History of Islamic Law* (Edinburgh: Edinburgh University Press, 1991).

Creel, H. G., "The Role of the Horse in Chinese History," *American Historical Review* LXX/3 (April 1965), 647–72.

Curtin, Philip D., *Cross-cultural Trade in World History* (Cambridge: Cambridge University Press, 1984).

Dale, Stephen F., *Islamic Society on the South Asian Frontier: The Mappilas of Malabar, 1498–1922* (Oxford: Clarendon Press, 1980).

"The Legacy of the Timurids," in Morgan and Robinson, eds., *The Legacy of the Timurids*.

Dani, Ahmad Hasan, *Thatta* (Islamabad: Institute of Islamic History, Culture and Civilization, 1982).

Danilova, L. V., "Torgovye Riady Iaroslavlia v kontse XVII v.," in Ustiugov, ed., *Voprosy Sotsial'no-Ekonomischeskoi Istorii i Istochnikovedeniia Perioda Feodalizma v Rossii*, 83–90.

Danvers, F. C. and Foster, William, *Letters Received by the East India Company from its Servants in the East* (London: Sampson, Low & Marston, 1896–1902), 6 vols.

Das Gupta, Ashin, *Indian Merchants and the Decline of Surat c. 1700–1750* (Wiesbaden: Fritz Steiner, 1979).

"A Note on the Shipowning Merchants of Surat c. 1700," in Lombard and Aubin, eds., *Marchands et hommes d'affaires asiatiques*, 109–15.

Dasti, Humaira, "Multan as a Centre of Trade and Commerce During the Mughul Period," *Quarterly Journal of the Pakistan Historical Society* XXXVII/3 (July 1990), 247–56.

Davidovich, E. A., *Istoriia Denezhnogo Obrascheniia Srednevekovoi Srednei Azii* (Moscow: Nauka, 1983).

"Klad serebrianykh Monet XVI v. iz Tadzhikistana," in D. B. Shelov, ed., *Numizmatika i Epigrafika* VIII (Moscow: Nauka, 1970), 67–80.

Klady Drevnikh i Srednevekovykh Monet Tadzhikistana (Moscow: Nauka, 1979).

"Materialy dlia kharakteristiki chekana i obrascheniia Sredneaziatskikh Mednykh monet XV v.," in D. B. Shelov, ed., *Numizmatika i Epigrafika*, V (Moscow: Nauka, 1965), 225–48.

Delouche, Jean, *Recherches sur les routes de l'Inde au temps des Mogols*, LXVII (Paris: École Française d'Extreme-Orient, 1968).

Demkin, A. V., *Russkoe kupechestvo XVII–XVIII* vv. Goroda Verkhne volzh'ia (Moscow: Nauka, 1990).

Deyell, John S., *Living Without Silver* (New Delhi: Oxford University Press, 1990).

Dickson, Martin, "Shah Tahmasp and the Uzbeks (The Duel for Khurasan with 'Ubayd Khan: 930–940 (1524–1540)," Unpublished Ph.D. dissertation, Princeton University, 1958.

Digby, Simon, "The Maritime Trade of India," in Raychaudhuri and Habib, eds., *The Cambridge Economic History of India*, I: *c. 1200–c. 1750*, 125–59.

Elphinstone, Mountstuart, *An Account of the Kingdom of Caubul and its Dependencies in Persia, Tartary and India*, repr. (Graz, Austria: Akademische Druck- u. Verlagsanstalt, 1969).

Emerson, John, "Chardin, Sir John," *Encyclopaedia Iranica* V, fasc. 3 (1991), 369–77.

  "Ex Oxidente Lux: Some European Sources on the Economic Structure of Persia between about 1630 and 1690," Unpublished Ph.D. dissertation, University of Cambridge, 1969.

Emerson, John and Floor, Willem, "Rahdars and their Tolls in Safavid and Afsharid Iran," *Journal of the Economic and Social History of the Orient* XXX (1987), 318–27.

Endicott-West, Elizabeth, "Merchant Associations in Yüan China: the Ortay," *Asia Major*, 3rd ser. II/2 (1989), 127–54.

Eskandar Beg Monshi, *History of Shah 'Abbas the Great* (Tarik-e 'Alamara-ye 'Abbasi), trans. by Roger Savory (Boulder, Colo.: Westview Press, 1978), 2 vols.

Evans, N. E., "The Anglo-Russian Marriage Negotiations of 1600–1603," *The Slavonic and East European Review* LXI/3 (1983), 362–87.

Evans, Peter B., Dietrich Roeschemeyer and Theda Skocpol, eds., *Bringing the State Back In* (Cambridge: Cambridge University Press, 1985).

Evers, Hans-Dieter, "Chettiar Moneylenders in Southeast Asia," in Lombard and Aubin, eds., *Marchands et hommes d'affaires asiatiques*, 199–219.

Farooqi, Naimur Rehman, *Mughul–Ottoman Relations* (Delhi: Idarah-i Adabiyet-i Delli, 1989).

Faroqhi, Suraiya, "Camels, Wagons and the Ottoman State in the Sixteenth and Seventeenth Centuries," in Suraiya Faroqhi, *Peasants, Dervishes and Traders in the Ottoman Empire* (London: Variorum Reprints, 1986), 523–39.

  "Seventeenth Century Periodic Markets in Various Anatolian *Sancaks*," *Journal of the Economic and Social History of the Orient* XXII/1 (1979), 32–80.

  Towns and Townsmen of Ottoman Anatolia, Trade, Crafts and Food Production in an Urban Setting, 1520–1650 (Cambridge: Cambridge University Press, 1984).

Fawcett, Charles, *The English Factories in India, 1670–77*, n.s. (Oxford: Clarendon Press, 1936–55), 4 vols. [a continuation of Foster, ed., *The English Factories in India*].

Ferishta, Muhammad Qasim, *History of the Rise of the Mahomedan Power in India . . .* , trans. by John Briggs, repr. (Calcutta: Editions Indian, 1966), 4 vols.

Ferrier (Gen.), J. P., *Caravan Journeys and Wanderings in Persia, Afghanistan, Turkistan and Beloochistan*, trans. by William Jesse (London: John Murray, 2nd ed., 1857).

Ferrier, R. W., "The Armenians and the East India Company in Persia in the Seventeenth and Early Eighteenth Centuries," *The Economic History Review*, 2nd ser., XXVI/1 (1973), 38–62.

  "An English View of Persian Trade in 1618," *Journal of the Economic and Social History of the Orient* XIX (1976), 182–214.

"Trade from the mid-14th Century to the End of the Safavid Period," in Jackson and Lockhart, eds., *The Cambridge History of Iran*, VI: *The Timurid and Safavid Periods*, 412–90.

Findley, Ellison, B., "The Capture of Maryam-uz-Zamani's Ship: Mughal Women and European Traders," *Journal of the American Oriental Society* CVIII/2 (1988), 227–28.

Fischer, W., McInnes, R. M. and Schneider, J., eds., *The Emergence of a World Economy 1500–1914* (Wiesbaden: Franz Steiner, 1986).

Fisher, W. B., ed., *The Cambridge History of Iran*, I: *The Land of Iran* (Cambridge: Cambridge University Press, 1968).

Flecker, James Elroy, *The Collected Poems of James Elroy Flecker*, ed. by J. C. Squire (London: Martin Secker, 1921).

Floor, Willem, "The Dutch East India Company's Trade with Sind in the 17th and 18th Centuries," *Moyen Orient and Ocean Indien*, xvie–xixie s., III (1986), 111–44.

Floor, W. M., "The Merchants (tujjar) in Qajar Iran," *Zeitschrift der Deutschen Morgen-ländischen Gesellschaft*, CXXVI/1 (1976), 101–35.

Foran, John, "The Long Fall of the Safavid Dynasty: Moving Beyond the Standard Views," *International Journal of Middle Eastern Studies* XXIV/2 (May 1992), 281–304.

"The Modes of Production Approach to Seventeenth Century Iran," *International Journal of Middle Eastern Studies* XX/3 (August 1988), 345–63.

Forster, George, *A Journey from Bengal to England through the Northern Part of India, Kashmire, Afghanistan, and Persia, and into Russia, by the Caspian Sea* (London: R. Faulder, 1798), 2 vols.

Foster, William, ed., *The English Factories in India, 1618–1669* (Oxford: Clarendon Press, 1906–27), 12 vols. [a continuation of Danvers and Foster, *Letters Received by the East India Company from its Servants in the East*].

Foust, Clifford M., *Muscovite and Mandarin: Russia's Trade with China and its Setting, 1727–1805* (Chapel Hill, N.C.: University of North Carolina Press, 1969).

Fragner, Bert, "Social and Internal Economic Affairs," in Jackson and Lockhart, eds., *The Cambridge History of Iran*, VI: *The Timurid and Safavid Periods*, 491–565.

Fraser, James B., *Narrative of a Journey into Khorasan in the Years 1821 and 1822*, repr. (New Delhi: Oxford University Press, 1984).

Fuhrmann, Joseph T., *The Origins of Capitalism in Russia, Industry and Progress in the Sixteenth and Seventeenth Centuries* (Chicago: Quadrangle Books, 1972).

Gaube, Heinz, *Iranian Cities* (New York: N.Y. University Press, 1979).

Gauthier-Pilters, Hilde and Dagg, Anne Innes, *The Camel* (Chicago: University of Chicago Press, 1981).

Gibb, H. A. R., ed., *The Travels of Ibn Battuta*, II (Cambridge: Cambridge University Press, 1936).

Gittinger, Mattiebelle, *Master Dyers to the World: Technique and Trade in Early Indian Dyed Cotton Textiles* (Washington, D.C.: The Textile Museum, 1982).

Goitein, S. D., *A Mediterranean Society* (Berkeley: University of California Press, 1967–88), 5 vols.

"The Rise of the Near-Eastern Bourgeoisie in Early Islamic Times," *Journal of World History* III/3 (1957), 583–604.

Golikova, N. B., *Astrakhanskoe Vosstanie 1705–1706 g.g.* (Moscow: Moscow University, 1975).

Ocherki Po Istorii Gorodov Rossii kontsa XVII–nachala XVIII v. (Moscow: Moscow University, 1982).

"Rostovshchestvo v Rossii nachala XVIII v i ego nekotorye osobennosti," in S. D. Skazkin, ed., *Problemy genezisa kapitalizma* (Moscow: Nauka, 1970).

Gomes, Leonard, *Foreign Trade and the National Economy, Mercantilist and Classical Perspectives* (London: Macmillan, 1987).

Gopal, Surendra, "Indians in Central Asia, 16th and 17th Centuries," Presidential Address, Medieval India Section of the Indian History Congress, New Delhi, February 1992 (Patna: Patna University, 1992), 1–21.

Indians in Russia in the 17th and 18th Centuries (New Delhi: Indian Council of Historical Research, 1988).

Grew, Raymond, "The Case for Comparing Histories," *American Historical Review* LXXXV/4 (Oct. 1980), 763–78.

Grewal, J. S., "Business Communities of Punjab," in Tripathi, ed., *Business Communities of India*, 209–24.

Guerney, J. D., "Pietra della Valle: the limits of Perception," *Bulletin of the School of Oriental and African Studies* XLIX/1 (1986), 103–16.

Guerney, J., "Rewriting the Social History of Late Safavid Iran," in Melville, ed., *Pembroke Papers, I: Persian and Islamic Studies in Honour of P. W. Avery*.

Habib, Irfan, "Agrarian Relations and Land Revenue: North India," in Raychaudhuri and Habib, eds., *The Cambridge Economic History of India*, I: *c. 1200–c. 1750*, 235–48.

An Atlas of the Mughal Empire (Delhi: Oxford University Press, 1982).

"Merchant Communities in Precolonial India," in Tracy, ed., *The Rise of Merchant Empires*, 371–99.

"Monetary System and Prices," in Raychaudhuri and Habib, eds., *The Cambridge Economic History of India*, I: *c. 1200–c. 1750*, 360–81.

"Population," in Raychaudhuri and Habib, eds., *The Cambridge Economic History of India*, I: *c. 1200–c. 1750*, 163–71.

"Potentialities of Capitalistic Development in the Economy of Mughal India," *Journal of Economic History* XXIX (1969), 32–78.

"The System of Bills of Exchange (*Hundis*) in the Mughal Empire," in Chandra, ed., *Essays in Medieval Indian Economic History*, 207–21.

"The Systems of Agricultural Production: Mughal India," in Raychaudhuri and Habib, eds., *The Cambridge Economic History of India*, I: *c. 1200–c. 1750*, 214–25.

"Usury in Medieval India," *Comparative Studies in Society and History*, VI/4 (July 1964), 393–417.

Haidar, Mansura, "Agrarian System in the Uzbek Khanates of Central Asia," *Turcica* VII (1975), 157–78.

Hanway, Jonas, *An Historical Account of the British Trade over the Caspian Sea . . .* (London: T. Osborne et al., 1753).

Hardy, Peter, *The Muslims of British India* (Cambridge: Cambridge University Press, 1972).

Hart, Simon, "Amsterdam Shipping and Trade to Northern Russia in the Seventeenth Century," *Mededelingen van de Nederlands Vereniging voor Zeegeschiedenis* XXVI (March 1973), 5–30.

Hasan, Aziza, "Mints of the Mughal Empire," in Chandra, ed., *Essays in Medieval Indian Economic History*, 170–98.

Hathaway, Jane, "A Twelfth-Century Partnership in Silk Trading: a Geniza Study," *Journal of Middle Eastern Studies* II/1 (1988), 24–37.

Hellie, Richard, *Enserfment and Military Change in Muscovy* (Chicago: University of Chicago Press, 1971).

Herbert, (Sir) Thomas, *Travels in Persia, 1627–1629*, repr. (Freeport, N.Y.: Books for Libraries Press, 1972).

Herzig, Edmund, "The Armenian Merchants of New Julfa, Isfahan: A Study in Pre-Modern Asian Trade," Unpublished Ph.D. dissertation, University of Oxford, 1991.

Herzig Edmund M., "Commercial Credit and Long-distance Trade: The Julfa Armenians in the Seventeenth Century," Paper presented at the "Workshop on the Political Economies of the Ottoman, Safavid and Mughal States during the 17th and 18th Centuries." Istanbul, Turkey, 16–20 June 1992.

Hillenbrand, Robert, "Safavid Architecture," in Jackson and Lockhart, eds., *The Cambridge History of Iran*, VI: *The Timurid and Safavid Periods*, 759–843.

Hittle, J. Michael, *The Service City, State and Townsmen in Russia 1600–1800* (Cambridge, Mass.: Harvard University Press, 1979).

Hodgson, Marshall, *The Venture of Islam*, III: *Gunpowder Empires and Modern Times* (Chicago: University of Chicago Press, 1974).

Holditch, T. H. (Capt.), "Geographical Results of the Afghan Campaign," *Proceedings of the Royal Geographical Society*, n.s. III (1881), 65–84.

Inalcik, Halil, "Capital Formation in the Ottoman Empire," *Journal of Economic History* XXIX/1 (March 1969), 97–140.

"The Hub of the City: the Bedestan of Istanbul," *International Journal of Turkish Studies* I/1 (1979–80), 1–17.

Ionnisiana, Ashota, *Armiano-Russkie Otnosheniia v Pervoi Treti XVIII veka*, II/1 (Erivan: Akademia Nauk, 1964).

Islam, Riazul, *A Calendar of Documents on Indo-Persian Relations, 1500–1750* (Karachi: Institute of Central and West Asian Studies, 1979), 2 vols.

Islamoğlu-Inan, Huri, *The Ottoman Empire and the World Economy* (Cambridge: Cambridge University Press, 1987).

Israel, Jonathan, *Dutch Primacy in World Trade, 1585–1740* (Oxford: Clarendon Press, 1989).

Issawi, Charles, "The Decline of Middle Eastern Trade, 1100–1850," in Richards, ed., *Islam and the Trade of Asia*, 245–66.

The Economic History of Iran, 1800–1914 (Chicago: University of Chicago Press, 1971).

Iukht, A. I., "Indiiskaia koloniia v Astrakhani," *Voprosy Istorii* no. 3 (1957), 135–43.

(Mir) Izzet Ullah, "'Travels beyond the Himalayas,' from *The Calcutta Oriental Quarterly Magazine*, 1825," in *Journal of the Royal Asiatic Society* VII (1853), 283–342.

Jackson, Peter and Lockhart, Laurence, eds., *The Cambridge History of Iran*, VI: *The Timurid and Safavid Periods* (Cambridge: Cambridge University Press, 1986).

Jagchid, Sechin and Symons, Van Jay, *Peace, War and Trade along the Great Wall* (Bloomington, Indiana: Indiana University Press, 1989).

Jain, L. C., *Indigenous Banking in India* (London: Macmillan, 1929).

Jarrige, Jean-François and Meadow, Richard R., "The Antecedents of Civilization in the Indus Valley," *Scientific American* CCXLIII/2 (August 1980), 122–33.

Jeannin, Pierre, *Merchants of the Sixteenth Century*, trans. by Paul Fittinghoff (New York: Harper & Row, 1972).

Jenkinson, Anthony, *Early Voyages and Travels to Russia and Persia*, ed. by Delmar Morgan and C. H. Coote (London: Hakluyt Society, 1886), 2 vols.

Joshi, Rita, *The Afghan Nobility and the Mughals 1526–1707* (New Delhi: Vikas Publishing House, 1985).

Kaempfer, Engelbert, *Am Hofe des persischen Grosskönigs 1684–1685* (Tübingen, Basel: Walter Hinz, 1977).

Kaufengauz, B. B., *Ocherki Bnutrennego Rynka Rossii Pervoi Poloviny XVIII veka* (Moscow: Akademiia Nauk, 1958).

Kaufmann-Rochard, J., *Origines d'une bourgeoisie russe (XVIe et XVIIe siècles)* (Paris: Flammerion, 1969).

Kayhan, Mas'ud, *Jughrafiya-yi mufassal-i Iran* (Tehran: Matba'ah-i majlis, 1311).

Kellenbenz, Hermann, "The Economic Significance of the Archangel Route (from the Late 16th to the 18th Century)," *Journal of European Economic History* II (1973), 541–81.

Keppel, George, *Personal Narrative of a Journey from India to England . . . in the Year 1824* (London: Henry Colburn, 1827), 2 vols.

Keyvani, Mehdi, *Artisans and Guild Life in the Later Safavid Period. Contributions to the Social-Economic History of Persia* (Berlin: Klaus Schwartz, 1982).

Khachikian, Ivan, "Le registre d'un marchand arménien en Perse en Inde et en Tibet (1682–1693)," *Annales: Économies, Sociétés, Civilisations* XXII (1967), 231–78.

Khan, Ahmad Nabi, *Multan History and Architecture* (Islamabad: Institute of Islamic History, Islamic University, 1983).

Khazanov, A. M., *Nomads and the Outside World*, trans. by Julia Crookenden (Cambridge: Cambridge University Press, 1984).

Kheirabadi, Masoud, *Iranian Cities, Formation and Development* (Austin, Tex.: University of Texas Press, 1991).

Kleis, W., "Die Karawanenwege in Iran aus Frühislamischer Zeit," in *Transition Periods in Iranian History* (Louvain, Belgium: Association pour l'avancement des études iraniennes, 1987), 141–49.

Koch, Ebba, *Mughal Architecture* (Munich: Prestel, 1991).

Kolff, D. H. A. and Van Santen, H. W., eds., *De Geschriften van Francisco Pelsaert over Mughal Indië, 1627 Kroniek en Remonstrantie* (s'Gravenhage, Netherlands: Martinus Nijhoff, 1979).

Koshman, L. V., "Manufaktura," in A. V. Artsikhovskii, ed., *Ocherki russkoi kultury XVII veka* chast' pervaia (Moscow: Moscow University, 1979), 105–21.

Kotov, F. A., *Khozhdenie kuptsa Fedota Kotova v Persiiu*, ed. by A. A. Kuznetsova (Moscow: Eastern Literature, 1958).

Kovrigina, V. A. and Marasinova, L. N., "Torgovlia, Puti i Sredstva Peredvizheniia," in A. V. Artsikhovskii, ed., *Ocherki russkoi kultury XVII veka* chast' pervaia (Moscow: Moscow University, 1979), 105–21.

Kozlov, Victor, *The Peoples of the Soviet Union*, trans. by Pauline M. Tiffen (London: Hutchinson, 1988).

Krader, Lawrence, *Peoples of Central Aisa* (Bloomington, Ind.: Indiana University Press, 1963).

Kroell, Anne, "Douze lettres de Jean Chardin," *Journal Asiatique* CCLXX/3–4 (1982), 295–338.

Labib, Subhi Y., "Capitalism in Medieval Islam," *Journal of Economic History* XXIX/1 (March 1969), 79–96.

Labrosse, Joseph (Ange de Saint-Joseph), *Souvenirs de la Perse safavide et autres lieux de l'Orient (1664–1678)* (Brussels: Université de Bruxelles, 1985).

Lal, Mohun, "A Brief Description of Herat," *Journal of the Asiatic Society of Bengal* III/25 (January 1834), 9–18.

Travel in the Punjab, Afghanistan and Turkistan to Balkh, Bokhara and Herat and a Visit to Great Britain and Germany (Calcutta: K. P. Bagchi, 2nd ed., 1977).

Lambrick, H. T., *Sind*, I (Hyderabad, Pakistan: Sindhi Adabi Board, 1964).

Lambton, A. K. S., "The Case of Hajji 'Abd al-Karim," in C. E. Bosworth, ed., *Iran and Islam* (Edinburgh: University of Edinburgh Press, 1971), 331–60.

Lambton, Ann K. S., "Persian Trade Under the Early Qajars," in Richards, ed., *Islam and the Trade of Asia*, 215–44.

Lane, Frederic C., ed., *Enterprise and Secular Change* (Homewood, Ill.: Richard Darwin, 1953).

Lane-Poole, Stanley, *The Coins of the Moghul Emperors of Hindustan in the British Museum*, repr. (New Delhi: Inter-India Publications, 1983).

Lansdell, Henry, *Russian Central Asia*, repr. (New York: Arno Press, 1970).

Leonard, Karen, "Indigenous Banking Firms in Mughal India: A Reply," *Comparative Studies in Society and History* XXIII/21 (April 1981), 309–13.

van Leur, J. C., *Indonesian Trade and Society* (The Hague: W. van Hoeve, 1955).

Liusternik, E. Ia., *Russko-Indiiskie Ekonomicheskie Sviazi* (Moscow: Eastern Literature, 1958).

Lombard, Denys and Aubin, Jean, eds., *Marchands et hommes d'affaires asiatiques* (Paris: Éditions de l'École des Hautes Études en Sciences Sociales, 1988).

Lowick, N. M., "Coins of Sulaiman Mirza of Badakshan," *The Numismatic Chronicle* 7th ser., V (1965), 221–37.

"More on Sulaiman Mirza and his Contemporaries," *The Numismatic Chronicle*, 7th ser., XII (1972), 283–87.

"Shaybanid Silver Coins," *The Numismatic Chronicle*, 7th ser., VI (1966), 251–330.

Lubimenko, I., "The Struggle of the Dutch with the English for the Russian Market in the Seventeenth Century," *Transactions of the Royal Historical Society*, 4th ser., VII (1924), 27–51.

Luzatto, Gino, "Small and Great Merchants in the Italian Cities of the Renaissance," in Lane, ed., *Enterprise and Secular Change*, 41–52.

Lyaschenko, Peter I., *History of the National Economy of Russia to the 1917 Revolution*, trans. by L. M. Herman (New York: Macmillan, 1949).

Ma'ani, Ahmad Golchin, *Karvan-i Hind* (Mashad: Astan-i quds-i razavi, 1969).

Maclagan, E. D., *Gazetteer of the Multan District 1901–1902* (Lahore: Civil and Military Gazette Press, 1902), 2 vols.

Maclean, Derryl, *Religion and Society in Arab Sind* (Leiden: E. J. Brill, 1989).

Manrique, Fray Sebastien, *Travels of Fray Sebastien Manrique, 1629–1643* (Oxford: Hakluyt Society, 1947), 2 vols.

Markham, C. R., "The Mountain Passes on the Afghan Frontier of British India," *Proceedings of the Royal Geographical Society*, n.s. I (1879), 38–62.

Masson, Charles, *Narratives of Various Journeys in Balochistan, Afghanistan and the Panjab*, repr. (Karachi: Oxford University Press, 1975).

Masters, Bruce, *The Origins of Western Economic Dominance in the Middle East, Mercantilism and the Islamic Economy in Aleppo, 1600–1750* (New York: N.Y. University Press, 1988).

Matley, Ian Murray, "The Population and the Land," in Edward Allworth, ed., *Central Asia. 120 Years of Russian Rule* (Durham, N.C.: Duke University Press, 1989), 92–130.

Matthee, Rudolph, "Anti-Ottoman Politics and Transit Rights: The Seventeenth-Century Trade in Silk between Safavid Iran and Muscovy," unpublished paper.

"Politics and Trade in Late Safavid Iran: Commercial Crises and Government Reaction under Shah Solayman (1666–1694)," Unpublished Ph.D. dissertation, UCLA, 1991.

Mauro, Frederic, "Mercantile Communities, 1350–1750," in James D. Tracy, ed., *The Rise of Merchant Empires* (Cambridge: Cambridge University Press, 1990), 255–86.

McChesney, Robert D., "Central Asia, vi. In the 10th–12th/16th–18th Centuries," in E. Yarshater, ed., *Encyclopaedia Iranica* V, fasc. 2, 176–93.

McChesney, Robert, *Waqf in Central Asia* (Princeton: Princeton University Press, 1991).

Mel'nikova, A. S., *Russkie monety ot Ivana Groznogo do Petra Pervogo* (Moscow: Finance and Statistics, 1989).

Melville, Charles, *Pembroke Papers*, I: *Persian and Islamic Studies in Honour of P. W. Avery* (Cambridge: Centre of Middle Eastern Studies, University of Cambridge, 1990).

Meserve, Ruth Ingeborg Vikdal, "An Historical Perspective of Mongol Horse Training, Care, and Management: Selected Texts," Unpublished Ph.D. dissertation, University of Indiana, 1987.

Michaud, Roland and Sabrina, *Caravan to Tartary*, trans. by Jane Brenton (London: Thames & Hudson, 1978).

Minorsky, V., ed. and trans., *Tadhkirat al-Muluk*, repr. (Cambridge University Press for the E. J. W. Gibb Memorial Series, 1980).

Misra, S. C. and Rahman, M. L., *The Mir'at-i-Sikandari* (Baroda: Department of History, University of Baroda, 1961).

Moosvi, Shireen, *The Economy of the Mughal Empire, c. 1595: A Statistical Study* (Delhi: Oxford University Press, 1987).

Moreen, Vera Basch, *Iranian Jewry During the Afghan Invasion* (Stuttgart: Frans Steiner, 1990).

Iranian Jewry's Hour of Peril and Heroism (New York–Jerusalem: American Academy for Jewish Research, 1987).

Moreland, W. H., *From Akbar to Aurungzeb, A Study in Indian Economic History* (London: Macmillan, 1923).

India at the Death of Akbar (London: Macmillan, 1920).

Morgan, David O. and Robinson, F., *The Legacy of the Timurids* (New Delhi: Oxford University Press for the Royal Asiatic Society, forthcoming, 1994).

Morgenstierne, G., "Afghan," in H. A. R. Gibb et al., eds., *The Encyclopaedia of Islam*, new ed. (Leiden: E. J. Brill, 1960), I, 216–21.

Moynihan, Elizabeth, *Paradise as a Garden: In Persia and Mughal India* (New York: Braziller, 1979).

Mukhamedzhanov, A. R., *Istoriia Orosheniia Bukharskogo Oazis* (Tashkent: Fan, 1978).

Mukminova, R. G., *Sotsial'naia Differensiatsiia Naseleniia Gorodov Uzbekistana v XV–XVI vv.* (Tashkent: Fan, 1985).

Murav'yov, Nikolay, *Journey to Khiva through the Turkoman Country* (London: Oguz Press, 2nd Eng. ed., 1977).

Murzaev, E. M., ed., *Srednaia Azia* (Moscow: Akademii Nauk, 1968).

Naqvi, H. K., *Urban Centres and Industries in Upper India 1556–1803* (London: Asia Publishing House, 1968).

Naqvi, Hamida Khatoon, "Urban Growth in Hindustan circa 1000–1550: An Exploratory Study," *Studies in Islam* XVI/3 (July 1979), 150–95.

Nikitin, Afanasy, *Khozhenie Za Tri Moria Afanasiia Nikitina*, ed. by Ia. S. Lur'e and L. S. Semenov (Leningrad: Nauka, 1986).

Nikitin, V. P. Nikitin, *Astrakhan' i ee Okrestnosti* (Moscow: Iskusstvo, 1981).

Öhberg, Arne, "Russia and the World Market in the Seventeenth Century," *Scandinavian Economic History Review*, II (1955), 123–62.

Pallas, P. S., *Travels Through the Southern Provinces of the Russian Empire*, trans. by Francis L. Bludgon (London: Longman & O. Rees, 1802–3).

Parker, W. H., *An Historical Geography of Russia* (Chicago: Aldine, 1968).

Pashkov, A. I., ed., *Istoriia Russkoi Ekonomicheskoi Mysli*, I (Moscow: State Publications of Political Literature, 1955).

Pearson, M. N., "Brokers in Western Indian Port Cities, their Role in Servicing Foreign Merchants," *Modern Asian Studies* XXII/3 (1988), 455–72.

Merchants and Rulers in Gujarat (Berkeley: University of California Press, 1976).

Pelenski, Jaroslaw, *Russia and Kazan. Conquest and Imperial Ideology (1438–1560s)* (The Hague: Mouton, 1974).

Perlin, Frank, "Proto-Industrialization and Pre-Colonial South Asia," *Past and Present* XCVIII (February 1983), 30–95.

Petrov, A. M., "Foreign Trade of Russia and Britain with Asia in the Seventeenth to Nineteenth Centuries," *Modern Asian Studies* XXI/4 (1987), 625–37.

Petrushevsky, I. P., "The Socio-Economic Condition of Iran Under the Ilkhans," in Boyle, ed., *The Cambridge History of Iran*, V, *The Saljuq and Mongol Periods*.

Postans, T., "Miscellaneous Information Relative to the Town of Shikarpoor in the Years 1840 and 1841" (India Office Library), 87–102.

Pottinger, Henry, *Travels in Beloochistan and Sinde* (London: Longman, 1816).

Punjab Government, *Attock District* XXIXA of Punjab District Gazetteers 1930 (Lahore: Government Printing Office, 1932).

Gazetteer of the Dera Ghazi Khan District, rev. ed., *1883–1884* (Lahore: Civil and Military Gazette Press, 1898).

Gazetteer of the Dera Ismail Khan District 1883–84 (Lahore: Arya Press, 1884).

Gazetteer of the Lahore District 1883–1884 (Calcutta: Calcutta Central Press, 1884).

Gazetteer of the Peshawar District 1897–1898 (Lahore: Civil and Military Gazette Press, 1898).

Raverty, Henry George, *Notes on Afghanistan and Baluchistan*, repr. (Quetta: Nisa Traders, 1982), 2 vols.

Ray, Rajat Kanta, "The *Bazar*: Indigenous Sector of the Indian Economy," in Tripathi, ed., *Business Communities of India*, 241–67.

Raychaudhuri, Tapan and Habib, Irfan, eds., *The Cambridge Economic History of India*, I: *c. 1200–c. 1650* (Cambridge: Cambridge University Press, 1982).

Raychaudhuri, Tapan, "Inland Trade," in Raychaudhuri and Habib, eds., *The Cambridge Economic History of India*, I: *c. 1200–c. 1750*, 325–59.

"Non-Agricultural Production: Mughal India," in Raychaudhuri and Habib, eds., *The Cambridge Economic History of India*, I: *c. 1200–c. 1750*, 261–307.

"The State and the Economy: the Mughal Empire," in Raychaudhuri and Habib, eds., *The Cambridge Economic History of India*, I: *c. 1200–c. 1750*, 172–92.

Riasanovsky, Nicholas V., *A History of Russia*, (New York: Oxford University Press, 1984).

Rich, E. E. and Wilson, C. H., eds., *The Cambridge Economic History of Europe*, VI: *The Economy of Expanding Europe in the Sixteenth and Seventeenth Centuries* (Cambridge: Cambridge University Press, 1967).

Richards, D. S., *Islam and the Trade of Asia* (Oxford: Bruno Cassirer, 1970).

Richards, J. F., *The Imperial Monetary System of Mughal India* (New Delhi: Oxford University Press, 1987).

"Mughal State Finance and the Pre-Modern World Economy," *Comparative Studies in Society and History* XXIII/21 (April 1981), 285–308.

Rickmers, W. Rickmer, *The Duab of Turkistan* (Cambridge: Cambridge University Press, 1913).

Rispler-Chaim, Vardit, "Insurance and Semi-Insurance Transactions in Islamic History until the 19th Century," *Journal of the Economic and Social History of the Orient* XXXIV/2 (June 1991), 142–58.

Robinson, J. A. (Capt.), *Notes on the Nomad Tribes of Eastern Afghanistan*, repr. (Quetta: Nisa Traders, 1980).

Roemer, Hans Robert, *Persien auf dem Weg in die Neuzeit: Iranische Geschichte von 1350–1750* (Beirut: Franz Steiner, 1989).

Roemer, H. R., "The Safavid Period," in Jackson and Lockhart, eds., *The Cambridge History of Iran*, VI: *The Timurid and Safavid Periods*, 189–350.

"The Successors of Timur," in Jackson and Lockhart, eds., *The Cambridge History of Iran*, VI: *The Timurid and Safavid Periods*, 98–146.

Röhrborn, Klaus Michael, *Provinzen und Zentralgewalt Persiens im 16. und 17 Jahrhundert* (Berlin: Walter De Gruyter, 1966).

Rose, H. A., *A Glossary of the Tribes of the Punjab and the North-West Frontier* (Based on the Census Report for the Punjab, 1883 by the late Sir Denzil Ibbetson, K.S.C.I. and the Census for the Punjab, 1892 by the Hon. M. E. D. Maclagan, C.S.I.) (Delhi: Punjab National Press, 1970), 2 vols.

Rossabi, Morris, "The 'Decline' of the Central Asian Caravan Trade," in Tracy, ed., *The Rise of Merchant Empires*, 351–70.

"The Tea and Horse Trade with Inner Asia during the Ming," *Journal of Asian History* XLII (1970), 136–68.

Roux, Jean-Paul, *Histoire des Grands Moghols, Babur* (Paris: Fayard, 1986).

Sakharov, A. M., "Rossiia i ee kul'tura v xvii stoletii," in Artsikhovskii, ed., *Ocherki russkoi kul'tury XVII veke* chast' pervaia, 5–24.

Savory, Robert, *Iran under the Safavids* (Cambridge: Cambridge University Press, 1980).

Schumpeter, Joseph A., *Imperialism and Social Classes* (New York: A. M. Kelley, 1951).

Schuster-Walser, Sibylla, *Das Safawidische Persien im Spiegel Europäischer Reiseberichte (1502–1722)* (Baden-Baden, Bruno-Grimm, 1970).

Schuyler, Eugene, *Turkistan, Notes of a Journey in Russian Turkistan, Kokand, Bukhara and Khuldja*, ed. by Geoffrey Wheeler, abridged by K. E. West (London: Routledge & Kegan Paul, 1966).

Sharma, G. D., "The Marwaris: Economic Foundations of an Indian Capitalist Class," in Tripathi, ed., *Business Communities of India*, 185–208.

Singh, Chetan, "Centre and Periphery in the Mughal State: The Case of Seventeenth Century Panjab," *Modern Asian Studies* XXII/2 (1988), 299–318.

Singh, Chettan, *Region and Empire: Panjab in the Seventeenth Century* (Delhi: Oxford University Press, 1991).

Singh, M. P., *Town, Market, Mint and Port in the Mughal Empire 1556–1707* (New Delhi: Adam Publishers, 1985).

Siroux, Maxime, "Les caravansérais routiers safavids," *Iranian Studies*, VII/1–2 (winter-spring 1974), 348–75.

Skinner, J. William, "Marketing and Social Structure in Rural China," *Journal of Asian Studies* XXIV (1964), 3–44.

Sladkovskii, M. I., *Istoriia Torgovo-Ekonomicheskikh Otnoshenii Narodov Rossii s Kitaem (do 1917 g.)* (Moscow: Nauka, 1974).

Sombart, Werner, "Medieval and Modern Commercial Enterprise," in Lane, ed., *Enterprise and Secular Change*, 25–40.

Spasskii, I. G., "Dengi i Denezhnoe Khoziaistvo," in Artsikhovskii, ed., *Ocherki russkoi kultury xvii veke* chast pervaia, 145–64.

"Gold Coins and Coin-like Gold in the Muscovite State, and the First Gold Pieces of Ivan III," *The Numismatic Chronicle*, 7th ser. XIX (1979), 174–84.

"Numismatic Research in Russia, the Ukraine, and Byelorussia in the Period 1917–1967," *The Numismatic Chronicle* XII (1972), 247–73.

The Russian Monetary System, trans. by Z. I. Garischina and L. S. Forrer (Amsterdam: Jacques Schulman N.V., rev. ed., 1967).

Spate, O. H. K., *India and Pakistan*, repr. (London: Methuen, 1960).

Spengler, Joseph, "Comment on [Irfan Habib's] 'Usury in Medieval India'," *Comparative Studies in Society and History* VI/4 (July 1964), 420–23.

Spuler, B., "Astrakhan," in H. A. R. Gibb et al., eds., *The Encyclopaedia of Islam*, new ed. (Leiden: E. J. Brill, 1960), I, 721–22.

"Central Asia from the Sixteenth Century to the Russian Conquests," in P. M. Holt, Ann K. S. Lambton and Bernard Lewis, eds., *The Cambridge History of Islam*, v/1a (Cambridge: Cambridge University Press, 1977), 462–502.

Steel, Richard and Crowther, John, "Journey of Richard Steel and John Crowther, from Ajmeer in India, to Isfahan in Persia, in the Years 1615 and 1616," in Robert Kerr, ed., *A General Collection of Voyages and Travels* (Edinburgh: Blackwood, 1824), IX, 206–19.

Steensgaard, Niels, *The Asian Trade Revolution of the Seventeenth Century, The East India Companies and the Decline of the Caravan Trade* (Chicago: University of Chicago Press, 2nd ed., 1974).

Steinmann, Linda K., "Shah 'Abbas I and the Royal Silk Trade, 1599–1629," Unpublished Ph.D. dissertation, New York University, 1986.

Stewart, C. E. (Col.), "The Country of the Tekke Turkomans, and the Tejend and Murghab Rivers," *Proceedings of the Royal Geographical Society*, n.s. III (1881), 513–46.

Subrahmanyam, Sanjay, "Persians, Pilgrims and Portuguese: The Travails of Masulipatnam Shipping in the Western Indian Ocean, 1590–1665," *Modern Asian Studies* XXII/3 (1988), 503–30.

The Political Economy of Commerce: Southern India, 1500–1650 (Cambridge: Cambridge University Press, 1990).

Subramanian, Lakshmi, "Banias and the British: the Role of Indigenous Credit in the Process of Imperial Expansion in the Second Half of the Eighteenth Century," *Modern Asian Studies* XXI/3 (1987), 473–510.

"The Eighteenth-Century Social Order in Surat: A Reply and Excursus on the Riots of 1788 and 1795," *Modern Asian Studies* XXV/2 (1991), 321–65.

Sukhareva, O. A., *Kvartal'naia Obschina Pozdnefeodal'nogo Goroda Bukhary* (Moscow: Nauka, 1976).

Taknet, D. K., *Industrial Entrepreneurship of the Shekhawati Marwaris* (Jaipur: D. K. Taknet, 1986).

Tandon, Prakash, *Punjabi Century* (Berkeley: University of California Press, 1960).

Tavernier, Jean-Baptiste, *Travels in India*, trans. and ed. by V. Ball (London: Macmillan, 1889), 2 vols.

   Travels in India, ed. by William Crooke (London: Oxford University Press, 2nd ed., 1925).

   Voyages en Perse, repr. (Paris: Editions Carrefour, 1930).

Tawfiq, Firuz, "Census I. In Persia," in E. Yarshater, ed., *Encyclopaedia Iranica* V, fasc. 2, 142–52.

Thackston, Wheeler, *A Century of Princes* (Cambridge, Mass.: Aga Khan Program for Islamic Architecture, 1989).

Thornton, Edward, *A Gazetteer of the Countries Adjacent to India . . .* (London: W. H. Allen, 1844), 2 vols.

Thrupp, Sylvia, *The Merchant Class of Medieval London* (Chicago: University of Chicago Press, 1948).

Timberg, Thomas, *The Marwaris* (New Delhi: Vikas, 1978).

Toposian, E. R., ed., *Iz Istorii Kultur'nykh Sviazei Narodov Srednei Azii i Indii* (Tashkent: Fan, 1986).

Tracy, James D., ed., *The Political Economy of Merchant Empires* (Cambridge: Cambridge University Press, 1991).

   The Rise of Merchant Empires (Cambridge: Cambridge University Press, 1990).

Tripathi, Dwijendra, ed., *Business Communities of India* (New Delhi: Manohar, 1984).

Tyan, Emile, *Histoire de l'organisation judiciaire en pays d'Islam* (Leiden: E. J. Brill, 1960).

Udovitch, A. L., "Commercial Techniques in Early Medieval Islamic Trade," in Richards, ed., *Islam and the Trade of Asia*, 37–62.

   Partnership and Profit in Medieval Islam (Princeton: Princeton University Press, 1970).

Ustiugov, N. V., *Voprosy Sotsial'no-Ekonomicheskoi Istorii i Istochnikovedeniia Perioda Feodalizma v Rossii* (Moscow: Akademii Nauk, 1961).

Vambery, Arminius, *Sketches of Central Asia*, repr. (Taipei: Ch'eng Wen Publishing Co., 1971).

   Travels in Central Asia: Being the Account of A Journey from Teheran Across the Turkoman Desert . . . , repr. (New York: Arno Press, 1970).

Van der Wee, Herman, *The Growth of the Antwerp Market and the European Economy* (The Hague: Martinus Nijhoff, 1961).

Verma, H. C., *Medieval Routes to India* (Calcutta: Naya Prakash, 1978).

Vernadsky, George, *A History of Russia, V/2: The Tsardom of Moscow 1547–1682* (New Haven, Conn.: Yale University Press, 1969).

Vernadsky, George, ed., *A Source Book for Russian History from Early Times to 1917*, I: *Early Times to the Late 17th Century* (New Haven, Conn.: Yale University Press, 1972).

Vigne, G. T., *A Personal Narrative of a Visit to Ghuzni, Kabul and Afghanistan*, repr. (Lahore: Sang-e-Meel, 1982).

Volonikov, V. G. and Khalfin, N. A., eds., *Zapiski o Bukharskom Khanstve*, ed. by P. I. Demezona and I. V. Vitkevitcha (Moscow: Eastern Literature, 1983).

Walder, G. C., *Gazetteer of the Lahore District 1893–1894* (Lahore: Civil and Military Gazette Press, 1894).

Wallerstein, Immanuel, *The Modern World System* (New York: Academic Press, 1974–80), 3 vols.

Washbrook, David, "South Asia, the World System, and World Capitalism," *The Journal of Asian Studies* XLIV/3 (August 1990), 479–508.

Watson, Andrew M., "Back to Gold and Silver," *The Economic History Review*, 2nd ser. XX/1 (1967), 1–34.

Willan, T. S., *The Early History of the Russia Company, 1553–1603* (Manchester: Manchester University Press, 1956).

Williamson, Oliver E. and Winter, Sidney G., eds., *The Nature of the Firm: Origins, Evolution and Development* (New York: Oxford University Press, 1991).

Wink, André, *Al-Hind: The Making of the Indo-Islamic World* (Leiden: E. J. Brill, 1990).

Index

'Abbas, Shah, 14, 16, 18, 19, 67, 75, 87, 88; currency, 29; economic policies, 5, 22, 23, 32, 388–39, 41, 42, 99; restructures Safavid state, 9

'Abbasi, 28–29

'Abd Allah Khan, 14; currency, 29, 30; economic policies, 20, 38, 42

Abu'l Fadl 'Allami: *A'in-i Akbari*, 15; *Akbar nama*, 33; describes Akbar's economic policy, 32, 34, 35, 36

Afghans (Pushtuns), 76; invade India, 131; Luharni Afghans in India, 53; as merchants, 45, 53, 61–67, 120; as Mughul officials, 54; residents of Bukharan dvor, 102; sack Isfahan, 129; threaten trade routes, 37, 52; *see also* Powindahs

Agarwals, 60; *see also* Marwaris

Agra, 25

Agrizhan or Indo-Tatar community, 102; socio-economic traits, 107

Ahmedabad, 37, 48, 132

Akbar, 5, 15, 41, 43; commercial and economic policies, 14, 25, 32, 33, 34, 36–38, 42, 53

Aleppo: Indian textile profits in, 72; commenda in, 120

Alexei Mikhailovich, 82; introduces copper currency, 83; sanctions trade mission to India, 90

'Ali Mardan Khan, constructs Peshawar caravansarai, 53

Amsterdam, as a world-economic center, 55, 130

Anbu Ram Mulin: principal "company man" in Astrakhan, 121–22; petitions tsar to trade in Europe and China, 128–29

Archangel, 110, 132; English and Dutch at, 2, 85, 95, 96; Indians petition to trade in, 122, 128; role in Russian trade, 78, 83; sales of Asian goods in, 109

Ardebil: religious and commercial center, 93; silk-producing center, 109

Armenian(s): archbishop's see in Astrakhan, 101; Herzig's study of, 4, 11; persecution of in Iran, 12; trade in Iran, 70, 74, 99; trade in Russia, 87, 97, 102 and n6, 105, 108

Arora caste, 66

asafoetida, 22

Ashrafi, 28

Asiatic despotism, Russian historiography of, 9–10

Astrakhan, 95; census of Indians in, 102, 112–17; commenda used, 66; commercial significance of, 78, 94; decline of Indian community in, 128–32; foreign merchants in, 85, 86; Indian Christian converts in, 107, 123; Indian commercial organization in, 112–17, 135; Indian diaspora in, 1, 3, 44; Indian loans in, 74; Indian and Muslim artisans in, 93; Indian settlement in, 77, 86–89, 97, 98, 99; Indo-Turkic (Agrizhan) population of, 107; Iranian links with, 67, 69, 105, 108, 110–17, 126–27; Khattris and Marwaris in, 59, 105; Multanis in, 57, 102; nature of Indian trade from, 108–12; Russian merchants in, 90, 91; Russian officials criticize Indians in, 131–32; Russian records of, 6, 58; socio-economic trait of Indians in, 105–8; status of Indian community, 12, 103–4; Turkic spoken in, 12; Vaishnavite ceremonies of Indians in, 106–7, 133

Attock (Atak-Banares): border between Hindustan and Kabulistan, 36, 133; customs at, 37

Aurungzeb, 8; Russian mission to, 92, 94

Babi Afghans, mediatory traders, 65; *see also* Powindahs

Babur: coinage of in Turan, 26; describes trade at Kabul and Qandahar, 61–63, 65; founds Mughul empire, 7–8; love of melons, 22

al-Badauni, 33

Bahawalpur, 60

baj and tamgha taxes, 35 and n97

Printed in Great Britain
by Amazon

18887295R00103